Junk Bonds

Junk Bonds
How High Yield Securities Restructured Corporate America

Glenn Yago

New York   Oxford
Oxford University Press
1991

Oxford University Press

Oxford   New York   Toronto
Delhi   Bombay   Calcutta   Madras   Karachi
Petaling Jaya   Singapore   Hong Kong   Tokyo
Nairobi   Dar es Salaam   Cape Town
Melbourne   Auckland

and associated companies in
Berlin   Ibadan

Copyright © 1991 by the Oxford University Press, Inc.

Library of Congress Cataloging-in-Publication Data
Yago, Glenn.
    Junk bonds : how high yield securities restructured corporate
America / Glenn Yago. p.   cm.
    Includes bibliographical references.
    ISBN 0-19-506111-X
    1. Junk bonds—United States.   2. Junk bonds—United States—Case
studies.   I. Title.
HG4963.Y34   1990   332.63′234—dc20   90-35876

9 8 7 6 5 4 3 2 1

Printed in the United States of America
on acid-free paper

Preface

This book is about one of the most important breakthroughs in the effort by U.S. industry to restructure itself in the face of global competition: high yield corporate securities. I will argue that in the late 1970s the color of the biggest blue chip stocks began to fade as investment grade companies steadily lost jobs and American industry faced a general competitive decline. I will show that as this was happening companies that raised funds in the junk bond market created jobs four times faster than the economy as a whole, experienced one-third greater growth in productivity, fifty percent faster growth in sales, and about three times faster growth in capital spending.

But while high yield bonds—usually referred to as "junk bonds"—were gaining popularity by reducing financial imitations on many firms, they were also generating considerable controversy that remains unsettled at this writing. Volatility in the stock market is accompanied by volatility in the bond markets, and most recent issues of high yield bonds have been withdrawn for lack of buyers. Whatever the outcome of this uncertain marketplace, the future of the junk bond market and restructuring in general will be based on the economic questions examined in this book and the evolving answers in the years ahead.

In writing this book I heard a parable about the political controversy surrounding such financing that had made its way around the junk bond market. The interpretation of this baseball analogy speaks volumes about the political economy of junk bonds and buyouts in our time. Imagine there was once a baseball team with the biggest and strongest players in history. For years, they always won. As baseball was played at that time, the sheer magnitude of the size and girth of the players determined who would win. Suddenly, the team started losing games. Puzzled by this turn of events, the owner went to the manager and asked how this could happen. How had their playing or the competition changed?

"Well, there are these new guys," said the manager. "They move fast and throw fast balls, curve balls, and sliders."

"Okay," replied the owner, "teach your guys to hustle and how to hit fast balls, curve balls, and sliders." Assuming that the manager could manage and the matter of losing would end, the owner turned on his heel and left.

As the weeks went by, the team kept losing. Once again the owner approached the manager, who confessed, "I'm sorry. I've got the biggest and strongest players. Buy they're also the dumbest players I've ever worked with. I've tried, but they just can't learn to move fast, hit curve balls and sliders, and compete the way the game is now being played. You've got only one choice if you want this club to win. Go to the Commissioner and change the rules. Slow the game down, get him to outlaw fast balls, curve balls, and sliders."

For nearly three decades after World War II, American business played slow, strong, and easy. Each year the largest corporations increased their employment, share of profits and sales, and concentrated their corporate power. By the mid-1970s, however, the great push and shove of international trade and technological change caused the largest American businesses to lose their competitive edge. As new foreign and domestic businesses showed up on the business playing field to compete, major corporations that had once relied on sheer size and strength to maintain their market share were suddenly losing ground to smaller competitors. Some were even facing takeover threats from companies a fraction of their size.

What corporate leaders had perceived as the preordained alignment of the economic universe—the primacy of large, diversified, multidivisional U.S. corporations in increasingly concentrated industries—changed. To resist that change, companies tried to learn new management styles and strategies. Corporate strategies of diversification ensued in the 1970s along with popular management theories. Business and policy fads abounded—Q factors, Z theories, and reaches for excellency and beyond were part of the vision to regain competitiveness.

But competitiveness is not found gained in the pages of a book skimmed at 30,000 feet. If anything, the theories and fads of the late 1970s and early 1980s were nothing more than part of the resistance to change, a way to rationalize a style of corpocracy that had long ceased to function properly. In spite of this, something was working in our economy during this period, something that would manifest itself in the robust economy and low unemployment that the United States enjoyed later in the 1980s. Greater access to credit and capital fueled an economic boom; the primary tool to capital access was the high yield bond. Junk bonds were not a fad and, despite some excesses, the concept behind them was fundamentally sound.

The concept behind junk bonds also represented a fundamental shift in the concept of the purpose of our capital markets. The old days, when credit markets were open only to investment grade companies, were also easy days. Companies were judged on past performance. If an entity had been profitable and nothing material had changed, then it was judged likely to continue to be profitable. A company was not downgraded until after some significant adverse event had occurred. Thus the American capital markets financed American companies on the basis of their past, not their future. And therein lies the true revolution caused by junk bonds: the concept that a company should be judged on its potential, rather than what it has previously accomplished.

A country that finances on the basis of past performance will never finance the future.

Acknowledgments

This book represents the cooperative and collaborative efforts of many people that have supported and assisted in my research efforts over the past years. Though very much a team effort, I accept individual responsibility for the accuracy and representation of the facts about the junk bond market and corporate restructuring as I have come to see them; however, the facts about this difficult, complex, and controversial market were never simple or straightforward to come by, analyze, or interpret. The 1980s were a period of enormous experimentation, creativity, and trial and error innovation in the financial and business worlds. During that period, tremendous economic value was created in new industries and technologies at the cutting edge of economic change. Since my research began in 1985, each new research project brought me into contact with other analysts, researchers, and financial and business practitioners from whom I have learned a great deal. Moreover, I was extremely fortunate to lead an extremely talented team of researchers that contributed to the various data and case study analyses covered in this book.

I have also learned a great deal from other researchers and writers in this area including Professor Edward Altman (New York University), Professor Michael Jensen (Harvard University), Professor Gregg Jarrell (Rochester University), Professor Robert Sobel (Hofstra University), Professor Mike Smith (University of Nottingham), Professor Frank Lichtenberg (Columbia

University), Professor John Pond (Harvard University), and Professor Don Siegel (SUNY-Stony Brook). Professional bankers and analysts in corporate finance at Drexel Burnham Lambert, First Boston, Morgan Stanley, Weiss Peck and Greer, Clayton and Dubillier, and Paine Webber helped me understand changes in the debt market and recapitalizations.

History will most likely confirm that anyone active in corporate finance, business, or economic research in either the academic or professional world owes an enormous intellectual debt to Michael R. Milken for his work in financial innovation. He always gave graciously of his time in answering numerous and difficult questions, and he was always accessible to explore tough issues that developed with the controversy surrounding the market that he helped create.

In research, as in most other endeavors, the final product is only as good as the people assembled to conduct the investigation. Dr. Charlene Seifert and Dr. Sen-Yuan Wu were key contributors to the work reported in Chapters 3-5. They also demonstrated great flexibility and skill as we shifted our research focus from labor to capital markets. Dr. Frank Lichtenberg and Dr. Don Siegel were worthy and helpful collaborators on the research project on leveraged buyouts from which Chapter 8 was derived. Rita Omark has served as a research and administrative assistant over the past two years and suffered through the enormous pressures of completing work assignments with nearly simultaneous deadlines in both the business and research spheres of my professional activity. Her efforts and patience are greatly appreciated. Jeff Tannenbaum worked tirelessly on data management and analysis and maintained a positive and humorous perspective when the tasks seemed insurmountable. Teri Sivilli provided exacting and demanding standards in her fact-checking and other editorial assistance. I had been led to believe by other authors that editors like Herbert J. Addison of Oxford University Press did not exist anymore—that is, editors that take genuine and constructive interest in the books they are responsible for publishing and the intellectual craftwork of their authors' trade. Mr. Addison's critical support and suggestions greatly improved the concept of crafting a number of potentially disjointed research projects into a meaningful book.

I am also grateful to Dean Gerrit Wolf of the Harriman School for Management and Dean Egon Neuberger of the School of Social and Behavioral Sciences at the State University of New York at Stony Brook for their support of the Economic Research Bureau. Thanks to Dr. Warren Ilchman, founder of the Rockefeller Institute of Government, I have greatly benefitted from participating in various research and policy debates as a Faculty Fellow of that Institute over the past years.

My greatest debt is to my wife and friend, Dr. Yudit Jung, who, while raising our children and faced with the challenges of her own demanding career, has tolerated the stress and strain associated with completing this book. She has supported my pursuit and the demands of diverse business and research projects with sound advice, constructive insight and her unique capability to reflect on events and people. Simultaneously, she kept our home intact. With everything in this world changing at incredible speed, it is the continuity of family and friends that sustain our work. I have been very lucky to have both over the past years. That continuity has been especially important in that my business experiences have informed my research, and vice versa. Specifically, my thanks are due to my business colleagues, Gilbert Scherer and Frank Fraccastoro, who have expressed ongoing support and interest in my research work even when it has sometimes taxed our business efforts.

Finally, I owe just about everything to my parents to whom I dedicate this book.

New York City
June, 1990

Contents

Junk Bonds

1

The Rhetoric and Reality of Junk Bonds

"Junk bonds," "securities swill," "toxic waste"—these are just a few of the names critics have developed for high yield securities. Yet despite the name-calling, corporate debt securities that have lost or never had investment grade ratings were the fastest growing financial instruments in the U.S. capital markets in the 1980s. They are still the most controversial.

The rhetoric surrounding high yield securities has been unprecedented. Frequently, the financial press and news media have linked these securities with risky ventures, defaults, unsavory business practices, hostile takeovers, and insider trading scandals. Few financial instruments have been as consistently maligned as junk bonds, leading the general public, corporate managers, educators, and legislators to view them with suspicion, if not outright contempt.

The association between high yield bonds and the wave of corporate restructuring has placed these securities and the people who craft and market them at center stage. Yet along with fame came the securities investigation of Drexel Burnham Lambert and Michael R. Milken, resulting in a settlement of $650 million by Drexel Burnham and the indictment of Milken. The subsequent bankruptcy of Drexel Burnham was the largest bankruptcy in Wall Street history.

As a researcher, I am in no position to evaluate the legal charges about technical violations of trading practices levied against firms or individuals active in the junk bond market. However, as an empirical investigator I have had the opportunity over the past years to assemble a unique body of evidence that sheds considerable light upon and evaluates the junk bond market, corporate restructuring, and their economic impacts. Indeed, this book contains the most comprehensive evidentiary record to date of the firms that have issued junk bonds and what they have accomplished with that funding.

Before I describe what I have discovered, however, it would be helpful to define some of the terms that are used in the book. The widely used pejorative term "junk" bonds, which so captured the public imagination, gives the securities a kind of generic status, with the added dimension of underscoring their status as noninvestment grade. Prior to the ascendancy of junk bonds, conservative institutional investors at insurance companies, pension funds, bank trust departments, and investment companies primarily invested only in *investment* grade credits. There are only 800 companies that have issued corporate bonds in the investment grade market. If all of the 23,000 U.S. companies with sales over $35 million were reviewed by bond rating agencies, only about 5 percent would qualify for investment grade ratings. These larger, older, more established businesses enjoy bond ratings of Aaa to Baa (under Moody's rating system) and AAA to BBB (under Standard and Poor's), and consequently are able to pay lower interest on their debt to investors.

A bond is considered *noninvestment* grade if it is rated Ba or lower by Moody's or BB or lower by Standard and Poor's (see Table 1-1). With the rise of the high yield market, 1,800 firms have tapped the public debt market. Using the criterion noted earlier, 95 percent of the firms with revenues over $35 million would be classified as *noninvestment* grade or "junk" credits and would be required to pay higher rates of interest on their bond issues. For that reason, noninvestment grade credits also go by the name of "high yield" since the interest paid on their securities relative to a comparable U.S. Treasury security is substantially higher than the interest on investment grade corporate bonds compared to those Treasuries.

Table 1-1. Corporate Bond Ratings Define the High Yield Market

Moody's		Standard and Poor's
Aaa		AAA
Aa	Investment Grade	AA
A		A
Baa		BBB
Ba		BB
B		B
Caa	High Yield	CCC
Ca		CC
C		C
D		D

Bond rating agencies in the past exercised a strong gatekeeping function in the capital markets, effectively excluding less established businesses without a substantial track record from access to capital. Since these smaller companies failed to qualify for investment grade ratings, they were essentially excluded from the public debt market until the early 1980s. In the prejunk world, these companies were at the mercy of dilutive and expensive stock offerings or costly commercial bank loans with restrictive covenants that could put them at a disadvantage to foreign competitors with a lower cost of capital and stymie their pursuit of changing markets and technologies.

The power of bond rating agencies, whose stated purpose was to protect investors, became legend, and consequently led to limited capital access for most firms. In some of my discussions in Washington, I found Congressional leaders who mistakenly thought that rating and credit analysis of bonds was done by government agencies and federally mandated.

Rhetoric

The dominant business theme of the 1980s was restructuring—either by putting together focused national or global companies in high-growth, innovative sectors of the economy or by taking apart large, diversified conglomerates in low-growth sectors. Prior to 1984, the high yield market concentrated almost exclusively on the former. Indeed, as we shall later see, for the whole decade, the majority of "junk" bonds were used for internal growth or strategic acquisition in these innovative sectors on the frontiers of technology that have provided services and products that were undreamed of by the consuming public a decade ago (e.g., cable television, cheap long distance service, cellular phones, personal computers, and the like).

It was not until high yield securities were applied to restructuring through deconglomeration and takeovers that hostilities against the junk bond market broke out, and much of the political storm over junk bonds was whipped up by large corporations that had seen the high yield market help smaller companies compete more effectively. Many of those same big businesses became takeover targets when faced with diminished market share and declining performance. The high yield market grew at the expense of bank debt, and high yield companies grew at the expense of the hegemony of many established firms. As Peter Passell noted in *The New York Times,* the impact was first felt on Wall Street, "where sharp elbows and a working knowledge of computer spreadsheets suddenly counted more than a nose for dry sherry or membership in Skull and Bones."

Over time, the accumulated evidence indicates that the building and rebuilding of firms and industries through takeovers, deconglomeration, and innovative restructuring provided benefits in terms of jobs, corporate efficiency, and international competitiveness. In the shortrun, however, the jobs of senior corporate managers disappeared. As the record shows, corporate managers vested by passive shareholders with effective corporate control did just about anything in their power to protect themselves against active investor groups that challenged them. They changed their corporate charter, adopted shark repellants, got fitted with golden parachutes, signed lock-up agreements, even forced their companies to swallow "poison pills." Calling for protective legislation became an easy way to avoid takeover threats. And calling the legislation "shareholder protection" instead of "management insulation" capped off their lobbying efforts with a stroke of linguistic genius.

By the mid-1980s, the takeover boom was in full swing, with T. Boone Pickens, Carl Icahn, and others waging major battles for corporate control. Often these so-called raiders took home substantial profits by selling their shares at prices inflated by the takeover bids, even if they failed to acquire the target companies. In fact, in many cases companies fought takeover bids by buying back their own shares at inflated prices from "raiders," a practice called "greenmail." Since many of these takeover bids were financed in part by high yield securities, "junk" bonds became associated with "greenmail," even though the securities themselves neither caused nor promoted the practice.

The real promoters of greenmail were frequently the managers of target companies, who saw premium repurchases of stock as the only way to protect their jobs, income, and independence. While the shareholders paid the piper, entrenched managers shifted the blame deftly to junk bonds, claiming that, but for the bonds, the companies never would have had to defend themselves.

This strategy was quite effective in rallying shareholders behind the managers. Unfortunately, it hid the fact that in many cases, managers had failed their shareholders on two important counts. First, by failing to maximize shareholder value, they had let their stock price languish well below the economic value of the company, virtually inviting outsiders to make an unsolicited bid. Second, by passing up the takeover offer, they had prevented their shareholders from realizing an attractive acquisition premium.

It is interesting that in cases where greenmail was not an issue and hostile offers succeeded (as in Ronald Perleman's Pantry Pride acquisition of Revlon in 1985), shareholders generally came away very happy. They had received added value for their investment, and the junk bonds that made the transaction possible were not cast as the culprit, but rather as the hero in the transaction.

The next round of rhetoric in the high yield market came when target companies and their legal and financial advisors began to complain about "bust-up shut-down junk bond takeovers," in which a company would be dismantled to pay off acquisition debt. Once again, the transactions were portrayed as sinister in the extreme. The popular picture, painted with the widest possible brush strokes, included a familiar company like Gulf Oil Corporation, Phillips Petroleum, or Disney Productions being attacked by sharks, allegedly funded almost exclusively with junk bonds. According to the portrayal, the raider's sole intention was to cannibalize the company, discarding or destroying the pieces on the way, provided the debt was repaid and the raider earned a handsome profit.

This portrayal of early takeover strategies contained an element of truth and an element of fiction. It was true that many raiders used junk bonds in funding their offers. But the fact that high yield debt generally accounted for a relatively small fraction (usually no more than 30 percent) of the total purchase price of acquisitions escaped the notice of the press. While divestitures were an integral part of takeover strategies, the assumption that key business units would somehow be destroyed or disappear into a black hole was wrong. Rather, the units were sold to willing buyers who felt they could add value or increase the unit's productivity and profitability. Not only would the pieces remain in operation, many would flourish under their new management and ownership structure. This occurred, for example, in the case of Omak Wood Products, which was divested from Crown Zellerbach after Sir James Goldsmith's takeover. With junk bonds, the union members acquired 60 percent of the stock, and through their controlling interest achieved better performance and more modernization than had been attained under Crown Zellerbach's control.

Total dismantling was not always the raider's aim. Often, the plan was to divest unprofitable units and rebuild the company around its more productive core businesses. In addition, the notion that dismantling a company is necessarily bad in itself, as shall be seen later, is a fiction. The Beatrice leveraged buyout, which was followed by at least eight major spin-offs and divestitures, proved to be one of the most successful transactions in history, for pre and postbuyout investors, for Beatrice itself, and for the businesses that were sold after the buyout.

Despite these factors, the rhetoric of "junk bonds," "sharks," "raiders," "bust-ups," "hostiles," "friendlies," and "white knights and squires," evoked such profound fear in the ranks of American business that controversy was inevitable. The press had a field day, and corporate managers joined in the public debate, hoping to turn fear and negative sentiments into protective legislation and court action.

Getting the Facts

As I watched this controversy unfold, I was particularly impressed by the vitriolic rhetoric. But because my job centers on empirical research, I also began to wonder about the underlying facts. While everyone seemed to have an opinion about junk bonds, no one seemed to be providing any evidence to support their claims. In fact, many of the claims were themselves vague, ambiguous, or simply blustering, though colorful, denunciations of the opposing view.

My previous research (supported by the National Science Foundation, the Research Foundation of the State University of New York, the AFL-CIO, the German Marshall Fund, and other foundations) had focused on plant closings and job loss, regional economic development planning, and economic adjustment strategies for state and local government. With support from the Securities Industry Association, I had compared my data on plant closings with merger and acquisition activity and, contrary to the conventional wisdom of the time, discovered that nonacquired plants, many owned by Fortune 500 firms, were the most likely to shut down. Ownership change through merger or acquisition was an alternative to, not a cause of, plant closings.

An obvious next step in the research agenda about corporate restructuring was to examine the links between changes in the capital markets and economic performance. My primary objective was to move beyond the rhetoric and get to the facts. Through observation and analysis, I wanted to demystify high yield securities and find out how businesses were actually putting them to use.

The most extensive data on the high yield market had been developed by the leading underwriter and market-maker in high yield securities, Drexel Burnham Lambert. In 1987, I submitted to them a proposal to support a university research project aimed at assessing the uses and effects of high yield securities. They provided access to their own data sets and other proprietary and public data about firm and industry performance. Later, I extended the project to examine leveraged buyouts and received additional support (from Drexel, the Securities Industry Association, and the Research Foundation of the State University of New York) to explore additional issues related to capital market changes presented in this book. In no instance did any of these parties seek to limit my access to data or to censor the analysis of findings of this book. Further details about the data and methods of this analysis are presented in the Appendix.

Reality

Misperceptions about Financing Change

While there are many more aspects to the high yield market than can possibly be covered in a single book, one important fact stood out clearly through all of my research. For the most part, junk bonds have been just the opposite of what most people assume. Despite what many people think, junk bonds have not primarily been used to fund hostile takeovers. Instead, their core application has been to generate economic value through aggressive business development strategies. Contrary to popular opinion, junk bonds were not the primary source of takeover funding. That honor belongs to bank debt and internally generated funds. Many people believe that junk bonds placed a crushing burden on leveraged buyouts, but the evidence suggests otherwise. It shows that additional debt gives managers added incentives to cut costs and improve performance in key operational areas.

Far from being the scourge of the capital markets or a "betrayal of capitalism," junk bonds have been associated with rapid growth in sales, productivity, employment, and capital spending. High yield firms have consistently outpaced their industries in these and other key performance areas. In light of the evidence, what looked like an ugly duckling turned out to be a swan. Far from undermining our economy, junk bonds promoted the economic objectives Americans value: efficiency, productivity, profit, and growth. The most degrading or destructive aspect of junk bonds has been the language used to describe them.

Democratizing Capital

With the growth in the *availability* of capital, junk bonds have created *access* to capital for small and medium-sized companies that had been economically disenfranchised from participating in the capital markets. High yield securities have helped promote the growth of companies that were previously excluded from the corporate bond market. In this regard, there is a continuity between junk bonds and past financial innovations that enhanced credit access. The expansion of farm credit drove agricultural productivity upward at the turn of the century, mortgage ownership made home ownership commonplace, and educational loans gave many the means to afford a college education. By creating access to the capital markets and carving new channels of finance to entrepreneurs, economic participation has increased. Basically, junk bonds applied the same logic that gave millions of Americans homes, automobiles, and higher education to provide loans for business ownership and development. Just as voting is elemental to political participation, access to credit finances asset building and ownership that is central to economic participation. As Nelson Peltz, who built Triangle Industries into one of the largest and most successful high yield firms put it succinctly, "the thing about capital is, if you don't inherit it, you have to borrow it."

In a very real sense, the high yield market democratized capital. Not only did high yield bonds make capital accessible to a broader range of companies, they also brought the benefits of capital to a much wider range of firms and people through market participation. Through employee and management equity participation, sponsored in part by high yield securities, companies used debt to extend the benefits of equity ownership to employees, including those who might otherwise be unable to invest in the companies where they work. Entrepreneurs, managers, and employees were financially empowered to buy or start businesses and pursue value-creating business strategies, new products and services were provided, and failing firms were restored.

Challenging Corporate Bureaucracies

The high yield market eliminated many of the advantages of corporate size. The political rancor surrounding junk bonds has been particularly strong and probably has more to do with fundamental realignment of economic power than it does with shifts in business strategy, changes in technology, or issues of insider trading. In essence, junk bonds gave many smaller businesses the access to capital, and hence to many of the privileges, once exclusively enjoyed by our nation's largest corporations. Junk bonds became an important agent of social and economic change. Capital access through junk bonds and debt gave small and medium-sized companies the market means to create wealth without government-mandated redistribution. Along with the growth of management and employee buyouts, the high yield market enabled democracy to enter the marketplace. Some called it "economic populism" or "social capitalism," others charged it was "business cannibalism" or "socialism." Senator Russell Long once commented that it reminded him of his father Huey's "Share the Wealth" program "without the Robin Hood."

Prior to the rise of the junk bond market, increased concentration of corporate power had been the dominant pattern since the turn of the century. Cashladen large corporations were, for the most part, the only ones that could acquire companies or finance large-scale expansion, given the barriers to entry in the capital markets before junk bonds. Widespread diversification ensued, as managers in cash-rich companies in low-growth or slowly declining sectors elected to retain cash flow within the company rather than distribute it to shareholders. For these managers, as Sir James Goldsmith has noted, "the bigger the business they run, the greater their prestige, rewards and power of patronage" (Financial Times, Nov. 11, 1989). This was proven by a number of studies that showed that public corporation managers tended to be compensated more on the basis of sales growth than increased rate of return on assets (Jensen and Murphy, 1989). Much of that cash flow in the 1960s and 1970s was used for nonrelated acquisitions, where managers paid large premiums for companies far from their core business (e.g., Goodyear's acquisition of Celeron and U.S. Steel's acquisition of Marathon Oil).

In developing an active market for corporate control and in financing the growth plans of entrepreneurial firms, high yield bonds enabled companies to restructure in a way in which the incentives of management, employees, and shareholders could become aligned, resulting in impressive operating improvements and productivity gains.

Financing High-Growth Innovation

Most of the proceeds of high yield financing went to industries with previously limited access to the capital markets who were blocked by conservative commercial bank lending practices. In the pharmaceuticals, chemical processing, computers, semiconductors, instruments, and electronics industries, where research and development are key, junk bonds helped create and popularize innovative products and services. Motion pictures, cable television, broadcasting, health care, social services, and communications are other sectors that have emerged as central to economic growth over the last decade and have utilized this new market effectively to grow and develop trade surpluses during an era of expanding U.S. trade deficits.

Restructuring Low-Growth Industries for Competitiveness

Buyouts and recapitalizations that occurred in food processing, textiles, apparel, paper, rubber and plastics, and retail trade restored and enhanced value. Most of these transactions were made possible by the growth of the high yield bond market. Low-margin, low-market-share producers were consolidated into higher-margin, higher-market-share competitors. Patterns of sales, operating, and employment decline were reversed.

When management or entrepreneurs bought companies with debt, they restructured the company by selling off subsidiaries that did not fit with the core objectives of the company, cut costs, and enabled active investors and manager- or employee-owners to guide the company. By focusing the company on its core business, by divesting businesses that fit better elsewhere and enabling those divestitures to be financed by other managers, employees, or entrepreneurs, by enhancing worker and manager compensation incentives, and by limiting the use of funds for dubious investments, companies in those sectors that utilized high yield financing experienced a return to competitive economic performance.

Rescuing Failing Companies

Junk bonds were also used in what had been their traditional market—recovering value through workouts and downgraded companies ("fallen angels"). When Consumers Power in Michigan was struck by the cost of an unbuilt nuclear power plant, high yield financing enabled the company to recover and expand into cogeneration and further utility expansion. Harley-Davidson had a similar experience with high yield securities after it had lost substantial market share to foreign competition. Seminole Kraft reopened a shut-down paper mill. Unimar International, a shipbuilding and ocean towing company, bought the assets of WFI industries out of bankruptcy and was recast as an employee-owned firm in one of the largest union-led buyouts ever.

Reintegrating Financial Structure and Corporate Strategy, Ownership, and Control

High yield debt fundamentally changed organizational behavior in companies and the relationship between financial and industrial institutions. Debt enabled change and focused managers and owners alike on what was truly important for the economic success of the firm. Managers slashed unprofitable investments, shrank overhead, and divested assets that were able to realize greater value outside the company.

Participation in substantial equity ownership (by managers, directors, and often also employees) began to reintegrate ownership and control in corporations. Through deconglomeration in low-growth industries and innovation and expansion in high-growth industries, the organizational structures of companies became decentralized. Less power was concentrated in corporate headquarters and decision making became more decentralized, moving toward the operating level.

The motivational benefits of equity participation were amplified through the implementation of performance-based compensation schemes. New corporate strategies of growth, recovery, and innovative competitiveness were made possible by corporate capital structures and financial plans in which high yield securities played a defining role. In short, high yield securities became the agent of change in decentralizing corporate power, enabling new and reconstructed firms to pursue new strategic objectives, and reintegrating ownership and control through new forms of financing and corporate organizations.

Plan of the Book

In Chapter 2, we examine the origins of junk bonds. High yield securities follow a long tradition of financial and credit liberalization that enabled rapid U.S. economic growth over the past two centuries. In each period of entrepreneurial expansion, new financial technologies were created that yielded higher returns and promoted capital access to industrial innovators. This chapter also examines the continuity of financial innovation in U.S. economic history and the origins of the junk bond revolution.

Chapter 3 analyzes the changing role of debt in corporate capital structure and the increased preference for debt as a means of lowering overall capital costs. Changes in financial regulation, foreign competition, and credit market demand will be detailed.

Chapter 4 describes how high yield securities are analyzed and how that market grew. Chapter 5 reports the results of extensive quantitative analysis of the use and impact of high yield securities by firms. Chapter 6 elaborates on these quantitative findings by detailing corporate strategies pursued by high yield companies across industrial sectors. Chapter 7 introduces the research and issues surrounding the growth of leveraged buyouts (LBOs). Chapter 8 presents the results of detailed prebuyout and postbuyout performance of forty-three LBO firms, charting changes in employment, sales, productivity, and capital spending. Chapter 8 goes into greater detail by providing extensive case histories of LBO transactions—including strategic LBOs, defensive LBOs, and divestitures and spin-offs. Chapter 9 moves from the firm to the plant level of performance evaluation of LBOs. In this chapter, findings from a detailed study of over 1100 plants involved in over 100 LBOs are presented. The results detail variations between LBO and non-LBO plants in productivity, employment, plant closings, and research and development.

Chapter 10 moves from the economics to the politics of the junk bond and buyout market. In this chapter, public policy responses to market changes are examined in detail. Chapter 11 reviews the contributions of the high yield market and details the recent shake-out and tiering of that market. This chapter also examines the prospects for future financial innovation and the challenges of economic change in the coming decade.

It is impossible to know for sure, but we still may be in the early days of high yield financing and the restructuring of the U.S. and global economy. In spite of their notoriety, junk bonds have only been used by 5 percent of all U.S. companies, leveraged buyouts comprise only 15-20 percent of all new business combinations, and employee stock ownership covers only about 10 percent of existing companies. Nevertheless, the old hierarchical, highly centralized, multidivisional firm is dead or on life-support. Many such firms pursued flawed acquisition strategies, maintained bloated overhead structures, and focused on old, high-volume, standardized production strategies when their markets required new, flexible, diversified business planning. These companies marshalled political support to insulate themselves from the inevitable forces of change as their economic strength atrophied.

The new corporate organization engendered by high yield financing currently takes many forms, from new start-ups and leveraged recapitalizations, buyouts, and buyins to turnaround buyouts, makeovers, and various forms of strategic alliances. Junk bonds introduced a new perspective to corporate finance and business planning and began a new age of increased participation by owners, managers, and employees in the benefits of economic change. As Michael Milken argued, "the point has always been to see the assets in the liabilities. To look beyond the debt and see what value really exists and how more can be created. The high yield market, both from the side of the investor and of the issuer, has always have been subject to the differences between perception and reality, form and substance." In the chapters ahead, I hope to sort out those differences and examine the strategies of firms that have used high yield financing and have been a part of the restructuring of corporate America.

The future of junk bonds is uncertain. By presenting a fair assessment of the past, I hope to inform the choices of how to best finance the future.

2

The Origins of Junk

To understand the high yield market today, it is important to know something about its history. Financial innovation has been an enduring trait of U.S. capital markets since their beginning. The rise of the junk bond market is only the most recent episode of the ongoing evolution of financial markets that reflects structural economic changes, business requirements for financing, and investor needs for higher returns on investment.

This chapter reviews changes in the bond market and the advances in credit analysis that led to new debt instruments that could be used to build and rebuild companies. Specifically, it reviews institutional changes in the financial markets engendered by junk bonds, and the role of Drexel Burnham Lambert in popularizing this new financial technology. Finally, it closes with a discussion of the role of leverage in corporate capital structure and evaluates the vulnerability of U.S. companies to greater debt exposure.

Like earlier financial innovations, junk bonds emerged during a period when U.S. economic conditions had gone awry and a widespread perception persisted that the country's business would have to be made over to be more competitive. In the public policy arena, debates over industrial policy versus supply side economics presented diametrically opposing solutions to a commonly perceived problem—the relative decline of U.S. competitiveness. Despite ongoing political deliberations over national economic policy approaches, the junk bond market developed as a highly microeconomic, firm- and credit-specific investment policy to reconstruct U.S. industry.

In what would come to be known as "the decade of restructuring," the 1980s saw a flood of new start-ups, takeovers, leveraged buyouts, divestitures, and spin-offs financed through new financial technologies. A new economic order took shape as corporate waste and inefficiency were cut dramatically. What started as a grass-roots economic upheaval among faltering Main Street businesses eventually became so comprehensive that it shook Wall Street and the corporate suites of America's largest companies. By the end of the decade, fully one half of the Fortune 500 had been restructured in one way or another, an explosion of entrepreneurship had created millions of new jobs and dozens of new industries, and the idea of reinventing existing companies in light of changing markets had become commonplace.

Reform and *reconstruction* are terms usually associated with periods of historical change in government policy. Yet they apply equally well to periods of change in business and industry. The worldwide pattern of restructuring in government and business that we observe today has clear precedents in earlier periods. In each era, financing change has required access to capital, whether the enterprise was building canals or railroads, bringing electricity to our cities, setting up nationwide retail chains, or funding research and development in the computer industry. Generally speaking, the risks and rewards of financing change have been higher than those in more established, though not necessarily more predictable, enterprises. Hence, the cost of securing funds for innovative projects or untested ventures has always been higher.

Today's headlines are not the first to define high yielding securities as junk. Yet, as in previous eras, today's financial markets are less concerned with headlines than with the profits that can be earned by matching investors seeking the highest returns with issuers seeking the lowest cost of financing. The fact that some of the issuers lack the size, history, or credit characteristics necessary for investment grade ratings is hardly surprising. American entrepreneurial history is largely composed of enterprises that started with little financial credibility.

Historical Background

Simply put, generic "junk" is high yielding debt. Young companies, and companies requiring new strategies and structures to survive, have always relied on high yielding debt. In fact, the high yield market is as old as the securities market itself and dates back to the earliest years of the Republic. As economist and historian Robert Sobel has detailed, perhaps the earliest junk securities in the United States were sovereign notes issued by Alexander Hamilton to redeem $80 million of foreign debt and secured by the anticipated sale of public lands to meet interest payments. The issuing interest rate was 6 percent, considerably higher than the going rate, but rose to 7 percent when the bonds fell during the early days of the Republic.

Many of our nation's best-known corporations were initially financed with "junk" bonds. In order to form U.S. Steel, J. P. Morgan was required to issue $225.6 million in mortgage bonds to Andrew Carnegie to purchase

Carnegie's steel company, and another $80 million to purchase and consolidate other steel manufacturing facilities.

In 1910, when Morgan had announced that 5 percent interest would draw money from the moon, William C. Durant, founder of General Motors, agreed to pay creditors 7 percent for refinancing that saved the company after a string of acquisitions inhibited cash flow and threatened to abort the automobile giant with an early bankruptcy. That same year, Charlie Flint was unable to sell stock in a new firm called Computing-Tabulating-Recording. Instead, he placed $7 million in 6 percent "junk" bonds with Guarantee Trust Company. By 1924, as the company developed, he changed the name to International Business Machines.

At times in history, financing ownership change has been the only method to insure that new management would abandon practices destructive to the economic value of the firm. Back in 1920, Charles Sieberling had bought a lot of rubber inventory for tire production at high cost. The world rubber market collapsed and so did Goodyear—almost. By 1921, Goodyear was on the edge of bankruptcy, with a book value of *minus* $44 a share and its common stock selling for around $5. Dillon Read, the firm's investment banker at the time, resorted to junk bonds. Under this plan, $97.5 million was raised for Goodyear at an average interest rate of 14 percent, nearly double the typical rates of the day. The offering increased working capital, refinanced bank debt, and retired merchandising debt. The creditors' committee, merchandisers' creditors' committee, and Dillon gained control of new management stock and took over the company. But the medicine worked—a hostile takeover financed by junk debt saved Goodyear.

Historical precursors of junk bonds are found in many varied forms of financial innovations of earlier decades. Tufano (1989) has detailed the large menu of alternative securities to finance America's infrastructure and industrial growth during the nineteenth and early twentieth century. In each era of financial innovation, the new securities allowed investors and issuers to reallocate risk, enhance liquidity, and reduce the costs of financing.

The motivation for these changes emanated from tax and regulatory changes, volatile inflation and interest rates, and changes in financial or information technology, all of which influence financial markets. In each era of economic change, financial innovations try to match the preferences of investors with the needs of issuers.

Economic growth, business failure, and new information about businesses shaped new financial instruments. Forms of secured credit (real estate, securities, physical assets) grew during the nineteenth century with the growth of canals and railroads. Unsecured debt obligations and small-denomination bonds grew during the first decades of this century as newer industries replaced railroads as major creditors and smaller investors entered the market.

Zero-coupon bonds, convertible bonds, preferred stock with proceeds tied to cash flow, and commodity-linked bonds were all innovations—along with changes in standard contract terms—that began in the early decades of twentieth-century industrialization and market expansion.

Business Development and Reconstruction

It is a fact of economic life that as businesses mature, they must either renew themselves or disappear. In the process, other industries will naturally emerge, providing products and services that support the demands of the current marketplace. While the growth of the automobile industry made saddle bags and buggy whips obsolete, it brought with it a new demand for tires, engines, transmissions, and axles, and created new markets for gasoline, insurance, and tourism. The development of new businesses and the re-creation of old ones are essential elements in periods of economic transition and are accompanied by waves of firm formation and job creation. These waves are often driven by fundamental economic, social, and technological changes in products, production processes, and distribution, or by progressive changes in transportation and communication.

Sobel (1989) has identified waves of corporate creation financed through different forms of high yield securities. From 1890 to 1910, communications and railroad infrastructure facilitated the creation of a national market. "United," "National," "Republic," and "American" began to appear in company names with increasing frequency as businesses shifted from local and regional to national customer bases. In order to take advantage of the opportunities of a huge domestic market, companies needed capital to grow. With few exceptions, however, the capital markets of the time were dominated exclusively by the security issues of railroads, telephone companies, or large public projects.

Changes in incorporation laws, the creation of a natural geographic market, and the availability of low-cost land and labor led to a rapid rise in firm formation. The only barrier to business development was access to affordable capital. With economic demand in place, investment bankers created a new financial product, industrial preferred stock, that was appropriate for newer firms. At the time, the investment community had no appetite for common shares of industrial start-ups or consolidations, in light of the perceived risks and the prevailing view of economic value. As Sobel explains:

> The conventional wisdom of the time held that a company was worth little more than the net asset value of its entire holdings, and that any part of its price above that was somehow illegitimate. Though today we recognize intangible assets and future prospects of a company are quite valuable, and that the price of stock should take these factors into account, to prudent investors of that day, this seemed tantamount to fraud.

While U.S. government securities were yielding less than 3 percent and high-grade railroad bonds were offering yields of less than 4 percent, industrial preferred stocks offered 7 percent dividend yields. These financial instruments resembled the perpetual bonds issued in the early nineteenth century, paying fixed amount of dividends and carrying no call provisions. The returns available from preferreds were substantially higher than from bonds of the same companies. Industrial preferreds were, in short, the high yield securities of the turn of the century.

Another form of high yielding nondebt investment that accompanied entrepreneurial growth emerged in the new-equity-issue market of the 1950s and 1960s. New incorporations and business combinations rose steadily during the post-World War II period. High-risk, speculative common stocks were issued, promising attractive capital gains. The number of shareholders increased nearly fivefold, from 6.5 million in 1952 to 30.9 million in 1970, and in 1968, price/earnings ratios rose to an all-time high.

Fallen Angels and Advances in Credit Analysis

By definition, nonrated or below-investment grade bonds have existed ever since the bond rating system began in 1909. Until World War II, junk bonds accounted for 17 percent of all publicly issued straight corporate debt. The greatest increase in high yield bonds occurred during the Depression, when the number of "fallen angels"—issues that were downgraded from their original investment grade rating—exploded. In order to measure the differences between different debt securities, the number of basis points (one-hundredth of a percent) is used to measure yield differences. From 1929 to 1934 the difference (or spread) between Aaa and Baa industrials ballooned from 38-111 basis points to 225-599 points. Nevertheless, the default rate for downgraded issues was low—no industrial issue over $20 million defaulted.

During the late 1940s and 1950s, scholars such as W. Braddock Hickman, T. R. Atkinson, and O. K. Burrell studied the paradox of low rated debt and its high risk-adjusted performance to develop a more precise measure of credit analysis.

Hickman had closely examined the rating systems and their impact on bond pricing. He found that during various points in the business cycle, lower rated bonds performed better than higher rated ones. He noted,

> errors in judgment committed by the rating systems arose from a failure to appraise accurately the earnings trend of the different industries and to allow fully for cyclical risks... issues in the high quality classes (including large issues of labor obligators) had the lowest default rates, promised yields, and loss rates; but the returns obtained by those who held them over long periods were generally below those on low-grade issues. (Hickman, 1958, p. 13)

Within the framework of traditional credit analysis at the time, differentials in bond yields were directly a result of default risk. The greater the variability of returns from a bond investment, the greater the risk. According to this "insurance theory" of yield differentials, investors were insured proportionate to their risk. But, based on empirical studies of the bond market, Hickman, Burrell, and others documented at length that this theory was incorrect. They first quantified the actual risk premiums paid to various bond investors. A risk premium is the extra yield (owning to various types of risk inherent in an investment) over the risk-free rate. For companies, this meant that they would pay investors a risk premium in the form of higher interest rates than those paid by U.S. Treasury notes to compensate for the higher default risk inherent in a private company.

What they found was that bond investors had been overinsured by the market for default risk. The risk premiums they calculated for high yielding, low-rated bonds were far greater than necessary to compensate for the actual risk of default. In other words, relative to other securities, "junk" bonds provided superior performance, even after accounting for their relative perceived risk. Hence, on a risk-adjusted basis, returns for downgraded securities far exceeded the returns of their investment grade counterparts.

The later application of this theory to the new issue junk bond market corresponds closely with the experience earlier observed by financial scholars tracking the junk bond market of the 1930s and 1950s, which was composed only of fallen angels. Throughout the 1980s, total returns from high yield bonds, even after losses, continued to exceed both Treasuries and investment grade bonds. Even during the falling junk bond market in the Fall of 1989, high yield securities traded at an average of 600-plus basis points over the U.S. Treasury rate. Even defaulted bonds continued to trade, which resulted in recovery value over time of 40-50 percent. In other words, defaults did not result in total loss, but investors generally were able to recover 40-50 percent of the bonds' value. Accordingly, the annualized loss rate for the high yield market was 1.4 percent, or less than the annual default rate (2.5 percent), reflecting the fact that even defaulted bonds retained value.

Corporate financial analysis was simultaneously evolving. Instead of viewing companies solely in terms of their static capital structure, Modigliani and Miller (1958) showed that the cost of capital should be understood in terms of the underlying real flows of income and expense, which seldom were apparent in traditional valuation criteria. Their work shifted valuation conventions from an equity analysis based primarily on book earnings to a more cash-flow driven investment perspective. Because cash is the fuel that drives a business, cash flow has become the most important financial statistic. Cash flow, of course, is calculated by adding noncash charges such as depreciation to net income after taxes. Net worth accounting alone could not explain the values present or potentially realizable within a firm. Consequently, investors shifted their focus away from the equity layer of the capital structure toward other layers of financing, namely debt.

Debt is classified generally in both junior and senior forms, depending on the priority accorded to the creditor's claim for repayment. Senior debt refers to that class which has priority repayment of both interest and principal over all other classes of debt and equity. Loans from financial institutions and certain high-grade debt securities such as mortgage bonds are senior debt. Since that debt is less risky, it is associated with a lower rate of interest compared with debt that has a more subordinated claim (various forms of junior debt).

In terms of economic theory, Modigliani and Miller demonstrated that, to optimize firm performance and growth, the corporate capital structure could and should seek the mix of debt and equity that best lowered the costs of capital. In terms of credit theory and analysis, Hickman, Burrell, and their colleagues empirically demonstrated that from the investor's perspective, the market created opportunities for higher returns on investment. From the standpoint of the issuer and the investor, these intellectual tools enabled the junk bond revolution to occur. With the oil shocks of the 1970s, interest rate spikes, inflation, the rise of global competition, and the faltering of U.S. economic dominance, the macroeconomic demands for new instruments to finance business restructuring were growing. The pieces of this financial-economic puzzle existed. Now, all that was necessary was for someone to put them together.

The Junk Bond Revolution

By the early 1970s, short-term floating-rate bank debt was the primary source of capital for corporations, especially those that failed to qualify for investment grade ratings. As inflation spiraled and interest rates rose dramatically, companies began to look for a more stable and cost-effective source of capital. Investors were also experiencing the effects of inflation and looking for ways to increase their returns. Conditions were ripe for financial innovators to create new products that would address the needs of companies seeking affordable fixed-rate funding and investors seeking higher yields. Together, these needs gave birth to the new issue junk bond market.

In the early 1970s, a young student at the Wharton School, the business school at the University of Pennsylvania, had carefully reviewed the studies by Hickman and combined them with his own research to form the analytic basis for what turned out to be the new issue high yield bond market. His name was Michael R. Milken, and his role in the subsequent development of the high yield bond market led the *Wall Street Journal* (in 1989, on its one-hundredth anniversary of publishing) to refer to him as "arguably the most important financial thinker of the century" and list him as one of the ten most important business leaders who shaped the century. *Life* magazine named him as one of the five people who transformed the decade of the 1980s.

Milken was able to demonstrate that the spreads between noninvestment grade and investment grade bonds had continued to widen since the mid-1950s. Accordingly, he realized that the rewards of a portfolio of high yield bonds far outran the risks.

After finishing his courses at the Wharton School, Milken began work in the Philadelphia office of Drexel Firestone. In 1973 he moved to the New

York office, and in the same year the firm was acquired by Burnham and Company. I. W. "Tubby" Burnham, who had started his investment firm during the Depression, recalled his first meeting with Michael Milken. "Mike worked away trading securities nobody else was interested in. I offered him $28,000 a year and increased the position that he could handle from $500,000 to $2 million. I allowed him to keep a dollar for every three he made. He doubled the position's value in a year. Our deal never changed."

By 1974, Fredrick H. Joseph joined the renamed Drexel Burnham Lambert from Shearson Hutton in order to remake the firm into a major player on Wall Street. He met Milken, who was already trading and recommending what he called "high reward bonds" to large institutional investors in insurance companies, pension funds, and banks. On Wall Street, however, these bonds were widely scorned as "chinese paper" and "junk"—designating their higher perceived risk and lower value relative to investment grade securities.

The step from creating a market of fallen angels and troubled securities to realizing that the same market might purchase securities for healthy, growing businesses wracked by interest rate volatility was a short one. As Joseph described it,

> Mike thought he could see some real potential there! Suddenly, all these companies that had never been able to raise any money were out there. We said to each other, "Maybe we could sell their bonds." Almost immediately we got the bonds going for Texas International. I remember someone in corporate finance asking me, "Do you really think Milken has the ability to sell them?"

The first step in realizing a new high yield market was to perceive that demand for such financial products existed. The competition in the corporate bond market was concentrated in those companies that were rated as investment grade, only 564 parent companies and perhaps an equal number of subsidiaries that were or could have been rated investment grade. That left 21,000 publicly traded firms (95 percent of the publicly traded companies) with over $35 million in revenues that were not served by the corporate bond market.

Milken noted the irony that the companies could sell their equity, but not their debt.

> So we had a willingness to invest in the companies of the future— particularly on the equity side, but not on the debt side. So I asked myself, why? Why—after factual information covering this entire century, showing that noninvestment grade bonds put out higher rate of returns, and showing that they are less volatile, less risky—why does this skepticism still exist?

The mid-1970s were a trying time for companies seeking financing and investors seeking returns. Interest rates were spiking in the 12 percent range. Many of the country's top companies were going bankrupt—Woolworth, W. T. Grant, Ryder, U.S. Industries, Con Ed, Western Union, and much of the airline industry. Simultaneously, newer, less established companies that were posting record profits and volume growth were getting squeezed by their traditional lenders. As Milken recalls that period,

> The banks and a number of other people put out the message they wanted to reduce their exposure to a particular industry. So if you called your loan officer in to say: "We want to reduce our exposure to industry X. How do you do it?" Well, one, the companies that are financially weak and can't pay you back, they can't give you any money back so it isn't going to do you any good to ask them for a repayment. The companies like Exxon of the world you don't want to pay you back; you like to have that name on your books as a positive. So who pays you back? Who allows you to reduce your loans outstanding? The young, vibrant companies of the future who have the financial wherewithal to pay you back. But what you've done is, you've eliminated their opportunity for growth and you've put a crimp on their plans for the next five to ten years because they no longer have capital. And this was a major, major thing that occurred in the mid-seventies (speech, Institutional Investor Conference, March 1988).

When trying to finance their companies and their plans, people that owned or ran public companies in the mid-1970s were faced with volatility of both interest rates and the price value of their shares. Recalling the film *Network* which was popular in the seventies, Milken notes,

> they (owners and managers) were sick and tired and they were not going to take it anymore. They were not going to have the future of their business based on whether they're going to win a beauty contest (in the stock market) every day of the week... and they wanted to protect themselves from volatile interest rate movements.

The solution to the problem was the selling of fixed-rate long-term debt:

> You know what your cost is: it's an insurance policy. You would have five, ten, twenty years to work out your plans. Your success will be dependent on your ability and the value of your plans, not on whether interest rates were going to go up and down the next week, and how the cost of your money might change, or whether you were no longer the favorite because some people didn't believe in your industry. This all occurred in the mid-seventies. What we saw and felt was a desire for corporations who lost the flexibility to finance, to put out permanent capital and reduce, not increase their risk.

From the investor side, a similar dynamic was under way. Tremendous volatility in the equity markets existed. As credit analysis shifted from accounting to economic criteria, a focus on cash-flow criteria for valuating a company enabled investors to perceive that they could move their investment dollars up the capital structure from equity to debt and get a higher rate of return. Even as equity values exploded, the rate of return for noninvestment grade bonds increased. In a new issue high yield market, new opportunities for investors were created as well. Speaking in 1988, Milken summarized why creating a market for junk bonds was of interest for investors,

> So now you have a vehicle that's far less volatile in terms of price movement. For example, governments have twice the price volatility of junk bonds. Obviously, stocks might be four times as volatile. You have a higher rate of return, and you're more senior in the capital structure.

The year of Drexel's first new issue high yield securities was 1977. By that year, junk securities had declined to only 12 percent of all corporate bonds. Until that year, noninvestment grade securities lacked a consistent, liquid market, so new issues of public debt were essentially limited to investment grade companies. Until that year, the only way corporate bonds could achieve junk status was by losing their investment grade rating through poor performance.

When a company's bond rating was lowered, its securities fell in price. The resulting increase in yield was often more than enough to compensate bond buyers for any increase in default risk. Unfortunately, many investors, including pension funds and other institutions, were forced by rules and regulations to limit their holdings to investment grade securities and jettison high yield bonds.

The junk bond revolution began in 1977, when Drexel began developing new issue high yield bonds. Seven deals were done that year for companies that had previously been shut out of the corporate bond market. Investors began to realize that, as Hickman had long ago studied and Milken demonstrated in his trading experience, if you took into account the risk associated with high yield securities (i.e., computed the risk-adjusted return), junk bonds could be excellent investments, outperforming investment grade bonds over time. Having developed the credit analysis tools for qualifying companies that would benefit from high yield investments, Drexel Burnham created distribution channels for these high yield bonds, and investors supported the market. This enabled companies to begin issuing bonds that were below investment grade from their inception. New issue junk bonds increased the proportion of high yield corporate financing back to prewar levels. Contrary to conventional wisdom, junk bonds were issued and marketed successfully by design and not just as fallen angels. The analytical breakthroughs by Hickman in credit analysis and Modigliani and Miller in corporate finance fused in the growth of the high yield market and the firms it sponsored.

As Michael Milken started recommending "high reward bonds" to his clients, he found it hard to escape the street language characterization of these securities as "junk." He viewed the use of that unfortunate moniker philosophically and with some humor,

> When you look back in history, you find that most things that are new are all rated junk.... Everything that seems to stand the test of time is junk. And particularly, everything someone else thinks of is junk. And I think this somewhat characterizes the way the junk bond market was greeted.

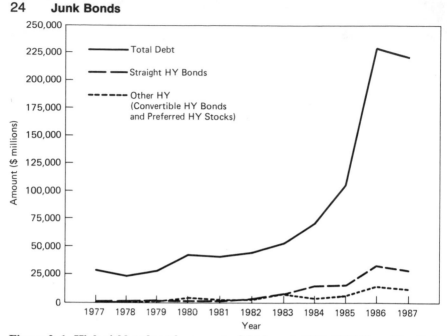

Figure 2–1. High yield and total corporate debt issued, 1977–1987 (Securities Data Company, Inc.)

By 1983, the amount of high yield securities began to rise sharply (Figure 2-1). Due to the growth of new noninvestment grade issues, by 1987 junk securities represented approximately 24 percent of all outstanding corporate

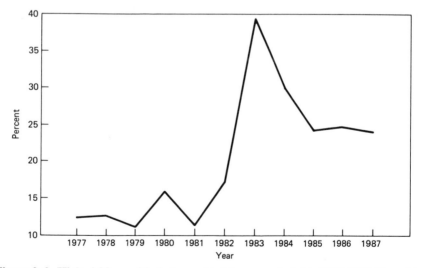

Figure 2–2. High yield securities' share of total corporate debt, 1977–1987 (Securities Data Company, Inc.)

debt (Figure 2-2). Less than one third of the total junk bond market consists of fallen angels (Rasky, 1986). It is important to note that increases in high yield debt follow rather than lead trends in increased corporate indebtedness.

As junk bonds outperformed their investment grade counterparts, confidence in the rating system as a determinant of bond value declined. The structure of corporate and personal taxes, increased capital needs for restructuring, and shifts in the relationship between outstanding debt and default risk attracted both issuers and investors to the junk bond market (Fridson and Wahl, 1987; Altman and Namacher, 1987; Pozdena, 1987; Schrager and Sherman, 1987).

The opening of the high yield bond market gave issuers affordable access to fixed-rate funding, without the covenants and restrictions associated with bank loans and private placements. By issuing high yield bonds, corporations could also avoid costly and dilutive common stock offerings. In short, the high yield market allowed noninvestment grade companies to raise funds faster, cheaper, and with fewer negotiations.

With greater flexibility and lower capital costs, issuers could more effectively respond to changing industrial and international trends. High yield firms found that they could deploy their assets toward new objectives, make better use of technological advances, and more flexibly adapt to competitive pressures.

Within a decade at Drexel, Milken raised $93 billion, and the junk bond market grew to nearly $200 billion, serving over 1,500 companies. Barry S. Friedberg, head of investment banking at Merrill Lynch, described Milken's contribution this way: "Let there be no doubt about it: No individual has done more in at least the last twenty-five years to alter the face of corporate finance." Boone Pickens once put it to me succinctly, "Give me 100 Michael Milkens on our team on the international economic playing field and we wouldn't have a U.S. budget or trade deficit." Michael Jensen, professor of business administration at Harvard University, said, "Today's high yield bonds are one of the most important innovations in recent financial history. What Milken did was dramatically show how to use the idea and apply it." As Milken himself sees it, "Junk bonds allow entrepreneurs outside the system to get capital to realize their dreams." Interestingly, in a world of finance characterized by quantitative methods, numerical minutiae, and concrete business plans, the first question Milken was to ask entrepreneurs and managers seeking to raise money when they visited his office concerned their ideas. "What are your hopes and dreams?" he would ask.

Milken's insight was not simply the product of refining and applying financial analysis, central as that was. Personally, he had seen his career develop through identifying the opportunities that emerged from the perceived discrepancy between accounting and economic criteria for evaluating business plans. "Business and society are intertwined," he often said. "The best businessmen, the best investor, has always been a social scientist. He has always been concerned with people; he's always tried to figure out what people want and what the people's needs are." Perhaps even more important than Hickman was Milken's fascination in the late 1970s with John Naisbitt's theories about the major trends shaping the future—the importance of human capital and the notion of knowledge as the scarcest and most important resource.

The purpose of high yield credit analysis and investment was to "add value" to the company. The ubiquitous mention of value creation in the high yield market refers not only to increasing the market value of the company. Indeed, market valuation is considered a reflection of more intrinsic advances in technology, distribution, or production. As Milken put it, "the value of a company and a business is the knowledge and wisdom and vision of its employees." Whether it was cellular communication, employees seeking to purchase a divested lumber mill, a bankrupt shipbuilding company, biotechnology, entertainment, or health care, Milken was most interested in businesses that were reconceptualizing their industry and redefining their business structure and strategy.

As we shall see, whole industries like cable television, entertainment, cellular communications, and health care were made over through the use of high yield financing. Companies like Chrysler, Quanex, Stone Container, and others recovered and redirected their corporate fortunes from decline to recovery.

Junk Bonds on the Defensive

Though initially conceived of for use by small, growing companies, the application of high yield financing enabled controversial takeovers in the airline industry, telecommunications, and manufacturing that restructured and refocused business development. How did this happen? How did this junk bond revolution result in such support while simultaneously generating such a political and prosecutorial backlash?

The positive experience of utilizing high yield securities for internal growth or strategic acquisition by small and medium-sized companies became widespread during the early 1980s. Despite later perceptions and reporting to the contrary, high yield securities were never primarily used for hostile takeovers. As we will see in Chapter 4, for the 1,100 high yield issues occurring between 1980 and 1986, less than 3 percent at most were used for hostile or unsolicited transactions. The U.S. General Accounting Office's study of the high yield market, covering data for 1985-1986 (at the peak of hostile takeovers) found that only slightly over 15 percent of the high yield securities were used for such transactions.

The insight that high yield financing could be used for hostile takeovers did not take place until November 1984. The first hostile takeover (of Electric Storage Battery by International Nickel) had taken place a decade earlier and involved no junk bonds at all. The concept of using junk bonds to finance hostiles originated not in Drexel's Beverly Hills high yield department, but among bankers in the corporate finance department in New York. Milken initially opposed the idea of pursuing the takeover market, but was encouraged to do so by his colleagues, who perceived it as a growing source of demand for new high yield issues.

The seeds of the political backlash against the high yield market that later haunted Milken and Drexel Burnham were sown during the early hostile takeover attempts against big oil companies in 1985. As we shall detail further in Chapter 10, the mobilization against takeovers and junk bonds began in earnest during Boone Pickens's attempt to acquire UNOCAL. In the process, Pickens instead acquired the unending enmity for himself and the high yield market of UNOCAL's CEO, Fred Hartley, and his colleagues in the largest oil companies and some of the largest corporations.

Analysts generally conceded that the oil companies were poorly run at the time and exemplified corporate bureaucracy and waste. Excessive executive perks (Hartley's corporate jet contained a grand piano) and the pursuit of negative-present-value projects, such as drilling oil while demand plummeted, were characteristic of oil-company performance. But it was not the economics of high yield securities or the need for ownership change to maximize market and economic values that was the issue.

The Business Roundtable, the public policy organization representing the Fortune Top 200 companies, the American Petroleum Institute, and other corporate interest groups representing big oil companies, quickly organized lobbying efforts against takeovers and high yield financing. The Securities and Exchange Commission was reported to have also been contacted, and the resulting investigative scrutiny led to indictments. Thirty-seven states passed antitakeover laws or regulations restricting high yield securities. Much similar legislation was introduced in Congress, leading to restrictions on Savings and Loan investments in high yield securities and other measures still under consideration.

In financing change, the high yield market generated market support for untried products, technologies, strategies, and management. As we have seen, "junk" financing represented a paradigmatic shift in credit analysis, corporate finance, and the definition of the role of financial institutions. Investment and control, management and ownership, and financing and industrial interests were reintegrated. The flexibility of these new financial instruments was reflected in the new entrepreneurial, nonbureaucratic companies that were market driven and not dominated by more hierarchical, tradition bound corporate organizations that had dominated the U.S. economy for most of this century. Between the pages of economic data to be reviewed in the next chapters, a new economic and organizational paradigm can be seen to emerge, one that would recast American business in the 1980s and would survive both a period of turmoil in the junk bond market and the demise of Drexel Burnham.

3

The Role of Corporate Debt

A variety of factors helped create favorable conditions for the rise of the high yield bond market (Perry and Taggert, 1987):

- Deregulation and competition forced banks to offer higher rates to depositors, making up for their increased costs by lending to corporations at higher rates.
- New regulatory standards for pension funds and institutions (e.g., ERISA) allowed money managers to pursue higher yield investments.
- Interest and inflation rate volatility made fixed-rate funding attractive to corporations, and gave investors strong incentives to seek higher yields.
- Increased international capital flows and securities registration changes expanded the capital markets and attracted international investors seeking high returns.

Since the opening of the high yield bond market in 1977, the composition of corporate debt has shifted away from bank loans and toward the capital markets (Figures 3-1 and 3-2). As commercial banks became less competitive, their share of total corporate debt fell by 8 percent, while the combined credit market share of corporate debt increased by over 13 percent.

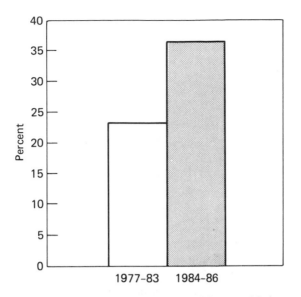

Figure 3–1. Credit market debt (bonds and other debt securities) as percentage of total sources of funds (bank loans, private placements, and credit market debt), 1977–1983 (Federal Reserve Flow of Funds Accounts)

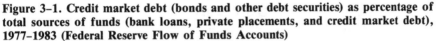

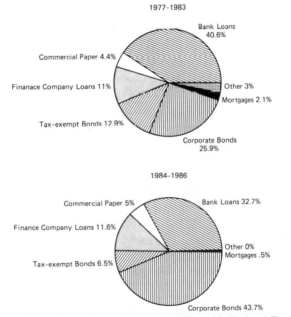

Figure 3-2. Composition of credit market debt, 1977–1983 (Federal Reserve Flow of Funds Accounts)

Comparing the composition of credit market debt in 1977-1983 with that in 1984-1986, we find that tax-exempt bonds as a source of capital decreased to 6.5 percent from 12.9 percent. Commercial banks became less responsive to businesses as a source of capital, as indicated by bank loan declines. Mortgages decreased slightly, to 0.5 percent from 2.1 percent. Finance company loans increased slightly, to 11.6 percent from 11.7 percent. Commercial paper also increased somewhat, to 5.0 percent from 4.4 percent. Corporate bonds, on the other hand, increased significantly, to 43.7 percent from 25.9 percent.

The Role of Debt in Corporate Capital Structure

Recent evidence about the performance of U.S. firms relative to their foreign competitors suggests that higher capital costs have been a significant element in the weakening of U.S. competitiveness. Many companies find it difficult to adapt to competitive pressures and changing market trends because banks will not extend credit, or because market conditions or the firm's size make equity offerings undesirable. These problems of capital allocation and their impact on corporate capital structures are reflected in macroeconomic terms in our national accounts. The U.S. rate of capital investment has traditionally been lower than that of our major trading partners. Net nonresidential fixed investments, or additions to productive capacity, have ranged between 1.5 percent and 2.9 percent of GNP. This figure is considerably lower than during the 1960s and most of the 1970s, and roughly half the level of investment by most EEC nations and Japan. Capital investment rates peaked in the mid-1980s and have since declined.

Even when capital is available, its costs may be prohibitive. The weighted average real cost of various investments was 10.7 percent in the United States according to the International Trade Commission (NIR) (1983) and Hatsopoulos (1983), but only 4.1 percent in Japan. In long-term research and development, the Japanese cost of capital was 2.4 percent, compared to 10.1 percent in the United States. Overall, U.S. firms faced capital costs that were 7-9 percent higher than their European and Japanese competitors.

Both the amount and the composition of debt have been strongly influenced by the relatively lower costs of debt capital. Corporate debt as a proportion of GNP rose from 34 percent in 1983 to 42 percent in 1987. Is this debt excessive? The question needs to be more precisely stated: Excessive to whom and for what purpose?

There are several commonly analyzed measures of the level of debt in the economy:

- The ratio of debt to domestic output for nonfinancial corporations
- Net interest as a share of gross cash flow (i.e., the amount of net cash generated by a business)
- The ratio of short- to long-term debt

From the early 1950s through the mid-1970s, corporations steadily increased their dependence on debt. While corporate debt ratios have also increased in the 1980s, they remain well below the levels of the mid-1970s. Net interest as a share of gross cash flow has grown, but is not substantially higher than it was in the seventies. Short- to long-term debt ratios have fallen as firms have sought more predictable financing and more efficient sources of low-cost capital (Bernanke and Campbell, 1988).

Relative to the underlying market value of the equity grown through debt, corporations do not appear overly leveraged (Bernanke and Campbell, 1988). Debt/equity ratios fell from 84 percent to 74 percent from 1983 to 1988. By this measure, Meltzer and Richard (1987) have shown that corporate debt peaked in the mid-1970s and has declined since then. Debt increases have resulted in equity growth and increased share prices. According to U.S. Department of Commerce figures on corporate profits, the capacity to service debt has remained relatively stable even though absolute levels of debt have risen. Interest coverage (income/interest payments) hovered between 6.2 and 6.4 from 1974 through 1986.

Relative to foreign corporations, U.S. companies also appear to be underleveraged. In the manufacturing sector, German and Japanese corporations averaged 66 percent and 64 percent of debt in their respective capital structures, compared to 30 percent for similar U.S. firms. Foreign manufacturers showed a lower after-tax cost of capital, increased volume and profitability growth rates, and reduced short-term pressures for share/price performance. As a percent of GNP, corporate debt is 100 percent in Japan, 70 percent in Germany, 65 percent in Canada, and only 42 percent in the United States.

Examining evidence from the oil and tobacco industries, Jensen (1986) showed that when cash flow was used to service debt, other value-increasing transactions ensued through changes in corporate strategy, acquisitions, product introductions, and development of new markets. In those industries, the weight of debt acted as an anchor, forcing management to maximize efficiency and productivity to meet interest payments. Or, as Merton Miller put it more bluntly, "By accepting such debt-service burdens, moreover, the managers are making a binding commitment to themselves and to the other residual equity holders against yielding to the temptations... to pour the firm's good money down investment rat holes" (Miller, 1988, p. 115).

Risk Assessment and the Financial Impact of High Yield Securities

As Hickman, Burrell, Milken, and others have noted, the standards used in assessing financial risk may fail to adequately reflect a company's economic prospects when taking competitive risks or entering new markets. Rating agencies such as Moody's or Standard & Poor's have developed their own criteria for determining whether or not a company will receive an investment grade rating. New companies may lack the size, capital structure, or history needed to qualify as investment grade. Companies that are entering new markets, introducing new products, or facing structural or strategic changes may be unable to document past performance and provide an adequate indication of future performance. As a result, such companies are typically denied investment grade ratings.

As an overall indicator of financial risk, investment grade ratings are not as reliable as many people assume. In some ways, junk bonds have proven to be superior investments.

- In examining variations between investment grade bonds and their relative default risk, Broske (1987) found that bond rating assignments were poor predictors of default probability.
- While default rates of junk bonds were relatively higher than for investment grade issues, the default rate has been skewed by significant bankruptcies (e.g., LTC, REVCO). When adjustments are made for the duration of the issue and the firm's underlying asset base, high yield bonds showed lower total risk (Altman and Namacher 1986).
- Blume and Keim (1987) found an annualized compound monthly rate of return of 11.04 percent for junk bonds compared to 9.6 percent for long-term Treasury bonds.
- Altman (1988) indicated that over time, yields for junk bonds have expanded while risks have remained unchanged.
- Pound (1988) showed that the markets provided firms raising new capital through debt issues with higher stock prices.
- Wharton Econometric Forecasting Associates (WEFA) (1988) found that except for consumer credit cards, the risk-adjusted return on high yield bonds has been consistently greater than on other types of assets generally held by thrift institutions. Similarly, a study by a regional bank showed that high yield corporate bonds outperformed commercial loans in a number of dimensions relevant to portfolio management—liquidity, asset/liability management, financial information, diversification, yield spreads, and credit quality.

A recent counterargument about the financial performance of high yield securities comes from a study of Asquith, Mullins, and Wolff (1989), which claims that default rates of junk bonds are substantially higher than those reported in earlier studies—34 percent of junk bonds sold in 1977 and 1978 wound up in default by 1988. The difference between this study and all previous default studies is not based on underlying data differences, but on the way those rates were calculated. The study confounds cumulative default risk with average annual default rates. The Asquith computation is based upon the default rate for 1977 and 1978 issues in ensuing years up to 1988. More commonly, default rates are computed as the volume of defaults versus all junk bonds outstanding, not just the fraction of a single year's issuance that defaulted.

Additionally, while the study examines default risk, it fails to consider subsequent returns. As discussed above, the returns of junk bonds have more than compensated for incremental lending risk. The study also fails to consider default recovery rates. Many defaulted bonds trade at near or above par. The average recovery rate for all junk bond defaults is approximately forty cents on the dollar. Finally, by taking issues only from 1977 to 1978, the Asquith study focuses on the junk bond market during early years of its learning curve. A disproportionate amount of bonds (32 percent) and subsequent defaults (34 percent) were concentrated in the oil and steel industries, sectors that were hit particularly hard by oil price shocks, foreign competition, and the 1980-1982 recession.

Nevertheless, during the severe downturn of the market during the fall of 1989, the widespread press reporting of the Asquith study continued to haunt all high yield securities and feed investors' fears. Actually, the study found a 3.4 percent *annual default rate* over a period of 10 years for a small group of high yield bonds (about 78 issues in a universe of over 1,500), which is only slightly higher than previous findings.

The default rate alone, however, is not necessarily the most significant event in the market history of bonds. Returns on investment are more critical. A follow-up study of the bonds in the Asquith study, by Marshall E. Blume and Donald B. Keim (1989), showed that because of significantly higher yields, those 78 bonds still returned 8.51 percent annually, or more than Treasuries or high grade corporate bonds (whose yield to maturities were 7.6 percent for intermediate Treasuries, 8.08 percent for long-term Treasuries and 8.43 percent for a composite of triple-A corporate bonds).

Regardless, concerns about the high yield market continued to focus on the ability of companies in that market to withstand an economic downturn. David Wyss, Christopher Probyn, and Robert de Angelis of Data Resources Inc., one of the nation's largest economic forecasting firms, attempted to model four different recessionary scenarios—including a "soft landing" of the business cycle, a deep inflationary recession, and a severe recession without inflation—for about 600 high yield companies, using the companies' balance sheet information. Under all scenarios, high yield bonds continued to outperform Treasuries, high-grade corporate bonds, CDs, and mortgage-backed securities. This modeling study is consistent with an earlier study by Stephen Waite and Martin Fridson (1989) which indicated that the concentration of junk bond issues by public firms and LBOs was mainly in those sectors where cash-flow volatility was lower and the ability to shoulder debt load was greater.

To be economically beneficial, debt issues must do more than reconfigure a company's financial structure. They must provide a positive contribution to the firm's operations, earnings, and long-range performance. They must enhance the company's value through successful strategies and investments.

To the degree that noninvestment grade securities are helping companies achieve these goals, they are indeed beneficial. Whether we utilize default risk or rate of return as the criterion, the quality of noninvestment grade securities appears to be understated by rating services. Moreover, the presence of high yield securities on a company's balance sheet does not appear to have a deleterious impact on equity value. In fact, evidence suggests that firms that raise new capital and put it to work consolidating their industry or aggressively pursuing opportunities are rewarded with higher stock prices (Pound, 1988).

In a later study of financial performance, Pound and Gordon (1989) found firms issuing high yield securities to have experienced increases in cash flow, earnings, dividend payments, sales, and capital spending. The firms' performance exceeded analysts' forecasts at the time of the issues. Price/earnings ratios (the current price of a stock divided by the current earnings per share, indicating market perception of future earnings) approximately doubled on the average, and price/cash-flow multiples (the multiple of cash flow calculated for the firm's market valuation) increased by about 10 percent, relative to their levels prior to the debt placements. Long-term and short-term profit growth also improved.

The Economic Effects of Leverage

To evaluate the impact of high yield financing on corporate performance, I needed more specific data and analysis. I wanted to investigate a number of questions that financial analysts could not answer, including:

- How do high yield issues change the way companies function?
- Do high yield bonds allow issuers to immediately expand employment, lease and equip new plants, or enter new markets?
- Did the funds go into research and development, or allow displacement of other funds for that purpose?
- How do high yield bonds affect the issuer's cost structure, sales, and market share expansion?

To address these questions, the study included a systematic examination of high yield companies, to assess their aggregate performance relative to industry figures. We also used individual case studies to document the specific effects of high yield financing on corporate performance and competitive positioning.

The impact of debt financing frequently transcends the effects seen on the balance sheet and income statement. The ultimate test of leverage is whether it can create economic value through firm growth and improved performance. Junk bonds have done more than simply provide capital. They've also helped companies enter new markets, succeed in new strategies, and attract additional funding from banks and equity investors. In the following chapters, we will examine the economic effects of high yield financing on new and existing firms in the public market and on businesses that have restructured through leveraged buyouts.

4

Analyzing High Yield Securities

For many industries, the 1980s were one of the most wrenching economic periods since the great Depression. An onslaught of foreign competition, high and volatile interest rates, a deep drop in economic activity, and a long but uneven expansion posed severe tests for many U.S. businesses.

At the same time, the 1980s held considerable promise for firms that were able to identify opportunities and mobilize their resources in productive directions. Whether firms pursued aggressive or defensive strategies, however, capital was critical to their success. As a result, a growing number of companies turned to the newly developed high yield bond market.

The use of high yield securities expanded rapidly. In 1980, 148 firms sold 161 high yield issues worth $5.35 billion (Table 4-1). Since then, the number of firms, number of issues, and the dollar value of issues all have grown together, with substantial variations from year to year. A major jump occurred in 1983, when the number of firms and issues almost doubled from 1982, and net proceeds grew by more than 250 percent—from $5.87 billion to $14.72 billion. In 1984, the number of firms and issues decreased slightly, but net proceeds continued to grow. Another big jump occurred in 1986, when new issuance leapt from about $21 billion to nearly $46 billion.

In the seven-year period from 1980 through 1986, 1,175 firms sold 1,742 issues of high yield securities, raising a total of $113.26 billion. During each of these years, there were substantially more issues than issuing firms, indicating that several firms had more than one issue in a year.

Table 4-1. The Growth of High Yield Securities, Number of Issuing Firms and Net Proceeds: 1980-1986

	1980	1981	1982	1983	1984	1985	1986	Total
No. of firms	148	116	125	215	168	283	423	1,478[1] (1,175)
issuing HY bonds	89	71	86	151	119	172	294	982[2] (755)
No. of	161	122	150	256	209	345	499	1,742[1]
issues	97	77	99	175	147	205	334	1,134[2]
Net Proceeds	5,350	3,689	5,867	14,724	16,325	21,309	45,996	113,261[1]
($ mil.)	3,106	2,644	4,360	9,960	11,565	11,505	24,212	67,352[2]

[1]Includes all publicly issued high yield securities.
[2]Includes only firms having available economic performance data for further analyses.

Numbers in parentheses are alternative counts of firms in which each firm is counted only once, no matter how many times it issued high yield bonds.

Source: Drexel Burnham Lambert, Inc.

The 755 high yield firms that will be described and discussed in Chapter 5 showed a similar growth pattern. Among these companies, eighty-nine firms sold ninety-seven issues for just under $3.11 billion in 1980. After a moderate dip in 1981, the annual issue amount grew almost continuously, with big leaps in 1983 and 1986. Altogether, these firms sold 1,134 issues from 1980 to 1986, raising $67.35 billion.

Use of Proceeds

What did high yield firms do with the funds they raised? To find out, we examined how all public firms issuing high yield bonds from 1980 through 1986 (Table 4-2). A full 73.70 percent of the proceeds were earmarked for corporate growth, and 21.90 percent were used for acquisition financing. Only 3.25 percent were used in unsolicited takeovers—disproving the popular myth that high yield securities are primarily used to fund hostile acquisitions. Secondary selling securities, or bonds that were purchased and later reissued, accounted for the remaining 1.16 percent of high yield bonds issued during the study period.

Lehn et al. (1986) found that junk bonds represented a relatively small portion of tender-offer financing. For 1985, the year of the study, junk bonds represented one sixth of all tender-offer financing, less than one quarter of financing against large targets, and less than one third of financing in hostile deals.

In the General Accounting Office's recent study of high yield bonds (1988), an examination of corporate takeover financing from 1985 to 1986 revealed that junk bonds represented only 12 percent of the total amount financed.

Table 4-2. Use of Proceeds by Year: All Firms Issuing High Yield Securities in 1980-1986

Year	Net Proceeds to Issuer	Corporate Growth				Acquisition Financing				Takeover Financing		Secondary
		General Corporate Purposes	Refinancing Bank Debt	Refinancing Other Debt	Recap.	Friendly Acqui.	Possible Future Acqui.	LBO	Refin. Acqui. Debt	Unsolicited Acqui.	Refin. Acqui. Debt	Selling Security Holders
1980 (N = 161)	5,350.3 (%)	2,391.9 (44.71)	2,162.7 (40.42)	402.3 (7.52)		7.0 (0.13)	42.6 (0.80)		252.6 (4.72)			91.0 (1.70)
1981 (N = 122)	3,689.2 (%)	2,296.1 (62.24)	1,012.4 (27.44)	99.1 (2.69)		17.8 (0.48)	104.3 (2.83)		159.4 (4.32)			
1982 (N = 150)	5,866.7 (%)	2,953.2 (50.34)	1,727.8 (29.45)	553.9 (9.44)		245.9 (4.19)	121.3 (2.07)		75.9 (1.29)			189.1 (3.22)
1983 (N = 256)	14,724.1 (%)	8,060.6 (54.74)	4,130.2 (28.05)	1,177.2 (8.00)	20.0 (0.14)	641.8 (4.36)	170.8 (1.16)		402.9 (2.74)			120.8 (0.82)
1984 (N = 209)	16,325.5 (%)	6,160.2 (37.73)	5,244.2 (32.12)	1,716.9 (10.52)		464.0 (2.84)	344.8 (2.11)	1259.3 (7.71)	1125.3 (6.89)			13.2 (0.08)
1985 (N = 345)	21,309.1 (%)	9,848.3 (46.22)	4,207.7 (19.75)	1,360.5 (6.36)	32.7 (0.15)	741.7 (3.48)	1027.1 (4.82)	1720.1 (8.07)	1914.1 (8.98)		183.8 (0.86)	273.0 (1.28)
1986 (N = 499)	45,996.2 (%)	14,468.4 (31.46)	7,857.6 (17.08)	5,037.9 (10.95)	546.8 (1.19)	5,525.6 (12.01)	1,781.5 (3.87)	655.0 (1.42)	6,000.2 (13.04)	2,413.8 (5.25)	1,087.5 (2.36)	622.2 (1.35)
Total (N = 1742)	113,261.1 (%)	46,178.7 (40.77)	26,342.6 (23.26)	10,347.8 (9.14)	599.5 (0.53)	7,643.8 (6.75)	3,592.4 (3.17)	3,634.3 (3.21)	9,930.4 (8.77)	2,413.8 (2.13)	1,271.3 (1.12)	1,309.3 (1.16)

Note: Dollar amounts are in millions.
N = number of issues.

Source: Drexel Burnham Lambert, Inc.

In short, while the use of junk bonds for takeovers varies with the study period and number of cases included, there appears to be nowhere near the level of use suggested by the popular press and political perception.

Within the segment of funds dedicated to corporate growth, 40.77 percent were used for general corporate purposes, including spending on plant construction, working capital, and asset purchases. Other uses included refinancing bank debt, 23.25 percent; refinancing other debt, 9.14 percent; and recapitalization, 0.53 percent.

In the acquisition category, refinancing acquisition debt had the largest share, 8.77 percent. This was followed by friendly acquisition debt, 6.75 percent; leveraged buyouts, 3.21 percent; and 3.17 percent for possible future acquisitions. In considering these figures, it is important to note that once a company has undergone a leveraged buyout, its private status removes it from the data on publicly owned companies considered in our study. Takeover financing included unsolicited acquisitions, 2.13 percent; and refinancing acquisition debt (usually bank debt) for takeovers, 1.12 percent.

To investigate the use of proceeds by industry, we analyzed data only for the 755 high yield firms that reported Standard Industrial Classification (SIC) codes and economic performance to COMPUSTAT. Hereafter, our analysis focuses only on this subset of all high yield issuers. The general pattern of fund allocation among these companies was similar to that for all high yield firms (Tables 4-3 and 4-4).

Overall, nearly half the proceeds, or 46.62 percent, was used for general corporate purposes, not reported to be earmarked for anything in particular. Another 26.26 percent went to refinance bank debt, and 9.84 percent was used to refinance other debt. Unfortunately, the data did not indicate when the bank or other debt was taken on, or for what purpose. Refinancing acquisition debt, however, was a separate category, and only 7.61 percent of high yield funding was used for that purpose.

In the acquisition category, 4.16 percent of funds were to be used in friendly acquisitions, and 2.71 percent were set aside for possible futures acquisitions. A mere 0.12 percent was earmarked for leveraged buyouts, though it should be noted that our study excluded private company issues.

In analyzing data by industry, we noticed a number of significant features:

- Insurance companies used a greater portion of their funds for friendly acquisitions (38.25 percent) than any other industry.
- The leaders in possible future acquisitions were business and professional services (11.71 percent) and communications (8.24 percent). Among communications firms, cable companies in particular have often grown by acquisitions.
- Nondurable manufacturers used 19.43 percent of their proceeds to refinance acquisition debt, well above the overall average of 7.61 percent.

Table 4–3. Use of Proceeds by Industry: Firms Issuing High Yield Securities in 1980-1986

Industry (2-digit SIC)	Issue Amount	General Corporate Purpose	Refinancing			Acquisition Financing				Takeover		N.
			Bank Debts	Other Debts	Recap.	Friendly Acqui.	Possible Future Acqui.	LBO	Refin. Acqui. Debts	Refin. Debts	Secondary Selling Sec. Holders	
Agricultural Products (01, 02)	177.0	31.4 (17.74)	97.6 (55.14)	48.0 (27.12)								4
Mining & Natural Res. Extraction	5,146.1	1,501.0 (29.17)	3,091.3 (60.07)	87.4 (1.70)		21.0 (0.41)	3.0 (0.06)		351.4 (6.83)		91.0 (1.77)	51
Construction (15-17)	255.2	98.4 (43.69)	117.6 (52.22)	6.7 (2.98)		2.5 (1.11)						7
Manufacturing, Durable	10,825.9	4,524.0 (41.79)	3,550.1 (32.79)	627.7 (5.80)	529.4 (4.89)	31.0 (0.29)	422.2 (3.90)		750.8 (6.94)	386.1 (3.57)	3.9 (0.04)	214
Manufacturing, Nondurable	6,354.7	2,353.7 (37.04)	1,539.2 (24.22)	732.1 (11.52)		358.3 (5.64)	25.5 (0.40)	41.2 (0.65)	1,234.5 (19.43)		70.3 (1.11)	84
Transportation (40-47)	4,461.8	3,381.1 (77.78)	619.2 (13.88)	169.5 (3.80)		77.8 (1.74)	111.6 (2.50)		1.5 (0.03)		101.0 (2.26)	58
Communications (48)	4,130.1	2,583.6 (62.56)	493.7 (11.95)	292.6 (7.08)		340.7 (8.25)	347.6 (8.42)		71.9 (1.74)			25
Public Utilities (49)	7,798.3	2,386.6 (30.60)	2,428.0 (31.13)	1,977.7 (25.36)					926.5 (11.88)		79.4 (1.02)	68
Wholesale Trade (50,51)	1,775.9	564.8 (31.80)	875.5 (49.30)	184.7 (10.40)			7.4 (0.42)		143.6 (8.09)			44
Retail Trade (52-59)	5,748.6	2,973.1 (51.72)	1,280.7 (22.28)	515.5 (8.97)		253.7 (4.41)	238.3 (4.15)		487.6 (8.48)			92
Finance (60-62, 67)	7,364.6	5,687.2 (77.22)	703.5 (9.55)	354.5 (4.81)	21.0 (0.27)	145.7 (1.84)	285.9 (3.62)	40.2 (0.51)	162.8 (2.06)		506.9 (6.41)	130
Insurance (63, 64)	1,854.8	502.7 (27.10)	25.0 (1.35)	371.7 (20.04)		709.4 (38.25)	47.6 (2.57)		198.4 (10.70)			20
Real Estate (65)	2,994.9	1,047.1 (34.01)	1,124.9 (37.56)	635.0 (21.20)		144.4 (4.82)	10.3 (0.34)		33.4 (1.12)			42
Business & Professional Services	1,813.6	664.7 (36.65)	634.2 (34.97)	158.9 (8.76)		100.0 (5.51)	212.3 (11.71)		43.7 (2.41)			44

Table 4-3 (continued)

Leisure & Repair Services	3,122.7	1,652.4 (52.92)	664.9 (21.29)	245.8 (7.87)	17.4 (0.56)	144.9 (4.64)	38.7 (1.24)		356.1 (11.40)		2.2 (0.07)	38
Health & Educational Services	3,016.8	1,444.7 (47.89)	440.9 (14.61)	222.7 (7.38)		470.1 (15.58)	77.8 (2.58)		360.8 (11.96)			61
Total	67,351.6,	31,396.5 (46.62)	17,686.3 (26.26)	6,630.5 (9.84)	567.8 (0.84)	2,799.5 (4.16)	1,828.2 (2.71)	81.4 (0.12)	5,123.0 (7.61)	388.1 (0.57)	854.7 (1.27)	982

Note: Only 755 firms with readily available performance data are included. All dollar figures are in millions. Numbers in parentheses are percentages (over issue amount).

Source: Drexel Burnham Lambert, Inc.

Table 4-4. Use of Proceeds by Industry: Manufacturing Firms Issuing High Yield Securities in 1980–1986

Industry (2-digit SIC)	Issue Amount	Refinancing				Acquisition Financing				Takeover		N.
		General Corporate Purpose	Bank Debts	Other Debts	Recap.	Friendly Acqui.	Possible Future Acqui.	LBO	Refin. Acqui. Debts	Refin. Debts	Secondary Selling Sec. Holders	
Lumber & Wood Products (24)	52.8	15.3 (28.98)	28.7 (54.36)	4.9 (9.28)							3.9 (7.39)	2
Furniture & Fixtures (25)	96.1	49.4 (51.40)	42.9 (44.64)	3.8 (3.95)								3
Stone, Clay, & Glass (32)	470.4	150.3 (31.95)	110.7 (23.53)	101.3 (21.53)					108.1 (22.98)			11
Primary Metal Industries (33)	1,040.0	302.7 (29.11)	506.5 (48.70)	226.5 (21.78)					4.3 (0.41)			15
Fabricated Metal Products (34)	1,178.6	506.6 (42.90)	213.0 (18.07)	80.3 (6.81)			177.3 (15.04)			202.3 (17.16)		17
Machinery, Except Electrical (35)	789.8	408.4 (51.06)	251.7 (31.47)	10.3 (1.29)			35.5 (4.44)		93.7 (11.72)			25
Electric & Electronic Equip. (36)	3,185.4	1,585.4 (49.77)	1,209.6 (37.97)	45.0 (1.41)			76.8 (2.41)		84.5 (2.65)		183.6 (5.77)	72
Transportation Equip. (37)	2,479.8	678.6 (27.37)	779.3 (31.43)	91.4 (3.69)	529.4 (21.35)	22.0 (0.89)	48.2 (1.94)		330.7 (13.34)			31
Instruments (38)	874.7	433.3 (49.54)	229.8 (26.27)	14.7 (1.68)		9.0 (1.03)			84.4 (9.65)		103.5 (11.83)	26
Misc. Manufacturing (39)	648.3	395.0 (60.93)	177.9 (27.44)	49.5 (7.64)					26.0 (4.01)			12
Food & Kindred Products (20)	1,461.6	789.8 (54.04)	172.8 (11.82)	206.5 (14.13)		201.9 (13.81)		41.2 (2.82)	49.2 (3.37)			18
Textile Mill Products (22)	376.4	117.9 (31.32)	162.5 (43.17)	20.0 (5.31)					36.1 (9.59)		40.0 (10.63)	8
Apparel (23)	195.7	46.5 (23.76)	117.3 (43.17)	22.7 (11.60)					9.2 (4.70)			7
Paper & Allied Products (26)	1,442.1	159.7 (11.07)	578.1 (40.09)	186.7 (12.95)					487.3 (33.79)		30.3 (2.10)	11
Printing & Publishing (27)	981.1	131.2 (13.37)	123.6 (12.60)	64.7 (6.59)			96.5 (9.84)	11.3 (1.15)	553.8 (56.45)			11

Table 4-4 (continued)

Chemicals & Allied Products (28)	444.6	250.4 (56.32)	71.7 (16.13)				33.0 (7.42)	2.0 (0.45)		87.5 (19.68)		12
Petroleum & Coal Products (29)	692.5	524.6 (75.75)	167.9 (24.25)									6
Rubber & Plastic Products (30)	760.7	333.6 (43.84)	145.3 (19.10)	231.5 (30.42)			26.9 (3.54)	12.2 (1.60)		11.4 (1.50)		11
Total Manufacturing	**17,180.6**	**6,877.7 (40.21)**	**5,089.3 (29.62)**	**1,359.8 (7.91)**	**529.4 (3.08)**	**389.3 (2.27)**	**447.7 (2.61)**	**41.2 (0.24)**	**386.1 (2.25)**	**1,985.3 (11.56)**	**74.2 (0.43)**	**298**

Note: Only 256 manufacturing firms with readily available performance data are included.
All dollar figures are in millions. Numbers in parentheses are percentages (over issue amount).

Source: Drexel Burnham Lambert, Investment Dealer's Digest

Among manufacturing industries, somewhat more went to refinance bank debt and acquisition debt than did among high yield firms in general (Table 4-4). Other significant findings include:

- The printing and publishing industry used a full 56.45 percent of its funds to refinance acquisition debt. Paper and allied products used 33.79 percent for the same purpose, followed by stone, clay, and glass (22.98 percent) and chemicals and allied products (19.68 percent).

- Fabricated metal products led the list of manufacturing industries in the percentage of money set aside for possible future acquisitions (15.04 percent). Instruments was second, with 9.65 percent.

- Recapitalizations took 21.35 percent of the proceeds raised by the transportation equipment industry.

- Fabricated metal products and electric and electronic equipment each used some of their junk bond dollars (17.16 percent and 5.77 percent respectively) to refinance debt incurred during takeovers.

Industry Distribution of High Yield Firms

High yield issuers were distributed across a wide variety of industries. Every major industry had several companies that relied on high yield financing during our study period. However, high yield financing was most intense in those sectors that were restructuring or growing the fastest: manufacturing, finance, and services.

As manufacturing firms faced a major influx of import penetration, many turned to the high yield bond market to retain or regain their competitive edge. In our study, 256 manufacturing firms issued high yield securities from 1980 through 1986, representing 33.91 percent of the 755 high yield firms we considered. Of these, 184 were in the durable goods sector; the other seventy-two manufactured nondurable goods (Table 4-5).

Among manufacturing industries with two-digit SIC codes, electric and electronic equipment was the most active sector, with 66 firms or 8.74 percent of the total. This heavy reliance on high yield debt reflects rapid, capital-intensive growth among computer hardware companies, instrument manufacturers, and related firms.

In industries outside of manufacturing, other forces were at work. Competition, deregulation, and massive restructuring helped draw 146 finance, insurance, and real estate (FIRE) companies to the high yield market. Of these, 105 were in finance, but real estate (twenty-five) and insurance (sixteen) were also well represented. The 146 participants in this sector represented 19.34 percent of the high yield firms in our study.

Service and miscellaneous industries followed, with 112 companies, or 14.84 percent of the total. This sector included health and educational firms, with forty companies (5.30 percent); business and professional services, with forty-

Table 4-5. Industrial Distribution of High Yield Securities by Number of Firms, Issues, and Issue Amount: 1980-1986

Industry (SIC)	Firms		Issues		Issue Amount	
	N	%	N	%	$ Mil.	%
A. Breakdown by Industry Group						
Agricultural Products (01, 02)	3	0.40	4	0.35	177.0	0.26
Mining & Natural Res. Extraction	35	4.64	60	5.29	5,146.1	7.64
Construction (15-17)	7	0.93	7	0.62	225.2	0.33
Manufacturing, Durable	184	24.37	228	20.11	10,825.9	16.07
Manufacturing, Nondurable	72	9.54	103	9.08	6,354.7	9.44
Transportation (40-47)	35	4.64	74	6.53	4,461.8	6.62
Communication (48)	16	2.12	32	2.82	4,130.0	6.13
Public Utilities (49)	36	4.77	102	8.99	7,798.3	11.58
Wholesale Trade (50, 51)	38	5.03	45	3.97	1,775.9	2.64
Retail Trade (52-59)	71	9.40	98	8.64	5,748.6	8.54
Finance (60-62, 67)	105	13.91	147	12.96	7,905.4	11.74
Insurance (63, 64)	16	2.12	24	2.12	1,854.7	2.75
Real Estate (65)	25	3.31	50	4.41	2,994.9	4.45
Business & Professional Serv. (73, 89)	41	5.43	46	4.06	1,813.6	2.69
Leisure & Repair Serv. (70, 72, 75-79)	31	4.11	47	4.14	3,122.7	4.64
Health & Educational Serv. (80, 8 2)	40	5.30	67	5.91	3,016.8	4.48
Total	**755**	**100.00**	**1,134**	**100.00**	**67,351.6**	**100.00**
B. Breakdown by 2-digit SIC for Manufacturing Industries						
Lumber & Wood Products (24)	2	0.26	2	0.18	52.8	0.08
Furniture & Fixtures (25)	2	0.26	3	0.26	96.1	0.14
Stone, Clay, & Glass (32)	10	1.32	11	0.97	470.4	0.70
Primary Metal Industries (33)	12	1.59	16	1.41	1,040.0	1.54
Fabricated Metal Products (34)	11	1.46	20	1.76	1,178.6	1.75
Machinery, Except Electrical (35)	23	3.05	27	2.38	799.8	1.19
Electric & Electronic Equip. (36)	66	8.74	75	6.61	3,185.4	4.73
Transportation Equip. (37)	26	3.44	34	3.00	2,479.8	3.68
Instruments (38)	22	2.91	27	2.38	874.7	1.30
Misc. Manufacturing (39)	10	1.32	13	1.15	648.3	0.96
Food & Kindred Products (20)	17	2.25	23	2.03	1,461.6	2.17
Textile Mill Products (22)	7	0.93	8	0.71	376.4	0.56
Apparel (23)	7	0.93	7	0.62	195.7	0.29
Paper & Allied Products (26)	8	1.06	17	1.50	1,442.1	2.14
Printing & Publishing (27)	9	1.19	12	1.06	981.1	1.46
Chemicals & Allied Products (28)	10	1.32	15	1.32	444.6	0.66

Table 4-5 *(continued)*

Petroleum & Coal Products (29)	5	0.66	7	0.62	692.5	1.03
Rubber & Plastic Products (30)	9	1.19	14	1.23	760.7	1.13
Total Manufacturing	**256**	**33.91**	**331**	**29.19**	**17,180.6**	**25.51**

Note: Only 755 firms with readily available performance data are included.

Source: Drexel Burnham Lambert, Investment Dealer's Digest.

one companies (5.43 percent); and leisure and repair services, with thirty-one companies (4.11 percent).

Wholesale and retail trade had almost as many high yield issuers, with 109 companies, or 14.43 percent of the total. Of these, seventy-one were retailers and about half that number were wholesalers.

There were eighty-seven companies, or 11.53 percent of the total, in transportation, communications, and public utilities that sold high yield issues from 1980 through 1986.

Industry Distribution of Junk Bond Financing

The distribution of high yield funding differed from the distribution of firms for two basic reasons:

- The size of individual issues varied with the nature of the project, its projected returns, and other company-specific factors.
- The number of issues varied among firms and industries.

The 755 companies for which extensive data were available raised $67.35 billion in 1,134 separate issues of high yield securities (Table 4-1). The average number of junk bond issues per company was 1.5, and the average issue size was $59.39 million.

Most of the high yield financing activity was concentrated in manufacturing. Companies manufacturing durables represented 24.37 percent of the issuing firms and raised 16.07 percent of the high yield proceeds (Table 4-3). The 9.54 percent of the high yield companies that were in nondurable manufacturing raised 9.44 percent of the high yield funds. Combined manufacturing accounted for 33.91 percent of the junk bond companies and 25.51 percent of all high yield funds raised. Other industries that showed concentrated levels of high yield financing included finance (11.74 percent), public utilities (11.58 percent), and retail trade (8.54 percent).

The percentage of proceeds was greater than the percentage of firms in several sectors—including mining, transportation, communications, insurance, real estate, and leisure and repair services. Significantly, public utilities raised 11.58 percent of all high yield funds, although they comprised only 4.77 percent of high yield issuers.

This concentration of high yield financing is not unexpected. All of these industries were undergoing massive restructuring (mining), rapid and capital-intensive expansion (communications), or both (public utilities).

The High Yield Index

To some extent, the distribution of high yield firms reflects the general importance of their industries within the economy. To investigate which industries disproportionately utilized junk financing relative to their position in the economy, we developed a high yield financing index, the *intensity index.*

This index compares the portion of high yield bonds issued in the industry with that industry's contribution to the gross national product. For example, nondurable manufacturing accounted for 8.46 percent of GNP and 10.23 percent of high yield issues among the companies we studied. Dividing the proceeds ratio by the GNP ratio gives a high yield index of 1.21, indicating that nondurable manufacturing participated in the junk bond market proportionately more than it did in the U.S. economy (Table 4-6). (The industrial grouping in the *Survey of Current Business* before 1982 was different from that after 1983. This discrepancy limited our analysis of GNP to the 1983-1986 period.)

Table 4-6. Junk Bond Intensity Index by Industry: 1983-1986

Industry (SIC)	Net Proceeds to Issuer		GNP of the Industry		Intensity Index
	$ Mil.	%(1)	$ Bil.	%(2)	(1)/(2)
A. Breakdown by Industry Group					
Agricultural Products (01, 02)	177.0	0.309	293.4	2.465	0.125
Mining & Natural Res. Extraction	4,122.5	7.202	507.1	4.261	1.690
Construction (15-17)	161.3	0.282	693.0	5.370	0.053
Manufacturing, Durable	8,605.0	15.033	1,983.3	16.666	0.902
Manufacturing, Nondurable	5,855.9	10.230	1,006.9	8.461	1.209
Transportation (40-47)	3,683.0	6.434	477.2	3.758	1.712
Communication (48)	2,947.6	5.149	374.6	3.148	1.636
Public Utilities (49)	6,547.4	11.438	408.5	3.433	3.332
Wholesale Trade (50, 51)	1,513.3	2.644	1,023.9	8.604	0.307
Retail Trade (52-59)	5,237.2	9.149	1,340.8	11.267	0.812
Finance (60-62, 67)	7,150.1	12.491	374.4	3.146	3.970
Insurance (63, 64)	1,758.8	3.073	209.4	1.760	1.746
Real Estate (65)	2,900.7	5.067	1,486.7	12.493	0.406
Business & Professional Serv. (73)	1,534.6	2.681	664.6	5.585	0.480
Leisure & Repair Serv. (70, 72, 75-79)	2,624.5	4.585	432.9	3.638	1.260
Health & Educational Services (80, 82)	2,422.8	4.233	707.7	5.947	0.712
Total	**57,241.7**	**100.000**	**11,900.4**	**100.000**	**1.000**

Table 4-6 *(continued)*

B. Breakdown by 2-digit SIC for Manufacturing Industries

Lumber & Wood Products (24)	52.8	0.092	80.6	0.677	0.136
Furniture & Fixtures (25)	96.1	0.168	45.2	0.380	0.442
Stone, Clay, & Glass (32)	441.1	0.771	97.2	0.817	0.944
Primary Metal Industries (33)	815.2	1.424	85.7	0.720	1.978
Fabricated Metal Products (34)	1,088.3	1.901	133.8	1.124	1.691
Machinery, Except Electrical (35)	624.8	1.092	215.3	1.809	0.604
Electric & Electronic Equip. (36)	2,231.9	3.899	490.0	4.118	0.947
Transportation Equip. (37)	2,143.9	3.745	312.3	2.624	1.427
Instruments (38)	539.8	0.943	353.7	2.972	0.317
Misc. Manufacturing (39)	571.1	0.998	106.6	0.896	1.114
Food & Kindred Products (20)	1,392.1	1.432	53.5	0.450	5.404
Textile Mill Products (22)	338.7	0.592	248.3	2.086	0.284
Apparel (23)	124.2	0.217	66.0	0.555	0.391
Paper & Allied Products (26)	1,401.8	2.449	79.3	0.666	3.677
Printing & Publishing (27)	946.8	1.654	120.9	1.016	1.628
Chemicals & Allied Products (28)	441.6	0.771	166.1	1.396	0.552
Petroleum & Coal Products (29)	554.4	0.969	235.4	1.978	0.490
Rubber & Plastic Products (30)	656.3	1.147	100.3	0.843	1.361
Total Manufacturing	**14,460.9**	**25.263**	**2,990.2**	**25.127**	**1.005**

Note: The intensity index is the ratio of the share of high yield issues accounted for by each industry relative to that industry's share of GNP during this period.

Source: Drexel Burnham Lambert; *Survey of Current Business,* Department of Commerce.

Finance and public utilities led in the disproportionate use of junk financing, with indices of 3.97 and 3.33 respectively. They were followed by insurance (1.75), transportation (1.71), mining (1.69), communications (1.64), leisure and repair services (1.26), and nondurable manufacturing (1.21)—all of which relied disproportionately on high yield bonds, perhaps as a result of capital intensity, deregulation, and industry restructuring.

These findings reflect the recent growth and restructuring activity in the U.S. economy. With an index of 3.97, finance was the most junk bond intensive sector. Many finance companies borrow or accept deposits in order to lend, so they take on debt to grow. Commercial banks, investment banks, and consumer finance companies are changing and expanding in response to deregulation, intense competition, and macroeconomic factors such as inflation and interest rate volatility.

Among manufacturing industries, we calculated the intensity index for two-digit SIC codes. The food and kindred products group was highest, with an index of 5.40, representing a disproportionately high level of high yield issues.

Fifteen food processing companies issued 2.4 percent of all net junk bond proceeds in 1983-1986, while the industry contributed less than 0.5 percent of the GNP.

Of the other seventeen manufacturing sectors, seven took on a disproportionate amount of high yield debt relative to their contributions to the economy. These sectors included paper and allied products (3.68), primary metals (1.98), fabricated metals (1.69), printing and publishing (1.63), transportation equipment (1.43), rubber and plastic products (1.36), and miscellaneous manufacturing (1.11). Each of these sections represented important characteristics of firms using high yield securities. They had relatively low levels of new investment prior to the high yield issue, the cash-flow volatility of the sector was relatively low, and new strategies were necessary to restructure and reposition the companies in global markets.

Summary: High Yield Bonds and Corporate Competitiveness

The findings presented in Chapter 5 suggest that high yield securities have been an effective tool to fund corporate growth. They have provided a flexible, cost-effective way for companies to purchase assets, expand product lines, and initiate new projects. They also have helped fund acquisitions that can increase a company's size and profit potential while improving its competitive position.

In response to increased competition, deregulation, and structural economic change, many companies are reorganizing, restructuring, and revising their corporate strategies. Capital is an essential part of this process, especially in capital-intensive industries such as manufacturing, finance, public utilities, and mining and natural resource extraction.

These industries have faced strong competitive and economic pressures; compared to other sectors, they tend to need greater amounts of capital to sustain productive growth. As a result, it is not surprising that they show more concentrated levels of high yield financing or disproportionate use of high yield securities relative to their economic output. Efficient access to large amounts of capital is essential for these companies to improve their profits, increase their productivity, and enhance their position in today's highly competitive markets.

5

The Impact of Junk Bonds on Industrial Performance

The most important question in the debate over junk bonds is what effect the securities have on corporate performance. To find what really happens, we examined the available data on employment, productivity, sales, capital investment, and capital spending. By comparing the performance of high yield firms with trends in individual industries and industry in general, we found that, overall, high yield financing has had a positive impact on corporations and the economy.

Current Research on Job Creation and Retention

Much of the research on high yield securities has centered on questions regarding job creation and retention, and related issues concerning corporate evolution and development. Claims that junk bonds are used largely for "bust-up shut-down takeovers" abound in the business press and some academic articles (Lowenstein, 1985; Lowenstein and Herman, 1986). Yet there appears to be no consistent evidence to support these claims.

In dealing with structural economic change, corporations must deal with the employment effects that result from changes in ownership, management, corporate direction, and technology. A widespread fear has been that such changes will result in continued job loss. But often the opposite occurs.

New ownership and new direction frequently lead to increased employment or improve the firm's ability to retain jobs.

The job-generation process was outlined in Birch's studies (1979, 1987), which showed that small plants were the major source of employment growth in the U.S. Birch and MacCracken (1981) compared independent and acquired firms in various stages of growth and decline. They discovered that a declining firm's fall was often arrested through acquisition, although growth was not necessarily enhanced through business combination.

Until recently, most research has only analyzed the growth rates of successful plants or firms, treating the employment growth process as independent of firm failure. Dunne, Roberts, and Samuelson (1987) analyzed employment growth in the manufacturing sector from 1967 to 1982. Unlike earlier investigators, they examined realized growth rates of both successful and failing plants. They reported that corporate failure and job loss vary systematically with plant size and age. According to the authors, net turnover and employment composition in existing plants tends to shift in response to changes in employment composition at the industry level. Their work suggests that to understand long-term job and industry growth, we need to appreciate both the process of job creation and the long-range factors that influence job retention.

Some recent empirical work suggests that changes in corporate structure and strategy can help preserve employment by increasing competitiveness. Paulus and Gay (1987) indicate that intensive restructuring activity is associated with greater productivity gains and can be used as a defensive response to competition from imports.

Lichtenberg and Siegel (1987) examined 19,000 manufacturing plants in 1972-1981; they found that companies tend to sell plants that lack a comparative advantage and that low levels of efficiency increased the likelihood of ownership change. They also found that companies that changed ownership through mergers, acquisitions, or divestitures showed increases in total-factor productivity. Moreover, in a follow-up study (1989), they found that changes in ownership resulted in a slashing of corporate overhead—a substantial reduction in administrative employment and in the ratio of administrative to production workers. Production employment actually increased after a takeover, and the differential between administrative and production wages actually decreased. In short, new owners of firms operated plants more efficiently.

The counterevidence generally cited comes from Ravenscraft and Scherer (1987, pp. 68-70), who found that the pretakeover accounting profits of target firms in ninety-five tender offers from 1957 to 1975 did not show a statistically significant difference from the corresponding profits of other firms in the same industries. Moreover, they found no evidence that the postmerger profitability of acquired assets in a larger sample of firms from 1950 to 1976 increased significantly in relation to premerger levels (Ravenscraft and Scherer, 1987, 101-3).

In fact, smaller companies and firms acquired by conglomerates that were not subsequently sold showed profitability declines, while other companies showed profitability increases. Critics have used these findings to suggest that acquisitions are unproductive and that the debt used to finance them could be put to better use.

A closer reading of the evidence, however, suggests an alternate interpretation that is more consistent with recent findings. For the most part, the evidence in Ravenscraft and Scherer's study stops in 1977, prior to the advent of the contemporary high yield market. An exception is some data on sell-offs that extend until 1981 and consist primarily of divestitures from the conglomerate acquisition wave that began in 1981 and was financed in part by high yield securities. This can best be characterized as deconglomeration, or the undoing of earlier mergers that had poor strategic and economic justification (Mitchell and Lehn, 1988).

Brown and Medoff's study (1987) of Michigan companies confirms that over time, mergers and acquisitions result in efficiency and employment gains. My own studies of plant closings in New York and New Jersey (1986) indicated that shutdowns could be attributed to restructurings in less than 2 percent of the cases. Bhide (1988) examined a sample of twelve hostile takeovers completed in 1985 and found no evidence of production loss caused by takeovers. Rather, the data showed that, between 1981-1985, or prior to the takeover, companies lost 4,000 to 5,000 jobs, or 7 percent per year, due to a lack of competitiveness. Post-takeover job loss was primarily due to corporate staff reductions, which averaged 200 to 300 jobs per company.

During the growth phase of an industry, small and medium-sized companies have an obvious advantage in creating jobs. Firms with appropriate financing, organization, and market strategy thrive (Birch 1987). The process of retaining jobs over time, however, appears to be more complex, particularly in mature or declining industries.

Ghemwatt and Nalebuff (1988) examined empirical evidence of decline in the soda-ash, steel castings, and integrated steelmaking industries. They found that larger firms with greater market share and less flexible plant and management structures shrank more rapidly than other firms during periods of industrial decline. The authors suggest that the disparity may be the result of cost differences related to firm size.

Other research shows that any mechanisms that hasten cost reductions in existing operations and allow for the introduction of new products or production processes can help revitalize companies and reverse the maturing of industry cycles (Abernathy, Hayes, and Clark, 1985).

Our review of current research on job creation and retention suggests the following general principles:

- Small and medium-sized firms provide the major sources of new jobs.
- The age and size of a firm is closely related to the number of jobs created and their duration.

- Financial restructuring is closely related to cost reductions, improved productivity, and increased employment.
- Larger firms experience faster shrinkage in dollar volume of sales and employment than smaller firms, because large firms have greater difficulty controlling costs and are less flexible in redeploying assets toward new products, production processes, or markets.
- Job retention in sectors facing increasing unemployment depends on the ability to reduce cost, improve productivity, and create management structures consonant with improved market strategies.

Employment Effects of High Yield Securities

If leverage helps firms maximize efficiency and growth, high yield firms should have higher-than-average levels of employment gain and retention. To test this hypothesis, we analyzed employment changes among those high yield issuers for which employment data were available, and compared them to changes in total industry employment.

To correct for the addition of new issuing firms, we studied high yield firms by using cohort analysis (i.e., analyzing the change in employment from the year the firm first issued a high yield security to 1986, the final year for which industry totals were available).

In each cohort from 1980 to 1985, high yield firms far and away outstripped industry rates of employment growth. The average annual increase in employment among high yield firms was 6.68 percent, compared to only 1.38 percent for industry as a whole (Table 5-1).

Table 5-1. Changes in Employment, High Yield Firms vs. Industry Totals

| Industry (SIC) | N | Average Annual Change, 1980-1986 | | | |
| | | High Yield Firms | | Industry Total | |
		Absolute	Percent	Absolute	Percent
A. Breakdown by Industry Group					
Agricultural Products (01, 02)	3	-0.518	-1.344	0.342	72.555
Mining (10-14)	28	1.556	2.887	-25.107	-7.215
Construction (15-17)	4	0.249	1.386	-6.205	-3.560
Manufacturing Durable (24, 25, 32-39)	148	-8.058	-0.892	-152.512	-2.199
Manufacturing Nondurable	69	-1.894	-0.411	-38.963	-1.001
Transportation (40-47)	28	23.527	6.992	113.922	11.369
Communication (48)	13	1.670	8.316	-1.455	-2.025
Public Utilities (49)	30	3.654	4.039	3.923	0.871
Wholesale (50, 51)	38	-4.823	-4.211	25.339	10.242
Retail (52-59)	62	60.001	13.848	187.586	6.303
Finance (60-62, 67)	45	7.308	10.263	16.320	7.944

Table 5-1 *(continued)*

Real Estate (65)	23	2.093	8.203	1.737	5.319
Business & Professional Serv. (73, 89)	33	5.917	7.823	22.567	12.121
Leisure & Repair Serv. (70, 72, 75-79)	25	11.257	14.125	27.970	8.271
Health & Educational Serv. (80, 82)	34	41.037	17.787	49.135	16.975
Total	**583**	**142.976**	**6.679**	**224.599**	**1.379**

B. Further Breakdown by 2-Digit SIC for Manufacturing Industries

Food & Kindred Products (20)	12	-0.418	-0.347	47.049	5.532
Textile Mill Products (22)	6	-3.516	-6.543	6.146	10.579
Lumber & Wood Products (24)	2	0.267	16.834	0.246	1.683
Furniture & Fixtures (25)	1	0.583	9.712	6.042	8.129
Paper & Allied Products (26)	8	5.138	6.773	6.296	1.609
Printing & Publishing (27)	7	0.379	1.430	13.402	4.433
Chemicals & Allied Products (28)	9	0.026	0.509	-29.873	-4.064
Petroleum & Coal Products (29)	5	-0.301	-1.533	-57.918	-5.079
Rubber & Plastic Products (30)	7	-5.294	-6.529	-24.066	-7.375
Stone, Clay, & Glass (32)	9	0.456	1.368	-2.176	-0.988
Primary Metal Industries (33)	9	-4.492	-2.760	-14.727	-2.251
Fabricated Metal Products (34)	11	3.459	10.008	-8.925	-1.922
Machinery, Except Electrical (35)	15	-1.161	-0.160	-25.947	-3.680
Electric & Electronic Equip. (36)	63	-0.658	-0.073	-20.866	-1.742
Transportation Equip. (37)	17	-5.850	-2.453	-99.544	-3.280
Instruments (38)	21	-0.663	-1.836	5.911	1.119
Misc. Manufacturing (39)	10	1.853	7.860	7.474	12.318
Total Manufacturing	**217**	**-10.192**	**-0.742**	**-191.476**	**-1.774**

Note: Absolute changes are in thousands of jobs.

Source: COMPUSTAT Data, Standard & Poor's Corp., 1980-1986.

From 1980 through 1983, industry as a whole experienced net job losses, while high yield firms showed relatively steady employment gains. In subsequent years, total industry employment improved, but not enough to match the rate of job creation among high yield firms. As a result, high yield firms added over 82 percent of the average annual job growth of all public companies reporting employment data in 1980 through 1986.

Health and educational services, leisure and repair services, retail trade, and finance were the industries within the high yield sector creating jobs the fastest, with average annual growth rates of 17.79 percent, 14.13 percent, 13.85 percent, and 10.26 percent respectively.

In communications, mining, and construction, high yield firms grew while their industries suffered considerable job loss. In other sectors, high yield firms grew considerably faster than their industry during the study period. High yield public utilities, for example, grew by 4.04 percent, compared to an industry growth rate of just 0.87 percent. In real estate, twenty-three high yield firms gained more jobs than the entire industry (2,093 versus 1,737 jobs per year), showing that investment grade real estate firms experienced net job loss. In agriculture, wholesale trade, transportation, and business and professional services, high yield firms had slower employment growth than their industries.

In manufacturing, job loss was evident in both high yield firms and the industry totals. In most sectors where this occurred, however, high yield firms experienced smaller rates of decline. Overall, job loss among high yield manufacturers was less than half the industry average (-0.74 percent versus -1.77 percent).

Five manufacturing sectors experienced job growth both at the industry level and among high yield firms. In three of these, high yield firms outperformed their industries' gains: lumber and wood products (16.83 percent versus 1.68 percent), paper and allied products (6.77 percent versus 1.61 percent), and furniture and fixtures (9.71 percent versus 8.13 percent). In both printing and publishing and miscellaneous manufacturing, high yield job creation fell behind the industry totals.

In fabricated metal products, in stone, clay, and glass, and in chemicals, high yield companies increased employment while their industries declined. In textiles, food and kindred products, and instruments, high yield firms lost jobs while their industries gained. And in primary metals, both the industry and high yield firms lost jobs, though the declines were slightly greater among high yield firms.

Disaggregating total employment effects, we found some interesting patterns among industries. Other than agriculture, where there were too few cases, high yield companies were relatively consistent in outperforming their industries (Figure 5-1). This was particularly evident in the following cases:

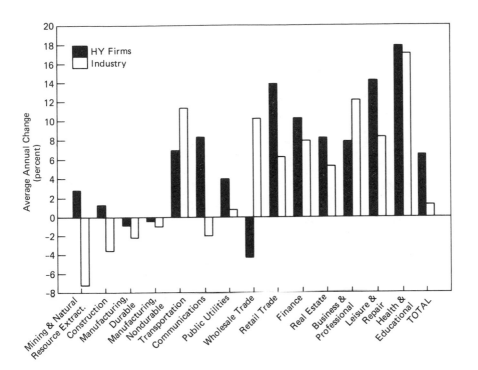

Figure 5–1. Changes in employment, 1980–1986 (Compustat Data, Standard & Poor's Corp., 1980–1986).

- Where employment grew in high yield companies but fell at the industry level (e.g., communications)
- Where employment grew faster among high yield firms than growth in the industry (e.g., retail and finance)
- Where employment shrank among high yield firms, but less than overall industry declines (e.g., manufacturing)

The Class of 1983: Annual Average Percentage Change of Employment by Cohort by Industry

To analyze the relationship between leverage and job growth further, we extracted those firms for which we had complete matching data for three years before and after high yield securities were issued. The analysis of the 1983 cohort, or the "Class of 1983," provides a broader and more explicit test of the employment effects of high yield financings.

We used similar cohort analysis to obtain detailed information on changes in sales per employee, sales, capital investment, and capital spending among firms that issued high yield securities in 1983. These before and after comparisons are detailed in later sections of this chapter.

Job Growth: Class of 1983, by Industry

The high yield firms in the Class of 1983 showed greater improvement in job growth than did industry in general. In the three years prior to their high yield issues, these firms had an average annual employment growth rate of 2.64 percent. After issuance, employment in the Class of 1983 grew more than twice as fast, at an annual rate of 7.75 percent (Table 5-2). In the industry totals, employment declined 1.01 percent in the 1980-1983 period, and expanded at an average annual rate of only 3.82 percent for the next three years.

High yield firms showed particular improvement in durable manufacturing, transportation, retail trade, and real estate. While industry averages also improved in several sectors after 1983, high yield companies showed a sharper upturn than the industry totals in durable manufacturing and transportation.

Job growth varied considerably between industries. In nondurable manufacturing, for example, employment in the high yield issuers contracted before issuance, and declined even faster thereafter. In the industry totals, nondurable manufacturing employment dropped before 1983 and after, but by a smaller amount.

In transportation, high yield employment shrank before 1983 and rose by more than 15 percent after high yield issuance. In the industry totals, transportation employment grew by about 11 percent per year before 1983 and at about the same rate after. In other words, high yield transportation firms underperformed their industry before, and outperformed it after, issuing high yield securities.

In retail trade, high yield firms and the industry totals showed parallel results. In both cases, employment growth rates after 1983 were more than twice those of the "before" period. In mining and natural resource extraction, employment declined before and after 1983 for both high yield firms and for the industry totals, but the downturn was sharper for high yield issuers. In health and educational services, the employment growth rate of high yield firms was higher than the industry totals both before and after 1983.

Manufacturing Industry Employment, Class of 1983

To examine the crucial manufacturing sector, we broke out data for manufacturing companies into two-digit SIC codes. Both high yield manufacturers and manufacturing in general showed employment declines prior to 1983. Employment dropped by 5.41 percent for high yield companies, and fell by 4.23 percent for the totals. Afterward, high yield firms continued to decline, but by so little as to be almost flat (i.e., by 0.08 percent). Total jobs in the manufacturing industry increased by 0.67 percent. The improvement between

Table 5-2. Changes in Employment: Firms Issuing High Yield Securities in 1983 vs. Industry Totals

		Average Annual Changes, Before and After Issuing Junk Bonds							
		High Yield Firms				Industry Total			
		Absolute Change		Percentage Change		Absolute Change		Percentage Change	
Industry (SIC)	N	1980-1983	1983-1986	1980-1983	1983-1986	1980-1983	1983-1986	1980-1983	1983-1986
A. Breakdown by Industry Group									
Agricultural Products (01, 02)	1	-0.933	-0.133	-2.504	-0.278	0.645	0.040	144.985	0.125
Mining & Natural Res. Estraction	8	-0.205	-1.531	-1.141	-15.616	-22.830	-27.384	-5.773	-8.657
Manufacturing, Durable (24, 25, 32-39)	25	-13.115	8.270	-7.062	5.632	-385.115	80.090	-5.743	1.345
Manufacturing, Nondurable	14	-4.330	-9.028	-3.128	-7.683	-61.685	-16.241	-1.573	-0.429
Transportation (40-47)	9	-2.121	37.179	-1.369	15.124	96.940	130.904	11.553	11.185
Communications (48)	1	2.268	1.631	66.109	16.171	1.028	-3.939	1.452	-5.503
Public Utilities (49)	11	1.370	0.579	2.552	1.006	1.227	6.620	0.272	1.470
Wholesale Trade (50, 51)	4	0.366	-0.451	4.743	-5.286	5.487	45.191	2.641	17.843
Retail Trade (52-59)	10	3.264	9.339	4.615	10.539	105.292	269.881	3.969	8.637
Finance (60-62, 67)	15	1.332	1.193	6.165	4.495	14.063	18.577	7.724	8.164
Real Estate (65)	7	0.778	3.174	17.665	32.612	0.898	2.575	3.432	7.206
Business and Professional Serv. (73, 89)	7	2.391	-0.047	20.984	1.470	13.949	31.186	9.249	14.992
Leisure & Repair Serv. (70, 72, 75-79)	3	0.539	0.296	4.875	3.322	14.280	41.659	4.920	11.621
Health & Educational Serv. (80, 82)	10	31.018	27.497	30.659	14.177	49.837	48.433	21.200	12.749
Total	125	22.622	77.968	2.637	7.750	-165.983	627.591	-1.009	3.821

Table 5-2 (continued)

B. Breakdown by 2-digit SIC for Manufacturing Industries

Food & Kindred Products (20)	1	0.113	0.164	111.742	39.901	22.546	71.552	2.920	8.144
Textile Mill Products (22)	2	-1.973	-3.983	-4.827	-12.307	1.469	10.823	2.982	18.177
Furniture & Fixtures (25)	1	0.567	0.600	10.986	8.438	3.758	8.326	5.936	10.321
Paper & Allied Products (26)	1	-0.533	-0.500	-6.079	-8.784	0.843	11.750	0.394	2.823
Printing & Publishing (27)	4	-1.637	-0.350	-7.078	-1.609	4.737	22.067	1.739	7.128
Chemicals & Allied Products (28)	1	-0.108	-0.147	-10.187	-20.366	-21.801	-37.946	-2.720	-5.409
Petroleum & Coal Products (29)	3	-0.424	-0.912	-3.436	-8.624	-42.616	-73.219	-3.397	-6.761
Rubber & Plastic Products (30)	2	0.233	-3.300	0.473	-6.544	-26.863	-21.268	-7.339	-7.412
Stone, Clay, & Glass (32)	3	0.400	0.100	7.075	1.382	-8.936	4.583	-4.561	2.584
Primary Metal Industries (33)	1	-8.767	3.667	-12.345	13.023	-46.874	17.419	-8.003	3.501
Fabricated Metal Products (34)	1	-0.200	6.967	-7.469	197.884	-34.270	16.419	-8.862	5.018
Machinery, Except Electrical (35)	3	-0.154	-0.163	-3.823	-5.517	-53.809	1.915	-7.740	0.380
Electric & Electronic Equip. (36)	11	-4.391	-4.601	-5.884	-7.134	-42.369	0.638	-3.546	0.061
Transportation Equipment (37)	2	-0.576	0.825	-5.161	8.241	-206.595	7.508	-6.856	0.297
Instruments (38)	2	0.005	0.209	1.130	18.081	-1.274	13.095	-0.244	2.481
Misc. Manufacturing (39)	1	0.000	0.667	3.630	8.025	3.593	11.356	7.815	16.820
Total Manufacturing	**39**	**-17.444**	**-0.758**	**-5.413**	**-0.075**	**-448.461**	**65.019**	**-4.229**	**0.670**

Note: Only 125 high yield firms with readily available employment data are included. Absolute changes are in thousands of jobs.

Source: COMPUSTAT Data, Standard & Poor's Corp., 1980-1986.

the before and after periods, however, was slightly stronger for high yield manufacturers than for total manufacturing.

Summary of Class of 1983 Findings

Using cohort analysis, we were able to track the impact of high yield financing on the Class of 1983's capacity to create new jobs, retain old ones, or manage employment reduction in the context of overall industrial job loss. Analyzing employment rates before and after junk bond issuance, we found that high yield companies increased their job growth after the issuing year by a substantial amount and showed slightly more improvement than the industry totals.

Productivity Effects of High Yield Securities

A popular charge against industrial restructuring in general and junk bonds in particular is that they are simply financial reshuffling or "paper entrepreneurism" and fail to create genuine value within the economy. Our study, however, suggested just the reverse. Often, restructuring involves transfers of ownership, new management and work practices, strategic acquisition of market share, or development of new production or distribution processes that improve cost efficiencies and redeploy assets toward higher rates of return.

As Table 5-3 indicates, the distribution of high yield financing parallels the distribution of mergers, acquisitions, and divestures throughout the 1980s. High yield financing has been concentrated in sectors that have faced deregulation or intense competition from abroad.

Table 5-3. Comparative Distribution of Corporate Restructuring and High Yield Financing: Summary Table, 1980-1987

Industry (SIC)	Share of Mergers, Acquisitions, or Divestitures	Share of Firms Issuing HY Bonds	Share of Output
Mining & Natural Res. Extraction	17.4	4.9	3.4
Manufacturing	40.5	33.71	22.2
Deregulated Industries:			
Transportation & Communications	10.4	6.96	6.4
Finance, Insurance, & Real Estate	18.2	19.60	4.4
SUBTOTAL	**86.5**	**65.17**	**36.2**
BALANCE OF U.S. ECONOMY	13.5	34.83	63.8

Source: Paulus and Gay (1987); Economic Research Bureau (1988); Industrial Productivity: BLS Productivity Index.

Table 5-4. Junk Bond Intensity, Productivity Change, and Restructuring Intensity

Industry (SIC)	Junk Bond Intensity Index	Change of Productivity Index	Restructuring Intensity Measure (RIM)
A. Breakdown by Industry Group			
Agricultural Products (01, 02)	0.125		
Mining & Natural Res. Extraction	1.690	33.95	5.8
Construction (15-17)	0.053		
Manufacturing, Durable (24, 25, 32-39)	0.902	8.55	1.5
Manufacturing, Nondurable	1.209	4.26	1.8
Transportation (40-47)	1.712	-0.62	0.8
Communications (48)	1.636	-34.78	0.9
Public Utilities (49)	3.332	22.82	0.9
Wholesale Trade (50, 51)	0.307		0.1
Retail Trade (52-59)	0.812	4.29	0.4
Finance (60-62, 67)	3.970	13.34	4.4*
Insurance (63, 64)	1.746		2.5
Real Estate (65)	0.406		0.1
Business & Professional Serv. (73, 89)	0.480		0.7
Leisure & Repair Serv. (70, 72, 75-79)	1.260	0.85	0.8*
Health & Educational Serv. (80, 82)	0.712		0.3
B. Breakdown by 2-Digit SIC for Manufacturing Industries			
Lumber & Wood Products (24)	0.136	3.25	2.2
Furniture & Fixtures (25)	0.442	3.00	0.4
Stone, Clay, & Glass (32)	0.944	7.33	0.9
Primary Metal Industries (33)	1.978	11.06	1.5
Fabricated Metal Products (34)	1.691	3.62	1.4
Machinery, except Electrical (35)	0.604	6.80	1.0
Electric & Electronic Equip. (36)	0.947	8.43	1.6
Transportation Equipment (37)	1.427	19.37	1.6
Instruments (38)	0.317	8.27	2.8
Misc. Manufacturing (39)	1.114		1.5
Food & Kindred Products (20)	5.404	6.04	3.8
Textile Mill Products (22)	0.284	6.31	1.2
Apparel (23)	0.391		0.9
Paper & Allied Products (26)	3.677	3.88	1.3

Table 5-4 *(continued)*

Printing & Publishing (27)	1.628		0.9
Chemicals & Allied Products (28)	0.552	-0.13	2.2
Petroleum & Coal Products (29)	0.490	25.33	0.4
Rubber & Plastic Products (30)	1.361	-13.08	0.8
Total Manufacturing	**1.005**	**6.25**	**1.6**

*Average of industries' RIMs in this industry group.

Note: The junk bond intensity index is the ratio of the share of junk bond (dollar amount) issuance for each industry relative to that same industry's share of GNP during 1983-1986. The change of productivity index is the difference of the industry's productivity (output per employee-hour, 1977 = 100) between 1983 and 1985. RIM is the ratio of the share of merger and acquisition activities accounted for by each industry relative to that same industry's share of U.S. output during 1980-1985.

Source: Drexel Burnham Lambert; COMPUSTAT, Standard & Poor's Corp.; Survey of Current Business, DOC; Worldwide Economic Outlook, Morgan Stanley; Productivity Measures, DOL.

Using the Bureau of Labor Statistics' productivity index, we found that in most industries where high yield financing and restructuring were intensive, productivity increases were considerable (Table 5-4). Mining, manufacturing, finance, and public utilities achieved substantial productivity increases. Transportation and communications had high levels of high yield financing, but their restructuring intensity was lower and they experienced productivity declines. Despite low levels of high yield financing and restructuring, retail trade firms achieved substantial productivity gains.

Among manufacturing industries, high yield financing, restructuring, and productivity increases were again closely associated. This pattern was particularly evident in primary metals, fabricated metals, transportation equipment, food and kindred products, and paper and allied products. With the exception of rubber and plastic products, wherever high yield securities were intensively used, productivity increases occurred.

Market Productivity: Sales Per Employee

The Bureau of Labor Statistics arrives at its productivity index by dividing an index of physical output by an index of employee hours expended on that output. While this provides a useful measure of productivity, detailed output data are available only for a limited number of industries.

To investigate a broader range of industries, we used sales per employee as an alternate measure of market productivity. During our study period, sales per employee grew faster in high yield firms than for industry totals (by 3.13 percent versus 2.41 percent) (see Table 5-5).

Table 5-5. Changes of Sales per Employee: High Yield Firms vs. Industry Totals

| Industry (SIC) | N | Average Annual Change, 1980-1986 | | | |
| | | High Yield Firms | | Industry Total | |
		Absolute	Percent	Absolute	Percent
A. Breakdown by Industry Group					
Agricultural Products (01, 02)	3	0.847	2.171	2.035	15.519
Mining & Natural Res. Extraction	28	-2.081	0.231	10.615	7.875
Construction (15-17)	4	5.727	8.424	-0.937	-0.219
Manufacturing, Durable (24, 25, 32-39)	157	3.978	5.209	7.100	7.940
Manufacturing, Nondurable	60	3.894	4.025	-2.088	-0.970
Transportation (40-47)	28	2.727	3.291	-0.470	-0.428
Communication (48)	13	19.537	18.282	19.311	16.334
Public Utilities (49)	30	8.227	3.297	9.007	4.151
Wholesale Trade (50, 51)	38	14.287	8.523	12.548	6.103
Retail Trade (52-59)	62	3.539	6.159	2.690	3.354
Finance (60-62, 67)	45	16.306	9.977	4.785	3.799
Real Estate (65)	23	-1.707	-0.122	14.252	9.269
Business & Professional Serv. (73, 89)	33	-0.521	-0.341	7.012	11.005
Leisure & Repair Serv. (70, 72, 75-79)	25	-1.576	-1.393	2.821	8.575
Health & Educational Serv. (80, 82)	34	2.208	7.638	0.854	2.431
Total	**583**	**2.798**	**3.127**	**2.705**	**2.405**
B. Breakdown by 2-digit SIC for Manufacturing Industries					
Food & Kindred Products (20)	12	3.350	5.275	-0.168	-0.133
Textile Mill Products (22)	6	4.855	8.602	2.849	6.727
Apparel (23)	5	1.088	3.690		
Lumber & Wood Products (24)	2	9.353	11.533	4.566	5.425
Furniture & Fixtures (25)	1	3.844	7.212	2.330	4.324
Paper & Allied Products (26)	8	7.000	7.129	6.411	5.734
Printing & Publishing (27)	7	3.376	5.967	5.853	7.411
Chemicals & Allied Products (28)	10	0.407	0.651	5.045	5.218
Petroleum & Coal Products (29)	5	-34.887	-6.975	0.198	0.683
Rubber & Plastic Products (30)	7	9.692	10.015	4.509	6.621
Stone, Clay, & Glass (32)	9	1.967	1.946	5.071	5.926
Primary Metal Industries (33)	9	3.184	2.822	2.205	2.606
Fabricated Metal Products (34)	11	4.122	5.405	4.777	6.241

Table 5-5 *(continued)*

Machinery, Except Electrical (35)	15	2.984	5.144	4.465	5.229
Electric & Electronic Equip. (36)	62	4.835	8.611	7.886	8.743
Transportation Equip. (37)	17	4.221	5.334	9.425	10.274
Instruments (38)	21	4.481	7.604	4.928	6.060
Misc. Manufacturing (39)	10	6.246	9.656	6.261	10.571
Total Manufacturing	**217**	**3.938**	**4.713**	**3.450**	**2.852**

Note: Only 583 high yield firms with readily available employment and sales data are included. Sales per employee are in thousands of dollars.

Source: COMPUSTAT Data, Standard & Poor's Corp., 1980-1986.

Compared to their industries, high yield firms had higher average annual growth rates of sales per employee in eight industry sectors and lower rates in seven. High yield companies outperformed their industries in construction, nondurable manufacturing, transportation, communications, finance, health and educational services, and wholesale and retail trade. High yield firms substantially underperformed their industries in mining, business and professional services, and real estate.

Within two-digit SIC manufacturing industries, sales per employee also grew faster in high yield companies than for the industry totals (by 4.71 percent versus 2.85 percent). These industries, however, were evenly split, with nine sectors where sales per employee grew faster in high yield firms and nine where the industries showed faster growth.

Sales per Employee: Class of 1983

According to the Class of 1983 analysis, the rate of growth of sales per employee of high yield firms was lower than industry totals in the "before" period (2.35 percent versus 5.27 percent), but better after the firms' 1983 issues (2.13 percent versus 1.89 percent) (see Table 5-6). Although the growth rate of sales per employee declined for high yield firms between the before and after periods, the reduction was considerably less than the decline in the industry totals.

For high yield firms, the industry groups were evenly split, seven and seven, between those where sales per employee improved after the 1983 issues, and those where it declined. In the industry totals, the rate improved after 1983 in six industries and declined in eight.

Within two-digit manufacturing industries, the results were even more dramatic. Before their 1983 issues, high yield firms increased sales per employee at a rate of only 0.78 percent. After issuance, that figure jumped sharply, to 7.38 percent. In the industry totals, the rate of increase dropped by more than half, from 6.99 percent before 1983 to 2.93 percent in the next three years.

Table 5-6. Changes in Sales per Employee: Firms Issuing High Yield Securities in 1983 vs. Industry Totals

		Average Annual Changes, Before and After Issuing Junk Bonds							
		High Yield Firms				Industry Total			
		Absolute Change		Percentage Change		Absolute Change		Percentage Change	
Industry (SIC)	N	1980-1983	1983-1986	1980-1983	1983-1986	1980-1983	1983-1986	1980-1983	1983-1986
A. Breakdown by Industry Group									
Agricultural Products (01, 02)	1	-0.508	1.964	-0.730	4.604	-2.092	6.162	20.279	10.759
Mining & Natural Res. Extraction	8	22.223	4.494	22.416	5.017	11.503	9.728	9.190	6.559
Manufacturing, Durable (24, 25, 32-39)	25	-0.720	7.655	-0.728	9.255	9.937	11.167	11.713	9.619
Manufacturing, Nondurable	14	1.609	7.967	1.778	7.573	4.167	-5.816	2.201	-2.446
Transportation (40-47)	9	7.660	-2.586	8.630	-2.248	-0.060	-0.878	-0.038	-0.810
Communication (48)	1	23.381	24.342	17.205	12.046	4.180	34.443	4.832	27.836
Public Utilities (49)	11	10.996	17.102	5.486	7.231	19.417	-1.428	8.658	-0.365
Wholesale Trade (50, 51)	4	12.271	17.485	6.476	8.265	13.412	3.108	7.064	1.768
Retail Trade (52-59)	10	2.305	2.312	4.958	4.738	2.317	3.265	3.082	3.856
Finance (60-62, 67)	15	13.485	18.465	10.126	10.650	1.126	8.443	1.618	5.979
Real Estate (65)	7	-25.886	-39.859	-7.923	-22.543	5.621	22.883	5.215	13.324
Business & Professional Serv. (73, 89)	7	2.561	14.011	5.164	15.991	5.366	8.658	9.886	12.125
Leisure & Repair Serv. (70, 72, 75-79)	3	5.537	-4.561	3.696	-4.433	3.430	1.658	11.668	2.812
Health & Educational Serv. (80, 82)	10	1.755	0.871	8.239	3.303	0.141	1.568	0.422	4.439
Total	125	1.953	1.943	2.347	2.315	6.092	2.363	5.269	1.889

Table 5-6 (continued)

B. Breakdown by 2-digit SIC for Manufacturing Industries

Food & Kindred Products (20)	1	22.692	38.907	35.075	47.011	-0.921	0.601	-1.127	0.878
Textile Mill Products (22)	2	2.990	6.586	6.279	10.978	-7.448	-4.640	-3.225	-2.357
Furniture & Fixtures (25)	1	2.335	3.353	4.916	9.508	2.263	2.398	4.497	4.146
Paper & Allied Products (26)	1	2.991	11.420	3.726	10.092	4.402	8.376	4.388	7.045
Printing & Publishing (27)	4	0.721	8.080	1.683	14.262	5.902	5.804	8.335	6.484
Chemicals & Allied Products (28)	1	15.355	32.477	7.724	9.978	12.438	4.208	11.465	3.049
Petroleum & Coal Products (29)	3	2.756	-26.068	1.348	-5.277	8.068	-7.671	2.054	-0.688
Rubber & Plastic Products (30)	2	-0.176	15.345	-0.133	17.173	5.605	6.309	9.878	8.621
Stone, Clay & Glass (32)	3	-2.299	6.032	-0.588	4.277	4.136	6.005	5.371	6.484
Primary Metal Industries (33)	1	-1.071	9.273	0.432	7.439	3.258	1.127	3.748	1.539
Fabricated Metal Products (34)	1	5.368	-3.282	5.336	-2.555	3.256	6.298	4.821	7.662
Machinery, Except Electrical (35)	3	-0.158	6.146	1.499	10.473	1.034	8.311	1.389	9.323
Electric & Electronic Equip. (36)	11	2.907	3.260	6.742	6.333	21.019	24.190	16.290	12.359
Transportation Equipment (37)	2	7.100	-0.185	12.293	0.309	10.755	11.399	15.147	10.902
Instruments (38)	2	4.924	-4.877	6.969	-4.477	3.133	6.723	4.294	7.824
Misc. Manufacturing (39)	1	-5.227	5.915	-8.464	18.210	-8.117	7.081	-10.573	13.869
Total Manufacturing	**39**	**0.564**	**6.878**	**0.784**	**7.381**	**8.859**	**4.169**	**6.989**	**2.934**

Note: Only 125 high yield firms with readily available sales and employment data are included.
Sales per employee are in thousands of dollars.

Source: COMPUSTAT Data, Standard & Poor's Corp., 1980-1986.

Among high yield manufacturing firms, performance improved between the before and after periods in eleven industries and declined in five. In the manufacturing industry totals, sales per employee performance was evenly split, with rates increasing in eight sectors and declining in eight.

Summary: Sales Per Employee

Using sales per employee as a proxy for productivity, we found that, overall, high yield firms outperformed the industry totals. In manufacturing industries, high yield companies outperformed industry totals by a more substantial margin. This result was consistent across the cohort analysis of all high yield companies and the "before and after" analysis of the Class of 1983.

In the Class of 1983 analysis, high yield firms showed higher rates of growth in sales per employee than did industry totals in the 1983-1986 period. Although sales per employee declined slightly for high yield firms between the before and after periods, the reduction was considerably less than that in the industry totals. High yield manufacturing firms showed a dramatic increase in sales per employee between the before and after periods of the Class of 1983 analysis, while manufacturing as a whole showed a sharp decline.

Sales Impact of High Yield Securities

Sales growth is a key indicator of a company's market position and competitive strength. In our analysis of sales performance, high yield firms showed an annual growth rate of 9.38 percent, compared to 6.42 percent for industry in general (Table 5-7).

Table 5-7. Changes in Sales: High Yield Firms vs. Industry Totals

| | | Average Annual Change, 1980-1986 | | | |
| | | High Yield Firms | | Industry Total | |
Industry (SIC)	**N**	**Absolute**	**Percent**	**Absolute**	**Percent**
A. Breakdown by Industry Group					
Agricultural Products (01, 02)	3	7.682	1.270	1.240	23.113
Mining & Natural Res.					
Extraction	29	174.129	1.462	-8.140	-1.434
Construction (15-17)	5	196.598	9.618	10.579	5.327
Manufacturing, Durable	158	3,957.541	7.006	658.251	8.705
Manufacturing, Nondurable	61	1,347.391	3.562	-96.557	-1.002
Transportation (40-47)	28	3,301.440	10.162	100.844	10.908
Communications (48)	15	681.987	28.531	192.147	17.288
Public Utilities (49)	30	1,778.682	7.317	113.374	6.010
Wholesale Trade (50,51)	38	820.910	5.282	76.571	11.841

Table 5-7 *(continued)*

Retail Trade (52-59)	63	5,736.610	21.751	261.189	10.061
Finance (60-62,67)	48	2,763.907	20.576	259.751	8.786
Insurance (63,64)	6	463.641	35.496	141.378	15.296
Real Estate (65)	24	331.061	10.107	8.182	14.973
Business & Professional Serv. (73,89)	33	318.600	8.727	34.109	20.394
Leisure & Repair Serv. (70,72.75-79)	27	905.237	15.506	4.296	1.923
Health & Educational Serv. (80, 82)	36	2,006.086	26.493	20.987	19.574
Total	**604**	**24,791.502**	**9.384**	**1,778.202**	**6.417**

B. Breakdown by 2-digit SIC for Manufacturing Industries

Food & Kindred Products (20)	13	329.584	5.771	37.159	5.467
Textile Mill Products (22)	6	75.366	2.865	7.680	7.004
Apparel (23)	5	30.577	3.920	9.144	10.214
Lumber & Wood Products (24)	2	50.633	30.804	7.118	5.634
Furniture & Fixtures (25)	1	54.250	14.703	5.268	12.740
Paper & Allied Products (26)	8	1,172.430	13.392	35.502	7.407
Printing & Publishing (27)	7	184.774	9.989	29.827	12.104
Chemicals & Allied Products (28)	10	29.962	1.871	22.683	2.939
Petroleum & Coal Products (29)	5	-692.934	-8.477	-241.491	-4.390
Rubber & Plastic Products (30)	7	217.632	2.878	2.112	1.162
Stone, Clay, & Glass (32)	9	167.730	5.451	7.897	4.998
Primary Metal Industries (33)	9	163.063	3.316	0.062	0.753
Fabricated Metal Products (34)	11	653.306	20.758	11.331	4.435
Machinery, Except Electrical (35)	15	242.339	5.977	136.303	8.310
Electric & Electronic Equip. (36)	63	1,368.088	9.129	227.728	12.300
Transportation Equip. (37)	17	692.639	4.468	224.460	9.362
Instruments (38)	21	139.518	8.273	31.605	8.085
Misc. Manufacturing (39)	10	425.974	25.081	6.480	13.345
Total Manufacturing	**219**	**5,304.932**	**5.573**	**561.694**	**3.778**

Note: Only 604 firms with readily available sales data are included.

Absolute changes for high yield firms are in millions of dollars; industry totals are in 100 millions of dollars.

Source: COMPUSTAT Data, Standard & Poor's Corp., 1980-1986.

In mining and nondurable manufacturing, industry sales decreased moderately (-1.43 percent and -1.00 percent), while high yield firms increased sales 1.46 percent and 3.56 percent respectively. In four other industries, high yield firms increased their sales twice as fast as their industries: retail trade (21.75 percent versus 10.06 percent), finance (20.58 percent versus 8.79 percent), insurance (35.50 percent versus 15.30 percent), and leisure and repair services (15.51 percent versus 1.92 percent). In agriculture, durable manufacturing, real estate, and business and professional services, the rate of sales growth was lower for high yield firms than for their respective industries.

Analyzing manufacturing separately, we found that high yield firms showed a 5.57 percent increase in sales, outperforming total manufacturing, which grew only 3.78 percent. High yield firms in lumber and wood products, fabricated metals, primary metals, and rubber and plastics grew at least twice as fast as did their respective industries, and in some cases, more then four or five times as fast. In both rubber and plastics and primary metals, high yield firms showed greater sales gains than their industries, showing that investment grade companies in these sectors had net sales losses.

By contrast, in textiles, apparel, printing and publishing, chemicals, machinery, electronics, and transportation equipment, sales growth was slower among high yield firms than in the industry at large.

Changes in Sales: The Class of 1983

Among firms that issued high yield securities in 1983, average annual sales growth after issuance (1983-1986) was almost twice the rate before issuance (1980-1983): 10.02 percent versus 5.10 percent. In the industry totals, sales growth rates improved between the before and after periods, but by a more modest margin (from 5.11 percent to 7.16 percent) (see Table 5-8).

Since agriculture and communications each had only one company in the Class of 1983 sales growth data, we excluded them from our industry comparisons. In seven of the remaining twelve industry groups, high yield firms outperformed their industry totals in annual percentage change in sales after 1983. These industries included durable and nondurable manufacturing, transportation, public utilities, retail trade, finance, and health and educational services.

The thirty-nine manufacturing firms in the Class of 1983 also showed a tremendous change in annual sales growth. Between the before and after periods, these companies reversed a declining sales trend, turning it into rapid positive growth (from -4.32 percent to -7.42 percent). While total manufacturing showed positive sales growth in both the before and after periods, the improvement was much less dramatic (from + 3.05 percent to + 4.41 percent). The issuance of high yield securities is therefore associated with increasing market share.

Table 5-8. Changes in Sales: Firms Issuing High Yield Securities in 1983 vs. Industry Totals

		Average Annual Changes, Before and After Issuing Junk Bonds							
		High Yield Firms				Industry Total			
		Absolute Change		Percentage Change		Absolute Change		Percentage Change	
Industry (SIC)	N	1980-1983	1983-1986	1980-1983	1983-1986	1980-1983	1983-1986	1980-1983	1983-1986
A. Breakdown by Industry Group									
Agricultural Products (01, 02)	1	-60.592	62.055	-3.260	3.945	-0.693	3.172	35.342	10.884
Mining & Natural Res. Extraction	8	179.930	-210.471	20.923	-17.377	2.323	-18.604	0.698	-3.565
Manufacturing, Durable (24, 25, 32-39)	25	-1,076.133	2,005.519	-7.312	15.676	384.462	932.041	6.050	11.360
Manufacturing, Nondurable	14	-208.928	-150.014	-1.212	-0.762	47.325	-240.438	0.734	-2.738
Transportation (40-47)	9	1,186.461	3,317.163	5.735	12.231	90.938	110.751	11.513	10.304
Communication (48)	1	476.842	642.424	94.423	29.580	137.514	246.781	15.705	18.872
Public Utilities (49)	11	907.318	1,144.026	8.269	8.245	176.580	50.169	9.638	2.382
Wholesale Trade (50, 51)	4	174.528	34.262	11.629	2.133	43.741	109.401	8.397	15.284
Retail Trade (52-59)	10	321.332	718.947	9.668	15.874	153.903	368.474	7.109	13.012
Finance (60-62, 67)	15	543.405	752.159	17.479	15.175	152.540	366.961	6.135	11.437
Real Estate (65)	8	94.561	0.651	8.752	0.427	3.080	13.284	8.455	21.491
Business & Professional Serv. (73, 89)	7	242.222	200.411	27.317	12.926	18.422	49.795	15.622	25.166
Leisure & Repair Serv. (70, 72, 75-79)	3	103.803	-36.275	13.641	-2.787	-7.205	15.797	-3.058	6.905
Health & Education Serv. (80, 82)	10	948.042	926.023	41.918	17.837	17.553	24.421	21.708	17.441
Total	126	3,832.791	9,406.880	5.100	10.018	1,220.483	2,032.006	5.108	7.163

Table 5-8 (*continued*)

B. Breakdown by 2-digit SIC for Manufacturing Industries

Food & Kindred Products (20)	1	16.534	56.633	244.161	66.006	11.065	63.253	1.760	9.173
Textile Mill Products (22)	2	34.861	-65.928	2.074	-2.433	-0.921	16.280	-0.653	14.662
Furniture & Fixtures (25)	1	41.621	77.209	16.016	18.338	3.508	7.027	10.566	14.914
Paper & Allied Products (26)	1	-33.841	-1.643	-3.328	0.803	19.409	51.594	4.806	10.008
Printing & Publishing (27)	4	-64.192	125.265	-6.056	12.113	20.290	39.363	10.194	14.013
Chemicals & Allied Products (28)	1	-14.169	-30.293	-3.568	-12.977	70.318	-24.952	8.367	-2.490
Petroleum & Coal Products (29)	3	-157.351	-637.369	-2.342	-13.338	-85.513	-397.469	-1.377	-7.402
Rubber & Coal Products (29)	3	9.230	403.319	0.312	8.993	3.370	0.855	1.753	0.570
Stone, Clay & Glass (32)	3	30.777	86.770	2.561	6.090	0.507	15.288	0.784	9.211
Primary Metal Industries (33)	1	-1,144.056	897.867	-15.600	19.656	-25.986	26.111	-3.990	5.496
Fabricated Metal Products (34)	1	-10.676	801.215	-3.497	179.340	-12.658	35.320	-4.160	13.030
Machinery, Except Electrical (35)	3	-10.807	0.536	-2.221	4.602	63.268	209.337	4.542	12.078
Electric & Electronic Equip. (36)	11	65.049	-66.309	2.220	-1.257	185.933	269.522	12.153	12.447
Transportation Equipment (37)	2	38.889	58.386	6.132	7.606	147.249	301.670	7.521	11.202
Instruments (38)	2	7.161	8.082	7.435	7.879	17.876	45.335	5.327	10.842
Misc. Manufacturing (39)	1	-94.092	141.763	-3.540	19.704	-1.418	14.378	-1.541	28.230
Total Manufacturing	**39**	**-1,285.061**	**1,855.505**	**-4.320**	**7.416**	**416.297**	**672.911**	**3.048**	**4.406**

Note: Only 126 high yield firms with readily available sales data are included.
Absolute changes in high yield firms are in millions of dollars; industry totals are in 100 millions of dollars.

Source: COMPUSTAT Data, Standard & Poor's Corp., 1980-1986.

High Yield Securities and Capital Investment

The cost, level, and allocation of capital are fundamental indicators of the future planning of firms and industries. As was noted in Chapter 2, capital investment rates in the United States have lagged far behind those of our major trading partners in Europe and the Far East.

In studying total invested capital, we examined the sum of long-term debt, preferred stock, minority interest, and common equity. We found that, overall, high yield firms showed a greater annual percentage growth in capital investment than industry in general (12.37 percent versus 9.85 percent) (see Table 5-9). This result is hardly surprising, since our study specifically singled out companies that had raised capital during the study period. Despite this selection bias, the variations in capital investment between high yield firms and industry at large remain highly instructive.

Table 5-9. Changes in Total Invested Capital: High Yield Firms vs. Industry Totals

| | | Average Annual Change, 1980-1986 | | | |
| | | High Yield Firms | | Industry Total | |
Industry (SIC)	N	Absolute	Percent	Absolute	Percent
A. Breakdown by Industry Group					
Agricultural Products (01, 02)	3	42.655	7.132	2.721	25.053
Mining & Natural Res. Extraction	29	1,214.453	10.159	23.507	5.493
Construction (15-17)	5	60.709	12.428	3.878	12.803
Manufacturing, Durable	158	1,722.733	5.639	369.191	10.169
Manufacturing, Nondurable	60	1,925.703	9.901	112.137	7.561
Transportation (40-47)	28	2,596.433	12.466	90.651	12.495
Communications (48)	15	590.386	20.160	114.481	7.393
Public Utilities (49)	30	5,568.645	11.438	237.497	7.733
Wholesale Trade (50, 51)	38	126.650	3.211	26.894	15.923
Retail Trade (52-59)	62	2,028.951	24.484	92.008	12.254
Finance (60-62, 67)	46	3,270.674	22.109	265.838	15.338
Insurance (63, 64)	6	440.667	36.323	2.553	10.000
Real Estate (65)	24	691.625	22.604	11.935	24.357
Business & Professional Serv. (73, 89)	33	465.861	17.066	12.831	16.684
Leisure & Repair Serv. (70, 72, 75-79)	27	1,165.863	18.541	11.319	5.352
Health & Educational Serv. (80, 82)	35	1,914.794	30.928	22.629	24.747
Total	**599**	**23,777.805**	**12.371**	**1,427.072**	**9.852**

Table 5-9 *(continued)*

B. Breakdown by 2-digit SIC for Manufacturing Industries

Food & Kindred Products (20)	12	276.740	13.053	17.672	7.053
Textile Mill Products (22)	6	13.328	1.190	4.060	8.079
Apparel (23)	5	47.328	15.713	5.240	13.420
Lumber & Wood Products (24)	2	30.946	52.396	4.134	4.211
Furniture & Fixtures (25)	1	31.733	23.217	2.295	12.269
Paper & Allied Products (26)	8	1,134.042	17.433	38.030	10.951
Printing & Publishing (27)	7	264.104	20.046	28.210	18.722
Chemicals & Allied Products (28)	10	105.777	12.897	15.575	3.346
Petroleum & Coal Products (29)	5	-44.757	-1.425		
Rubber & Plastic Products (30)	7	129.142	3.397	3.351	3.531
Stone, Clay, & Glass (32)	9	79.077	3.753	2.467	2.473
Primary Metal Industries (33)	9	-812.920	-11.979	7.698	2.454
Fabricated Metal Products (34)	11	453.175	21.627	11.194	7.663
Machinery, Except Electrial (35)	15	250.478	11.159	113.365	11.334
Electric & Electronic Equip. (36)	64	1,341.277	17.264	141.930	14.445
Transportation Equip. (37)	16	1.402	0.586	81.178	9.271
Instruments (38)	21	158.451	12.257	27.816	11.011
Misc. Manufacturing (39)	10	189.113	28.021	4.115	16.012
Total Manufacturing	**218**	**3,648.437**	**7.158**	**508.329**	**9.432**

Note: Only 599 firms with readily available capital invested data are included.
   Capital invested for high yield firms are in millions of dollars; industry totals are in 100 millions of dollars.

Source: COMPUSTAT Data, Standard & Poor's Corp., 1980-1986.

Among high yield firms, the most rapidly growing rates of invested capital were in nonmanufacturing sectors such as insurance (36.32 percent), health and educational services (30.93 percent), retail trade (24.48 percent), real estate (22.60 percent), and finance (22.11 percent).

In insurance, high yield issuers increased their total invested capital over three times as fast as their industry did (36.32 percent versus 10.00 percent). High yield firms in leisure and repair services also more than tripled their industry's investment rate (18.54 percent versus 5.35 percent). In communications, high yield companies increased their capital investment more than twice as fast as their industry did (20.16 percent versus 7.39 percent). High yield firms also outpaced their industries in retail trade, health and educational services, business and professional services, finance, public utilities, mining, and nondurable manufacturing.

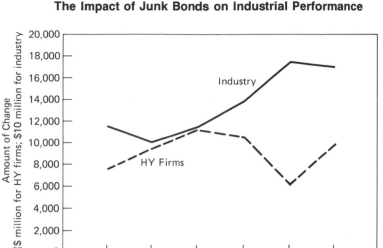

Figure 5–2. Annual change in total invested capital—firms that issued high yield securities in 1983 vs. industry totals (Compustat Data, Standard & Poor's Corp., 1980–1986).

Capital Investment: Manufacturing

Among high yield manufacturing firms, the rate of capital investment was slower than for manufacturing as a whole (7.16 percent versus 9.43 percent). This finding should be understood in light of the declines in investment in primary metals (-11.98 percent) and in petroleum refining (-1.43 percent). In the vast majority of manufacturing sectors, high yield firms outperformed their industries in growth of average annual capital investment.

Capital Investment: The Class of 1983

Unlike other variables, capital investment has an immediate and noticeable impact in the year companies issue high yield securities. The high yield Class of 1983 increased its investment to its peak of $11.2 billion in that year (Figure 5-2), while industry levels of capital investment followed a more secular pattern.

As Table 5-10 indicates, industry as a whole increased its rate of capital investment between the before and after periods (from 9.60 percent to 10.54 percent) while among the issuers in the high yield Class of 1983, the rate of capital investment declined (from 14.60 percent to 9.19 percent). Since high yield firms invest capital during the year of issue, it is not surprising that the post-1983 growth rate is relatively smaller. In most industries, the high yield firms in the Class of 1983 slowed their investment rates after absorbing the new financing. Three major industries had greater capital investment after

Table 5-10. Changes in Total Invested Capital: Firms Issuing High Yield Securities in 1989 vs. Industry Totals

		Average Annual Changes, Before and After Issuing Junk Bonds							
		High Yield Firms				Industry Total			
		Absolute Change		Percentage Change		Absolute Change		Percentage Change	
Industry (SIC)	N	1980-1983	1983-1986	1980-1983	1983-1986	1980-1983	1983-1986	1980-1983	1983-1986
A. Breakdown by Industry Group									
Agricultural Products (01, 02)	1	-36.564	99.397	-4.502	18.766	0.672	4.770	28.380	21.726
Mining & Natural Res. Extraction	8	680.139	-790.100	33.999	-28.338	53.954	-8.380	19.729	-1.578
Manufacturing, Durable (24, 25, 32-39)	25	531.702	-453.231	9.523	-2.277	270.729	513.386	8.490	12.169
Manufacturing, Nondurable	14	301.394	-138.661	4.689	-1.880	83.309	130.487	6.544	8.273
Transportation (40-47)	9	624.962	3,404.117	5.996	21.250	23.644	55.927	11.644	18.803
Communications (48)	1	822.164	360.251	98.415	12.052	124.906	104.055	8.880	5.906
Public Utilities (49)	11	4,136.189	2,903.001	14.619	7.382	259.989	215.004	9.351	6.116
Wholesale Trade (50, 51)	4	58.963	31.479	13.660	5.385	9.041	44.748	6.872	24.973
Retail Trade (52-59)	10	231.897	463.527	23.349	22.563	64.452	111.964	10.942	13.577
Finance (60-62, 67)	15	348.956	1,278.675	11.614	25.800	167.325	364.352	12.508	18.168
Real Estate (65)	8	290.305	514.376	31.342	25.621	6.003	17.868	18.552	30.162
Business & Professional Serv. (73, 89)	7	238.540	207.386	46.392	15.767	8.119	17.544	13.952	19.416
Leisure & Repair Serv. (70, 72, 75-79)	3	120.719	44.620	8.962	3.489	8.319	11.981	13.785	13.563
Health & Educational Serv. (80, 82)	10	1,063.299	868.423	53.533	16.591	21.365	23.893	31.489	18.005
Total	126	9,412.664	8,793.259	14.603	9.187	1,101.87	1,607.598	9.599	10.539

Table 5–10 (continued)

B. Breakdown by 2-digit SIC for Manufacturing Industries

Industry									
Food & Kindred Products (20)	1	22.165	18.005	160.614	21.117	11.910	23.435	5.043	9.064
Textile Mill Products (22)	2	14.874	-71.789	1.897	-8.350	0.132	7.989	0.462	15.697
Furniture & Fixtures (25)	1	23.052	40.415	24.398	22.036	1.612	2.978	10.569	13.969
Paper & Allied Products (26)	1	-1.236	-27.959	-0.087	-4.755	25.976	50.084	8.980	12.922
Printing & Publishing (27)	4	-9.942	107.421	-0.936	17.728	12.399	44.021	11.290	26.154
Chemicals & Allied Products (28)	1	21.455	-63.238	11.847	-34.038	31.938	-0.789	6.799	-0.107
Petroleum & Coal Products (29)	3	113.455	-167.120	6.935	-9.457				
Rubber & Plastic Products (30)	2	140.624	66.019	5.447	2.131	0.954	5.748	1.168	5.894
Stone, Clay, & Glass (32)	3	49.781	-59.342	5.321	-2.753	4.044	0.890	4.066	0.880
Primary Metal Industries (33)	1	131.378	-1,689.730	5.445	-55.628	6.746	8.650	2.148	2.760
Fabricated Metal Products (34)	1	18.429	474.376	20.829	139.440	4.443	17.944	3.540	11.787
Machinery, Except Electrical (35)	3	24.647	-4.732	18.088	-2.353	89.581	137.148	10.722	11.945
Electric & Electronic Equip. (36)	11	367.054	581.445	31.158	23.331	110.864	172.996	14.134	14.756
Transportation Equipment (37)	2	18.105	57.267	7.488	16.692	27.982	134.374	3.853	14.690
Instruments (38)	2	21.812	-0.219	37.396	0.805	25.746	29.887	11.879	10.143
Misc. Manufacturing (39)	1	-122.556	147.290	-30.642	3,810.607	-0.288	8.519	-1.059	33.084
Total Manufacturing	**39**	**833.096**	**-591.892**	**6.853**	**-2.939**	**354.038**	**643.872**	**7.914**	**11.095**

Note: Only 126 high yield firms with readily available capital investment data are included.
Invested capital for high yield firms are in millions of dollars; industry totals are in 100 millions of dollars.

Source: COMPUSTAT Data, Standard & Poor's Corp., 1980-1986.

the issue than before: finance (25.80 percent versus 11.61 percent), transportation (21.25 percent versus 6.00 percent), and agriculture (18.77 percent versus -4.50 percent). Within manufacturing, only in printing and publishing, fabricated metals, and transportation equipment did high yield firms increase their rate of capital investment after their 1983 issues.

High Yield Securities and Capital Expenditures

While data on invested capital reflects a company's changing capitalization, data on capital expenditures shows the actual amount spent on construction or acquisition of property, plant, and equipment. This figure is a key indicator of a firm's growth and response to changing market trends.

Overall, high yield firms showed an annual growth rate in capital expenditures that was more than twice that of U.S. industry as a whole (10.61 percent versus 3.83 percent). (see Table 5-11). High yield firms outstripped the growth rates of their respective industries in durable and nondurable manufacturing, transportation, communications, retail trade, real estate, business and professional services, leisure and repair services, and health and educational services.

Table 5-11. Changes in Capital Expenditures: High Yield Firms vs. Industry Totals

| | | Average Annual Change, 1980-1986 | | | |
| | | High Yield Firms | | Industry Total | |
Industry (SIC)	N	Absolute	Percent	Absolute	Percent
A. Breakdown by Industry Group					
Agricultural Products (01, 02)	3	1.241	3.603	0.182	12.386
Mining & Natural Res. Extraction	29	-245.674	-7.344	-10.775	-7.310
Construction (15-17)	5	-0.184	1.442	-0.012	5.279
Manufacturing, Durable	159	249.249	6.276	26.614	6.015
Manufacturing, Nondurable	61	417.184	15.532	-9.691	-0.529
Transportation (40-47)	28	1,274.891	26.178	10.033	8.973
Communications (48)	15	153.117	29.284	24.509	9.539
Public Utilities (49)	30	49.622	1.897	10.683	2.980
Wholesale Trade (50, 51)	37	-53.503	-1.535	0.270	3.112
Retail Trade (52-59)	63	323.654	26.979	14.884	13.443
Finance (60-62, 67)	34	46.247	19.750	3.173	29.918
Real Estate (65)	22	56.086	27.144	0.589	21.961
Business & Professional Serv. (73, 89)	33	174.166	29.554	2.633	23.174
Leisure & Repair Serv. (70, 72, 75-79)	26	357.953	22.443	6.982	17.708
Health & Educational Serv. (80, 82)	36	376.300	32.827	2.415	9.712
Total	581	3,180.349	10.605	82.489	3.830

Table 5-11 *(continued)*

B. Breakdown by 2-digit SIC for Manufacturing Industries

Food & Kindred Products (20)	13	39.792	17.049	2.025	6.432
Textile Mill Products (22)	6	5.158	10.363	0.580	15.432
Apparel (23)	5	6.211	37.897	0.097	6.311
Lumber & Wood Products (24)	2	1.382	82.472	0.305	9.003
Furniture & Fixtures (25)	1	3.739	37.501	0.162	20.973
Paper & Allied Products (26)	8	370.124	33.375	2.365	4.157
Printing & Publishing (27)	7	65.167	37.780	2.028	14.979
Chemicals & Allied Products (28)	10	12.403	17.389	2.681	2.600
Petroleum & Coal Products (29)	5	-87.918	-20.344	-21.927	-3.415
Rubber & Plastic Products (30)	7	6.245	10.890	2.460	16.428
Stone, Clay, & Glass (32)	9	-26.021	-2.991	-0.542	-2.304
Primary Metal Industries (33)	9	-29.453	-4.066	-1.515	2.816
Fabricated Metal Products (34)	11	127.022	102.077	0.441	6.925
Machinery, Except Electrical (35)	15	1.220	4.042	-0.762	-0.834
Electric & Electronic Equip. (36)	64	85.284	6.967	13.114	8.030
Transportation Equip. (37)	17	67.764	8.102	13.125	8.233
Instruments (38)	21	-0.813	1.511	1.957	5.651
Misc. Manufacturing (39)	10	19.127	31.623	0.328	14.530
Total Manufacturing	**220**	**666.433**	**9.694**	**16.923**	**2.086**

Note: Only 581 firms with readily available data are included.
Absolute changes for high yield firms are in millions of dollars; industry totals are in 100 millions of dollars.

Source: COMPUSTAT Data, Standard & Poor's Corp., 1980-1986.

High yield firms in agriculture, construction, public utilities, wholesale trade, and finance had lower growth rates in capital spending than did their industries. In mining and wholesale trade, high yield firms actually experienced declining levels of expenditures.

Capital Expenditures: Manufacturing

As we noted earlier, high yield issuance was primarily concentrated in the manufacturing sector. Manufacturing firms have faced a critical demand for retooling and modernization in the face of increasing import penetration. During our study period, 220 high yield manufacturing firms accounted for 39.38 percent of the increases in capital spending of all publicly traded manufacturing firms. The annual growth rate of capital spending among high yield manufacturers was more than four times that of total manufacturing (9.69 percent versus 2.09 percent).

Table 5-12. Changes in Capital Expenditures: Firms Issuing High Yield Securities in 1983 vs. Industry Totals

Industry (SIC)	N	Average Annual Changes, Before and After Issuing Junk Bonds							
		High Yield Firms				Industry Total			
		Absolute Change		Percentage Change		Absolute Change		Percentage Change	
		1980-1983	1983-1986	1980-1983	1983-1986	1980-1983	1983-1986	1980-1983	1983-1986
A. Breakdown by Industry group									
Agricultural Products (01, 02)	1	-4.378	4.060	-11.306	14.741	-0.077	0.441	-0.965	25.737
Mining & Natural Res. Extraction	8	49.653	-183.687	23.870	-31.154	-12.312	-3.457	-6.975	-4.968
Manufacturing, Durable (24, 25, 32-39)	25	27.883	252.383	4.313	28.781	-4.634	28.157	-2.170	13.981
Manufacturing, Nondurable	14	-106.015	15.576	-13.114	3.599	1.618	-29.644	1.593	-4.477
Transportation (40-47)	9	222.738	2,215.285	12.884	61.088	3.577	12.664	8.289	22.866
Communications (48)	1	208.533	104.497	89.980	15.324	20.728	28.533	9.596	10.014
Public Utilities (49)	11	780.358	-643.900	18.527	-12.035	28.417	-7.050	7.192	-1.232
Wholesale Trade (50, 51)	4	-0.892	-1.218	1.049	-4.258	0.031	1.065	2.928	17.414
Retail Trade (52-59)	10	108.400	18.229	89.117	6.588	5.418	12.334	9.972	15.277
Finance (60-62, 67)	11	1.325	14.907	3.098	17.617	0.941	5.417	16.020	45.925
Real Estate (65)	8	7.042	92.541	11.950	49.516	-0.046	1.225	2.640	41.282
Business & Professional Serv. (73, 89)	7	90.925	201.585	49.372	34.475	1.183	4.082	14.677	31.671
Leisure & Repair Serv. (70, 72, 75-79)	3	-114.551	-4.039	-18.427	10.901	0.357	2.973	2.886	14.897
Health & Educational Serv. (80, 82)	10	246.859	92.576	59.509	8.218	1.108	3.723	5.100	14.323
Total	122	1,517.882	2,178.795	14.223	13.660	46.309	60.462	3.248	3.668

Table-12 (continued)

B. Breakdown by 2-digit SIC for Manufacturing Industries

Industry									
Food & Kindred Products (20)	1	10.493	-5.467	7,655.918	149.361	-0.001	0.940	1.106	33.708
Textile Mill Products (22)	2	9.074	-15.033	9.762	-6.389	0.398	0.355	12.917	13.067
Furniture & Fixtures (25)	1	5.202	2.276	54.788	20.215	0.106	0.218	17.267	24.679
Paper & Allied Products (26)	1	-18.832	1.931	-29.548	17.250	-0.173	3.858	-0.256	7.631
Printing & Publishing (27)	4	-0.266	23.078	4.233	56.542	0.183	0.998	6.534	21.819
Chemicals & Allied Products (28)	1	-7.488	1.587	-4.943	18.697	-0.544	4.700	-14.810	218.879
Petroleum & Coal Products (29)	3	-63.510	-32.846	-19.136	-12.867	1.653	-45.507	2.117	-8.946
Rubber & Plastic Products (30)	2	-35.485	42.326	-13.900	21.024	0.155	4.766	2.025	30.830
Stone, Clay, & Glass (32)	3	-46.753	6.079	-18.220	4.094	-1.284	-0.359	-17.431	-9.914
Primary Metal Industries (33)	1	12.200	-27.067	7.432	-11.526	-0.877	1.494	-3.664	53.483
Fabricated Metal Products (34)	1	-0.449	207.612	-9.518	1,516.143	-0.555	0.425	-16.384	45.889
Machinery, Except Electrical (35)	3	-2.023	-0.292	4.254	9.125	-2.523	0.085	-15.670	1.367
Electric & Electronic Equip. (36)	11	52.460	57.459	41.252	23.846	0.192	21.226	0.404	15.711
Transportation Equip. (37)	2	5.215	5.353	20.189	13.721	0.589	4.494	2.163	13.091
Instruments (38)	2	0.221	0.354	7.762	22.765	-0.311	0.042	-6.474	2.665
Misc. Manufacturing (39)	1	1.810	0.508	13.333	17.409	0.029	0.533	4.639	34.396
Total Manufacturing	**39**	**-78.132**	**267.959**	**-4.888**	**17.974**	**-2.962**	**-1.733**	**0.542**	**0.587**

Note: Only 122 high yield firms with readily available data in capital expenditures are included.
Absolute changes for high yield firms are in millions of dollars; industry totals are in 100 millions of dollars.

Source: COMPUSTAT Data, Standard & Poor's Corp., 1980-1986.

Nine high yield groups had annual growth rates in capital spending that were more than twice the rates in their respective industries, including: fabricated metals (102.08 percent versus 6.93 percent); lumber and wood (82.47 percent versus 9.00 percent); apparel (37.90 percent versus 6.31 percent); printing and publishing (37.78 percent versus 14.98 percent); paper and allied products (33.38 percent versus 4.16 percent); miscellaneous manufacturing (31.62 percent versus 14.53 percent); chemicals (17.38 percent versus 2.60 percent); food and kindred products (17.05 percent versus 6.43 percent); machinery (4.04 percent versus -0.83 percent).

Capital Spending: Class of 1983

Although the 122 high yield firms in the Class of 1983 declined slightly in their rate of capital spending between the before and after periods, their rate of capital spending after issuance was over three times higher than for industry in general (13.66 percent versus 3.67 percent) (see Table 5-12).

Within manufacturing, high yield firms far outperformed industry levels of capital spending after 1983 (17.97 percent versus 0.59 percent). In fact, high yield firms managed to reverse declining levels of capital spending from the pre-issue period, moving from -4.89 percent to + 17.97 percent. During our study, capital spending growth for manufacturing in general remained essentially flat, moving from 0.54 percent to 0.59 percent.

Summary: Overall Industrial Performance

Our analysis shows that high yield securities had a positive impact on corporate performance across a wide range of accepted performance measures. High yield firms evidenced a greater capacity than U.S. industry in general to create new jobs, retain old ones, and successfully manage employment reductions in industries that were losing jobs.

The distribution of high yield securities parallels the distribution of restructuring activity, which is closely associated with productivity growth. According to the Bureau of Labor Statistics productivity index and our own data on sales per employee, high yield firms generally tend to show faster growth in productivity than industry in general.

Sales is another critical indicator of corporate performance and competitiveness. High yield firms showed faster sales growth than did industry in general, and high yield manufacturing firms outpaced total manufacturing in their rate of sales growth.

High yield firms were increasing their total capitalization faster than industry in general is. More important, they were spending their capital on new products, processes, and productivity enhancements to take advantage of new opportunities and improve their position in highly competitive markets. The rate of capital spending among high yield firms was more than twice the industry totals. Within manufacturing, where capital needs and competitive pressures are greatest, high yield firms increased capital spending more than four times as fast as did the manufacturing sector as a whole.

These findings about the competitive economic performance are consistent with recent findings about the financial performance of high yield firms as well. Pound and Gordon (1989) found that high yield issuers increased cash flow, profit earnings, and dividend payments, as well as sales, and also increased capital spending generally and by more than was expected at the time their debt securities were issued. Price/earnings ratios approximately doubled on average, and price/cash-flow multiples relative to levels prior to one-debt placements increased by about 10 percent.

The next chapter studies specific corporate strategies, detailing the steps taken to achieve the results just described. We will see how the new financial structures of high yield companies enabled them to pursue growth strategies.

6

High Yield Companies in Focus

In assessing the impact of high yield financing on corporate performance, aggregate industry and economic data can help us identify general trends. But to learn how particular companies have benefited from the use of high yield financing, we need to look at the companies individually.

In this chapter, we describe actual cases of high yield companies and the strategies they have pursued to maximize the value of their assets, labor force, products, and markets. Our examples show how businesses have responded to the pressures of economic change by modifying their strategies, adopting new technologies, and changing their supply and distribution channels. The companies studied also show how high yield issuers have responded to increasing competition in both domestic and international markets.

In developing data on these companies, we reviewed publicly available sources of corporate information—annual reports, 10-K and 10-Q filings, investment research, press releases, and public statements by the companies or their officials. We also interviewed research analysts, corporate finance experts, and corporate officials.

After our study was completed, many of the companies underwent rapid business changes that are not reflected in this book. We have included three important transactions that were completed shortly after our study was published. Triangle Industries was acquired by Central Jersey Industries, Continental Cablevision completed its acquisition of American Cable, and Charter Medical went private in September of 1988.

A common story appears to repeat itself throughout the case studies. In utilizing the high yield market, firms not only went beyond traditional sources of capital, they also created functions that went beyond traditional industrial categories. Stone Container, a manufacturer of corrugated box containers, for example, was able to consolidate a number of low-margin, low-market-share box producers into a high-margin, high- market share operation that modernized and reopened obsolete plants.

Hovnanian Enterprises is a high yield firm that may accurately be placed in the real estate industry. Yet the company has moved into several complementary areas to shape demand and ensure continued growth. Today, Hovnanian designs high-density housing developments (professional services), applies innovative construction methods (construction), and helps its customers secure home financing (financial services). Each of these functions has helped Hovnanian capitalize on opportunities in the real estate industry and more effectively serve its customers.

Worthington Industries, a steel products manufacturer, is another company that used high yield financing to move beyond traditional industrial categories. Traditionally, manufacturing firms achieved economies of scale by expanding to include all stages of production. Over time, however, many production facilities became costly overhead structures. When firms saw that they could achieve substantial cost savings by outsourcing parts production to specialized producers, Worthington filled the need by becoming a niche manufacturer of production service rather than a producer of a single product.

The list goes on. Our case studies showed that high yield firms commonly demonstrate one or more of the following characteristics:

- The ability to define firm strategies based on industrial diseconomies of scale
- The capacity to move beyond traditional goods and service areas, providing complementary products and services that offer added value to consumers
- Flexible organization of management, production, and distribution
- Specialization of products and services
- Application of advanced technologies to mundane goods and services
- Integration of marketing and production
- The pursuit of financial flexibility through innovative financing and balance sheet management
- Responsiveness to demographic and economic shifts that affect market composition and demand

Durable Manufacturing

Quanex

Throughout the 1980s, steel was the yardstick against which industry problems were measured. According to *Business Week,* U.S. steel producers lost $12 billion from 1982 to 1986. With the increased use of plastics, alloys, and other metals, total demand for steel declined. At the same time, global overcapacity, cheap currencies, and the need to earn foreign exchange intensified international competition and led many foreign steel producers to expand their exports to the United States. To remain competitive, U.S. steel companies had to invest in modernization and productivity-improving technologies. But financing these investments has not always been easy.

Quanex has always been known for high-quality steel and good service. When the oil industry collapsed, Quanex's revenues fell; this coincided with Quanex's expansion movement, resulting in financial difficulties for the company.

Determined to stay on course technologically, Quanex was in the midst of constructing a large, new steel bar plant in Fort Smith, Arkansas, when oil prices started to tumble in 1982. Since Quanex was a major supplier of tubular products to the oil industry, its business and cash flow also fell. More capital was needed to complete construction of the new plant, but banks were not forthcoming with cash. So, instead of opening and contributing to Quanex's cash flow, the partly finished plant was simply a drain on the company's resources.

When traditional banks were unwilling to finance the completion of the plant, Quanex went to the high yield market. In 1984, it sold a $125 million mortgage bond against the Arkansas plant and another facility already operating in Michigan. The funds helped open the Fort Smith plant, and workers are now producing steel there with state-of-the-art technology. By the end of our study period, 1986, Quanex had positive cash flow and was very profitable. Moreover, the company had already retired $45 million of the bonds through open market purchases and an exchange offer.

Now that Quanex is in a solid financial and manufacturing position, the company can effectively compete with both foreign and domestic steel producers.

Worthington Industries, Inc.

If any company has rolled with the punches to the steel industry, it has been Worthington Industries. In the late 1980s, Worthington ranked number 370 in the Fortune 500, and led the pack of steel companies, with a 10 percent return on assets. It was also number one in ten-year growth in earnings, and in earnings per share.

Headquartered in Columbus, Ohio, the thirty-two-year-old company has emphasized fundamentals. Employee councils meet monthly with plant mangers, and the company operates on a system that gives hourly workers the opportunity to become foremen. As a result, Worthington has a highly motivated workforce and an enviable record of waste reduction. Other factors that have contributed to the company's performance include strong financials, solid marketing, a reputation for high quality and on-time delivery, and managers who understand their customers, products, and markets.

In recent years, several of Worthington's major customers, including auto companies and household appliance manufacturers, have been restructuring. Increasingly, these manufacturers are turning to outside suppliers for parts, products, or subassemblies. This move toward outsourcing allows the manufacturers to more effectively respond to cost pressures, volatile foreign exchange rates, market and financial trends, and even the cost, quality, and service weaknesses of their own operations.

Worthington is well positioned to profit from this move toward outsourcing. As customers downsize their operations, Worthington and other outsourcers can grow. The company's sales rose consistently from 1980 to 1987. After a $35 million high yield issue in 1981, its employment declined for one year and later climbed from a low of 3,700 workers to 5,700 in 1985.

The 1981 issue was used to refinance bank and other debt. By offering more favorable terms, the high yield issue provided the company with better cash flow in the following years. As *Fortune* pointed out in its April 25, 1988, issue, Worthington has always been prudent in its debt management by imposing tight limits on borrowing and by requiring that return on investment cover interest expenses from the day of the issue. From 1982 to 1987, Worthington's net earnings grew steadily, from $19.15 million to $42.15 million. Over the same period, the rate of sales and revenue growth almost quadrupled, from 2.2 percent to 8.6 percent, with even stronger performance in 1984 and 1985. Meanwhile, the company strengthened its financial condition by steadily reducing the percentage of debt in its total capitalization, from 44 percent in 1982 to just 16 percent in 1987.

Triangle Industries, Inc.

Originally, Triangle Industries was a relatively small manufacturer of electrical wire, vending machines, currency changers, and jukeboxes. By 1987, it was the world's largest packaging company, with annual sales of $4.3 billion.

Strong management, strategic acquisitions, and high yield financing were critical elements in the company's transformation. In the early 1980s, Triangle tried to expand its business lines by acquiring Brandt, Inc., a manufacturer of coin-sorting and currency-changing products. Although Triangle failed in its attempt, it later acquired an interest in Central Jersey Industries, which was the successful bidder for Brandt.

Prior to 1985, Triangle had raised $176.5 million in two high yield bond issues. The company was looking for acquisitions, and in March of 1985, it took an interest in National Can. At the time, National Can was going through a reorganization and actively soliciting bids. An Employee Stock Ownership Plan had offered to buy the company, but management stated that it would work with another bidder who could offer a higher price. Triangle successfully outbid the ESOP, and acquired National Can for $421 million.

National Can's efficiency and manufacturing know-how had made it the lowest cost producer of two-piece beverage cans in the industry. But many perceived the acquisition as imprudent, since it increased Triangle's debt to more than $800 million on an equity base of approximately $50 million. With a debt-to-equity ratio of 16:1, the company was substantially overleveraged by conventional standards.

To make matters worse, the rise of plastics and other packaging materials was taking its toll on the glass container and metal can business, creating overcapacity and the need to restructure. For many companies, innovation and cost-cutting took on critical importance. Triangle was also taking innovative steps to strengthen its market position. Perhaps the most dramatic was its decision to acquire American Can Packaging in 1986.

Although not as efficient as National Can in metal can manufacturing, American Can was much stronger in performance plastics. The acquisition gave Triangle a synergistic pair of can manufacturers and a more diversified product line to offer its customers. The two companies were merged to form American National Can Companies, to combine National Can's efficiency and manufacturing know-how with American Can's prowess in research and development.

How did these acquisitions affect the company's performance? Just eighteen months after the "imprudent" acquisition of National Can, Triangle's stock price was up sixfold, and the company had increased its equity to approximately $500 million. By the end of 1987, Triangle had more than 115 manufacturing facilities in thirty-nine states and fifteen foreign countries. Employment, which was only 2,250 in 1984, had grown to over 24,000.

The rapid growth of Triangle Industries would have been impossible without high yield financing. The company's leadership and strategic diversification have helped protect earnings in both strong and weak markets. And in 1988, Central Jersey Industries purchased Triangle, in a transaction designed to benefit the shareholders of both companies.

Brunswick Corporation

Brunswick is America's oldest leisure products producer, tracing its origins to 1845. Company officials boast about Brunswick's being the best at what it does: a leader in marine power, fishing, bowling, retail bowling, chemical-injector pumps for the energy business, and door-opening equipment for subways and buses.

It was not always that way. After some unwise diversifications in the 1970s, Brunswick slipped into lethargy. But in the early 1980s, it staged a comeback. In 1981, Brunswick issued $60 million of convertible subordinated debentures, with net proceeds going to general corporate purposes. Basically, the funds were used to strengthen the firm's capital base and provide the flexibility it needed to pursue a back-to-basics strategy founded on quality, efficiency, and restructuring.

By shedding its Sherwood Medical division, Brunswick got back to being a leisure company. Although it already had a leading market share in practically all areas, the company was intent on increasing productivity and market penetration.

Brunswick's dedication to quality was absolute, even when it cost millions of dollars to recall, rebuild, or retool products. The company also focused attention on international sales by promoting bowling in the 1988 Summer Olympics and the 1991 Pan American Games.

Brunswick also believes in making the most of its existing assets through aggressive restructuring. To increase profits in its bowling centers, the company closed underutilized facilities and clustered remaining centers. And rather than move its Mercury Division south in search of cheaper labor, Brunswick renegotiated labor contracts and improved the flexibility and productivity of its plants in the north.

In late 1986, Brunswick purchased Bayliner Marine Corp. and Ray Industries, companies that had pioneered the transformation of the power boat industry with automation, high volume, and low-cost production. Brunswick is also a leader in the upper-priced boat market, which accounted for about three quarters of the company's 1986 profits.

Investment has been an important part of Brunswick's strategy. R & D spending, plant investments, and capital expenditures in general have all moved up strongly since the hard times in the early 1980s. R & D expenditures were $25.5 million in 1981; they rose sharply to $46.1 million in 1986. Investment in plant almost doubled, from $242 million in 1983 to $463 million in 1986. Over the same period, employment grew from 18,400 to 26,800.

Through acquisitions, consolidations, efficiency improvements, and careful attention to quality, Brunswick is showing excellent results, and giving its customers the products they want at prices they can afford.

Town & Country Jewelry Manufacturing Corporation

In the 1950s, Bill Carey was visiting retailers, selling bags of rings. He took Town & Country public in June of 1985. In its first year as a public corporation, it had sales of $71.6 million and posted a net income of $4.2 million. In 1987, Town & Country's sales had increased to $149.8 million, and net income had grown to $7.7 million.

The Town & Country story is the story of an entrepreneur who recognized trends in the global economy, and used acquisitions and backward integration to build a large, multinational jewelry company. In 1988, the company was manufacturing jewelry for the middle market and retailing jewelry to the top end. By aggressively emphasizing quality and low cost, the company had built an excellent reputation throughout the industry.

Town & Country became a retailer in 1980, when it acquired the Little Switzerland chain of duty-free shops in the Caribbean, which sold watches, crystal, china, high-quality jewelry, and gifts. In 1988, Town & Country owned eighteen such shops throughout the Caribbean, and store sales were growing at a rate of over 30 percent per year.

The company also owned Anju Jewelry, Ltd., in Hong Kong, a designer and manufacturer of fine jewelry and one-of-a-kind items. In 1986, Town & Country acquired Gold Lance, Inc., a Houston-based maker of school rings and incentive awards, and Verilyte, a domestic manufacturer of engraved jewelry. In 1987, the company acquired Kan Jewelers, retailers in Aruba and Curacao.

In June 1985, Town & Country issued subordinated notes, common stock, and warrants with net proceeds of $40.2 million to the company. The proceeds were used to refinance bank debt that was taken on for working capital and acquisitions. Access to the high yield market gave Town & Country a clear advantage in its efforts to consolidate the fragmented jewelry-manufacturing and retail portions of its business. As the company continues to grow, it will recognize additional savings from central purchasing, marketing, and inventory control, which will help the company remain efficient and competitive.

The company has also built plants in the Pacific to keep costs down. It expanded its Hong Kong facilities in 1987 and decided to double the work force in its Bangkok factory, which opened in 1986 and was profitable by the end of 1987. To effectively manage import fees, product prices, and currency values, Town & Country can shift production from one facility to another. Meanwhile, the company has increased its exports to Japan and other nations, to expand its global market penetration.

Town & Country's performance has been strong in every sector. Retail sales were $37.9 million by 1986, and up about 23 percent in 1987. By 1988, retail sales made up almost one third of the business. Manufacturing growth was even stronger than retail growth in 1987, surpassing $100 million from just $70.8 million the previous year.

The company is achieving its goal of becoming a one-step supplier for the jewelry industry. As the industry has become more consolidated over the years, Town & Country has taken advantage of the opportunity to supply larger national chain accounts with its products.

Nondurable Manufacturing

Stone Container Corporation

The corrugated and solid fiber box industry is a pervasive part of American life. Practically 100 boxes per person were shipped in 1985. Almost 90 percent of the industrial and consumer goods transported in the United States used some form of corrugated or solid fiber container, divider, or cushioning. In value of shipments, corrugated boxes run a close second to metal containers. And in recent years, corrugated boxes have gained share in the packaging market at the expense of wooden shipping containers, pallets, and metal drums.

The box industry's central role in industrial activity makes it vulnerable to industry cycles, and box shipments are considered a leading indicator of economic activity. The high cost of transport keeps exports at less than 1 percent of total shipments. So the industry's primary sensitivity is to domestic rather than foreign economic trends.

Rather than succumb to the threat posed by the plastics industry, box manufacturers have joined forces with plastics companies, creating laminated containers for liquid, semisolid, and liquid-suspended products. The laminates provide special benefits, including thermal insulation, moisture retention, and package strength.

The box industry had a severe setback during the economic downturn of 1981-1982. As sales plunged, companies were forced to seek new ways to increase productivity and cut costs. Although shipments increased as the economy recovered, the industry has continued to stress efficiency through automation and computerization, emphasizing higher-speed machinery and lower energy costs.

Stone Container has taken unique advantage of these industry cycles to become the nation's largest linerboard producer. When overcapacity made some competitors' plants unnecessary, Stone would buy and upgrade them, improving productivity and reducing energy costs. When the next upturn came, the company would use its profits to pay down debt and make new acquisitions.

Since banks are not fond of this cyclical strategy, Stone has made extensive use of the high yield securities markets to finance its extraordinary growth. The company issued $350 million of high yield securities in 1985, and another $200 million of subordinated securities the following year.

Primarily a linerboard company, Stone tries to emphasize its strengths. When it purchased Southwest Forest Industries in April of 1987, it acquired timberlands, sawmills, and plants specializing in linerboard, newsprint, veneers, and plywood. Stone spun off most of the lumber assets into Stone Forest Industries and retained the newsprint and linerboard assets and timberlands.

Stone's acquisition of Seminole Kraft shows how the company's growth strategy can inject new vitality into a dormant facility. The empty linerboard plant was located ten miles from Jacksonville, Florida, and had once employed 600 people. Stone purchased and upgraded the facility for $100 million. The plant was reopened, and in 1988, over 475 people were working there.

Stone Container's aggressive growth has kept employment booming. In 1982, the company had 3,500 employees. By 1987, that figure had jumped to 18,800. Yet hardly any of Stone Container's growth would have been possible without high yield financing. Unlike bank loans, the issues carry few covenants that would restrict acquisitions or prevent taking on additional debt. Stone has used its high yield proceeds to pay down bank debt and continue its acquisition program. A $200 million convertible bond and preferred stock issue of April 1986 has already been converted. And the company used the $350 million it raised in May of 1985 to pay down acquisition debt.

Doskocil Companies, Inc.*

The food processing industry has always had to respond to changing consumer tastes, but today those tastes are changing faster than ever before. Companies that have anticipated or stayed abreast of these changes have flourished; those that have failed to keep up have languished. Companies that supply food retailers must compete with other processors on the basis of quality and price. To win contracts, they need to keep their costs at rock bottom while providing outstanding quality and impeccable service. Since contracts do not last forever, growth may also depend on a company's ability to broaden its customer base and extend its product line. At Doskocil, putting these elements together has resulted in rapid growth.

While pizza makers like Pizza Hut, Godfather's, and Domino's fight it out at retail, they all come together at Doskocil, the leading supplier of quality food products to the pizza industry. In 1987, pizza making was a $15 billion industry, and pizzas were a specialty in 11 percent of the nation's restaurants. From its home base in Hutchinson, Kansas, Doskocil prepares precooked meat and dry sausage according to the highest quality standards, and ships its products to pizza chains, independent makers, restaurants, and institutional food service operations throughout the United States, Canada, and Japan.

Since food processing is a highly competitive industry, Doskocil had to be quick, aggressive, and imaginative to gain and retain its market share lead. Designing and developing its own equipment helped the company sharpen its competitive edge by keeping costs low and quality high.

Doskocil is a high-tech food processing company that is determined to stay on the leading edge of technology. By the end of 1986, the company had acquired Golden Harbor Seafoods, Inc., a start-up blue crab processor that provided Doskocil with innovative processing technology and an entry into the growing seafood market.

---

*In 1990, Doskocil filed for Chapter 11 protection from its creditors. This action (stemming from losses in its Wilson foods subsidiary acquired in 1988) was not a result of the performance of its core businesses.

In the highly competitive food processing industry, financing is critical for capital investments and strategic acquisitions that provide economies of scale in production and distribution. Doskocil issued $34.9 million of high yield securities in 1983, using the proceeds for internal restructuring, to build their sales and marketing staff, and to position the company for future acquisitions.

In 1985, Doskocil acquired Stoppenbach, Inc., for $40 million, supplying $428 million in cash, $4 million in common stock, and $8 million in convertible subordinated debentures. By combining its sausage division with Stoppenbach, Doskocil became the nation's largest maker of pepperoni and other meat supplied to the pizza industry. In the first full year following the acquisition, Doskocil's sales more than doubled, from $105.7 million in 1985 to $233.9 million in 1986.

Acquisitions like Stoppenbach and Golden Harbor are only possible because Doskocil has access to appropriate funding. While the company has used bank debt as part of its acquisition strategy, Doskocil issued $56 million of senior subordinated debentures in 1987 to repay bank loans, reduce interest payments, improve liquidity, and prepare for possible future acquisitions.

Rymer Company

While Doskocil expanded its existing food processing business, Rymer Company restructured itself into food processing from the bottom up. The company, originally known as Kroehler Manufacturing Company, emerged from bankruptcy in 1983 with only one claim to fame: It was the world's largest manufacturer of parking meters.

Parking meters provided a steady flow of business, but few opportunities for dramatic growth. So Kroehler's executives decided to change the company's direction. Building on the assets and cash flow of the parking meter business, they used high yield securities to fund a series of acquisitions and create a large, efficient food processing company. The transition was completed in 1987 when, with the food processing business on solid footing, the parking meter business was sold.

In 1983, Kroehler executives bought a company and a name. Since then, Rymer has grown internally and through selective acquisitions, expanding its market share in precut, frozen portions of beef, and later in chicken and seafood. It has built its business on a reputation for product consistency and by nurturing the entrepreneurial spirit of its acquired companies.

By 1988, Rymer provided over 100 million meals annually, mostly to family restaurant chains. Processed meats were still the company's main products, but chicken and seafood output were rapidly growing. Sales had skyrocketed, growing over sixteenfold since Rymer was acquired, from $22.2 million in 1983 to $374.4 million in fiscal 1987.

Rymer's biggest advances came in recent years. After raising $75 million in the high yield markets in early 1985, the company acquired four businesses between October 1985 and October 1986: H&N Foods, which provides high-quality chicken portions; Murry's, a specialty retailer of frozen processed foods, with 135 outlets; and two small seafood companies. Largely as a result of these acquisitions, Rymer's employment jumped from 495 in 1985 to 3,600 in 1986. Yet acquisitions have not accounted for all of Rymer's growth. In December of 1986, the company established Rymer International Seafoods to import and distribute specialty seafood products.

Communications and Media

Tele-Communications, Inc.

In 1988, Tele-Communications, Inc. (TCI) was the nation's largest cable company, with interests in cable television systems serving 8.3 million basic subscribers in forty-seven states. TCI is also the largest television company and one of the top five media companies in the U.S. Founded in the 1950s, the company has weathered the cable industry's cycles of expansion and contraction, growing primarily through asset purchases. It has investments in other cable companies, including United Artists Communications, United Cable, and Heritage Communications.

Originally, the cable business was a retransmission business. If you lived in New York City or in the mountains, where clear reception was not available, cable offered access to regular network programming. In the early 1970s, Tele-Communications overextended itself, and almost went bankrupt. But it worked through its problems and survived. Then, in the late 1970s, Home Box Office came along, giving consumers a new reason to subscribe. Instead of just retransmitting network shows, cable now offered full-length, uncut movies. This revitalized the industry and positioned it for rapid growth by selling entertainment with innovative programming in movies, music, and sports.

Tele-Communications did not participate in the franchising boom for cable distributors. While cities were granting franchises to other companies, TCI was making sure that its own house was in order by consolidating internal operations and marketing. By the mid-1980s, the company was ready and strong. Other companies had promised uneconomic frills that made system construction and operation too expensive. As they began to face difficulties, TCI was able to purchase several cable systems at low prices, growing from fourth place to first place in number of subscribers.

In 1988, there were 44 million cable subscribers in the United States. TCI and its affiliated companies had over 8 million subscribers, or nearly 20 percent of the total, and more than twice as many as TCI's nearest competitor. In May of 1988, TCI's stock had a market value of $4-5 billion and was considered by many to be the best in the business. The price of the company's class A stock had grown over tenfold since the beginning of 1980, increasing from about 2 1/4 to trade in the mid-20s in the first half of 1988.

The company has been financially innovative, using different kinds of financing appropriate to its various stages of growth. During the recent industry shakeout, TCI relied on high yield securities to finance many of its acquisitions. The company raised $120.7 million in 1982, $148.6 million in 1983, $220 million in 1986, and $250 million in 1987. Now that the company and industry are mature, TCI has ready access to bank financing.

TCI's goal has always been to maximize shareholder value, and the company developed its financial strategy accordingly. In this very capital-intensive business, with high cash flows, the company's stated objective is to show no earnings, except when it sells a cable system. By showing zero profit, TCI minimizes taxes and maximizes asset value per share. The company's strategy is to acquire properties at below market cost and improve operations through management efficiencies and economies of scale, using the debt markets to leverage up the company as much as possible. The approach is similar to the real estate business, where companies use their cash flow to take out big mortgages and sustain further growth.

Continental Cablevision, Inc.

Continental was started by two Harvard Business School professors in the early 1960s. Over the years, the company has used various legal forms and financing strategies, depending on what was most appropriate at the time. It began as a limited partnership because cable systems initially have high construction costs, low revenues, and losses that could be passed on to limited partners. When a system matures, it has high depreciation charges. After Continental's growth improved and it needed access to public credit markets to finance acquisitions, the company went public.

Toward the end of 1985, the company began to feel that its assets were undervalued by the market, so it went private in a leveraged buyout financed with bank debt and high yield bonds. Dow Jones owned 25 percent of the company when it was public and still holds about a fifth of the stock, even though Continental is private.

The cable industry grew rapidly in the early 1980s as franchises were granted. Then came a period of heavy construction. Now that virtually all of the franchises have been bought and most construction is completed, growth can only come by signing up more customers for a company's own franchises or by acquiring other companies.

Acquisitions have been important to Continental, and early on, they had to be financed by high yield bonds. Bank debt was either unavailable or came with so many restrictions that growth was constrained. By 1988, Continental had 1.5 million subscribers, placing it among the nation's top five cable companies. Another 500,000 subscribers were added with the acquisition of American Cable.

While acquisitions provide some economies of scale, their primary benefit is providing growth opportunities. Continental is committed to the cable business for the long haul. They want to be operators, to buy and run cable systems. The acquisition of American Cable offered the company growth opportunities in Florida and California, and an undeveloped franchise.

As Continental has grown, its asset values have increased to $2,000 per subscriber, compared to $1,000 just a few years ago. With bank financing now available, Continental was able to borrow $600 million to complete the acquisition of American Cable.

Real Estate

Hovnanian Enterprises, Inc.

Housing has always been a feast-or-famine business, populated mainly by small, local builders who scrambled busily when times were good and hibernated when activity slowed. The housing business is a classic cyclical, fragmented industry.

Hovnanian is a farsighted, pathbreaking company in an industry known for its myopia. Careful planning, a willingness to take calculated risks, and the ability to build quality housing at low prices have all combined with the proper financing to create one of the strongest and most profitable companies in the homebuilding business. Even with a Northeastern regional focus, Hovnanian sold 3,241 condominiums during the fiscal year ending February 28, 1987, moving up from fourth place to become the second largest builder of attached houses in the country. Its work is concentrated in New Jersey, Florida, and New York, where housing prices and profit margins are high.

Hovnanian is one of the nation's fastest-growing homebuilders. From 1980 through 1987, the company's employment grew at an average rate of 33.9 percent a year, compared to 17.6 percent for the entire industry. In 1982, the company employed 280 people. By 1986, that figure had grown to 660, more than doubling in just four years. Hovnanian's sales more than quadrupled from 1980 to 1986, increasing from $59.7 million to $287.1 million. And in 1987, Hovnanian ranked number forty-seven in the *Forbes* list of the 200 best small companies in America.

New Jersey-based Hovnanian offers a complete package of services: design, construction, sales, mortgage banking, and financing. The company has also acquired 49 percent of a builder in North Carolina, and has begun a project in New Hampshire.

Hovnanian provides a high-quality product for the low end of the housing market, or quality homes for "average people." Its reputation is so good that many of their projects sell out as soon as they open, and well before construction actually begins. In some cases, people have camped out at the entrance to the sales offices on the night before they opened to ensure they got on the list to buy a Hovnanian home. The people who run Hovnanian are smart developers and land buyers, good builders, and good marketers. They sell quality at the right price, and their construction is cost-effective.

Hovnanian generally purchases land, or renewable options on land, before a housing boom begins in a particular area. This has proved to be a farsighted strategy, but too risky for traditional lenders, so Hovnanian has had to rely on high yield debt and equity to finance its growth. The company sold its first high yield bond offering in 1982. It went public in 1983, raising $13 million, and it sold another high yield offering in 1984. These financings allowed Hovnanian to buy land in promising areas and establish its own financing operations. In 1988, the company had options on enough land to support 20,000 housing units, or over five years of building at their 1986 rate.

Hovnanian's continued expansion has depended on the availability of low-cost debt and equity financing. The company sold 700,000 shares of common stock on June 9, 1986, and occasionally sells commercial paper.

Energy and Utilities

Occidental Petroleum Corporation

When oil prices fell sharply in the early 1980s, Occidental Petroleum Corporation moved aggressively to cut costs across the board. The company was so successful that it began applying its managerial talents to restructuring firms in other basic industries.

In 1988, Occidental was active in a variety of industrial sectors. The company explored for, developed, produced, and marketed crude oil and natural gas products. It also had interests in natural gas transmission, coal, commodity chemicals, petro-chemicals, plastics, fertilizers, and food processing.

In May of 1988, Occidental acquired Cain Chemical, Inc., which operates a balanced, integrated olefins business with chemical plants, pipeline systems, and storage facilities located along the Gulf Coast of Texas. Cain broadened Occidental's existing chemicals business by providing ethylene feedstock and a line of plastic products complementary to Occidental's PVC business. The acquisition made Occidental a major domestic producer of ethylene and derivative products.

Restructuring has been an important part of Occidental's success. The company has demonstrated an ability to manage its assets for maximum cash flow, as the following examples amply demonstrate.

Cities Service. Occidental acquired Cities Service in 1982 for $6 billion. In 1988, the net residual cash investment was $1.2 billion, after asset sales, cash flow from operations, and the benefits of a capital loss carry forward. At year-end 1987, Cities Service had proven reserves with an estimated notional value in excess of $2.25 billion.

Cano Limon Field. After discovering a major oil field in the interior of Columbia, Occidental moved to develop it rapidly. As work proceeded, Occidental began to seek co-investors, and in 1985, the company sold a 25 percent interest in the Cano Limon Field to Royal Dutch Shell for $1 billion, of which it had received $900 million by mid-1988. In that year, Occidental sold an additional 6.5 percent interest to Repsol Exploration for $272 million, which implied a value of $4.2 billion for Occidental's remaining 18.75 percent interest.

Diamond Shamrock Chemicals. Diamond Shamrock Chemicals was acquired in 1986 for $860 million. After asset sales and cash flow from operations, Occidental's effective investment at the end of 1987 was only $90 million. Operating earnings from these assets were expected to be at least $80 million in 1988.

IBP. As a result of IBP's initial public offering and associated dividend to Occidental, the book value of Occidental's investment in IBP is only $20 million. Yet in 1988, the market value of its remaining 51 percent interest in this meat-packing business was approximately $300 million.

Cain Chemical. Cain was acquired at 4.2 times estimated 1988 cash flow, and was expected to significantly increase Occidental's earnings and cash flow, even after taking acquisition costs into consideration.

Through strategic acquisitions, divestitures, and restructuring, Occidental has been able to reduce costs in its various divisions and become a leader in each of its markets. The company now enjoys an investment grade rating earned through strong management, tight control, and successful operation of its many businesses.

Banking and Finance

Coast Savings & Loan Association

In the late 1970s and early 1980s, the thrift industry underwent fundamental changes when rate ceilings were eliminated on interest paid on deposits. Coast Savings and Loan Association successfully met the challenges facing the thrift industry with a four-part restructuring strategy.

First, Coast worked to significantly increase the sensitivity of its assets to interest rate fluctuations, and more closely match the interest rate sensitivities of its assets and liabilities. By the end of 1987, adjustable-rate loans, other floating-rate loans, and match-funded loans accounted for 90 percent of Coast's loan and mortgage-backed securities portfolio. The estimated mismatch between its earning assets and costing liabilities had been reduced to 5.1 percent of total assets.

Step two in Coast's strategy was to diversify the thrift's sources of funds, using both domestic and international capital markets. From 1984 through 1987, Coast raised approximately $1 billion in capital, including $169 million from its initial public offering of common stock, from a $125 million collateralized Eurodollar financing, and from two redeemable preferred stock offerings by a financing subsidiary that totaled $250 million.

Step three was to develop significant sources of noninterest income, including real estate development, syndication, and management activities. Coast has pursued this objective through Coast Fed Properties and National Partnership Investments Corp. By 1987, Coast reported earnings from its real estate activities of $19.5 million. In addition to its real estate activities, Coast acquired Data Line Service Company, which provides full data processing services for over 100 financial institutions.

Fourth and finally, Coast worked to significantly increase its capital to support growth. From year-end 1983 to year-end 1987, Coast's regulatory capital grew from $157 million to over $1 billion, with excess regulatory capital of $676 million on December 31, 1987. This growth was achieved in part through two issues of subordinated capital notes, totaling $250 million, and a $150 million issue of convertible subordinated debentures. In addition, Coast converted to stock ownership in 1985 in the largest conversion of that year. Finally Coast acquired $299 million of regulatory capital in connection with its acquisition of Central Savings in 1987.

How did Coast's four-part strategy pay off? Excluding gains on sales of loans, securities, and branch offices, Coast's pretax earnings increased from a loss of $34.9 million in 1983 to income of $50.4 million for 1986 and $92.2 million in 1987. By the end of 1987, Coast was the fourteenth largest thrift in the United States, with assets of $12 billion.

Columbia Savings & Loan Association*

Columbia Savings & Loan has been even less traditional than Coast. While most savings and loan associations have ventured cautiously into their new-found regulatory freedom to diversify away from home mortgage lending, Columbia has sprinted into the daylight.

It has used a new instrument for the savings and loan industry—high yield securities—on both sides of its balance sheet. Columbia supplemented its capital base and rapidly growing deposits by selling $200 million of high yield securities. Then it purchased a portfolio of high yield bonds to complement

---

*In March 1990, Columbia reported losses from the fourth quarter of 1989 and the first two months of 1990 which had left the thrift insolvent as of February 28, 1990. The losses were due to declines in the value of its high yield portfolio. Much decline in the high yield markets in 1989 and 1990 can be traced to Congress' restrictions on thrift ownership. By forcing S & Ls to sell their high yield paper, thereby putting pressure on bond prices, solvent institutions were compelled to mark down their inventories to artificially depressed prices, thereby impairing their capital and driving them into insolvency. Ironically, through the Resolution Trust Corporation, the Federal Government will likely emerge as the owner of one of the largest high yield portfolios in America.

its other loans. The high yield securities it purchased generally had shorter maturities than its other loans. That allowed Columbia to achieve a closer match between deposits and loans, and avoid the trap of supporting long-term loans with short-term deposits that can be withdrawn on short notice.

The first two of Columbia's high yield issues were sold simultaneously in 1984. Each issue was for $50.0 million, with one carrying a variable rate and the other a fixed coupon of 15.624 percent. In 1986, the thrift again went to market, with two $50 million issues of convertible subordinated debentures. One issue yielded 7.0 percent, and the other, which carried put options, had a coupon of 7.25 percent.

While these issues have helped Columbia meet its capital needs, investing in high yield bonds has provided other important benefits. With high yield securities, Columbia can earn anywhere from three to five percentage points more than it could from Treasuries or Ginnie Maes. When these spreads are multiplied by the billions of dollars in a thrift's portfolio, they become a primary source of profits. In addition, bonds in the portfolio are liquid and can be sold as conditions warrant. They are not albatrosses around the neck of an S&L, as mortgages used to be. And while the bonds may carry certain risks, so do mortgages and commercial loans.

Columbia has also kept expenses to a minimum. During our study period, its expense ratio ran about 1.5 or 2 percent. The thrift is tough on costs and has a smaller staff than many others, in part because it does not make the same types of loans. Columbia had ten people doing investment research, rather than fifty doing traditional loan analysis.

The results have been impressive. Assets grew from $1 billion in 1981 to $10 billion in 1986, and Columbia earned an average of 60 percent on equity during that same period. Aggressive marketing helped spur this growth. Columbia reached out to stockbrokers, for example, and received $3.4 billion in deposits routed through them, or about 65 percent of its total. Moreover, the thrift has not forsaken more common ways of taking long-term loans off its books. It sells issues of mortgage-backed securities on a regular basis, as well as mortgage pass-through securities.

To protect itself against the public perception that its practices are risky, Columbia has kept its capital ratios high—twice as high as required by regulators. It also set reserves aside against any future liquidity problems.

The Health Care Industry

Charter Medical Corporation

Charter Medical has been a pioneer in the treatment of mental illness. At a time when psychiatric care was relatively unfashionable for the public as well as for Wall Street, Charter set out to become one of the first national chains of psychiatric hospitals. Charter recognized the severe problem of underbedding for mental diseases, as well as the need to overcome the stigma attached to this type of care.

Charter Medical has also been innovative in its choice of therapeutic methods. It has participated in the trend away from treating mental illnesses in large institutions that rely primarily on drug therapy. Instead, Charter has focused on private or campuslike hospitals that provide several types of therapies and treatments for many different kinds of mental illness and patients in all age groups. Charter has applied modern management techniques and innovative product development and marketing skills to a sector of the health care industry where innovations have lagged behind need.

The company has grown rapidly. It began as a hospital management company, but now earns 70 percent of its total revenues from mental health care. The company's employment has grown steadily during our study period, from 5,500 in 1980 to 13,400 in 1986. In 1988, Charter Medical's employment reached 16,000.

In 1980, the company had fifteen facilities and $162.09 million in revenue. By March 31, 1988, Charter had expanded to sixty-seven psychiatric hospitals and thirteen general hospitals in twenty-four states, England, and Switzerland. In 1987, revenues reached $813 million, growing at a 23-percent compound annual rate over the previous five years.

Growth at such a rapid pace required leverage and the freedom to take on additional debt. The choices available to Charter, as to other small, growing companies, were banks, insurance companies, venture capitalists, and high yield securities. Banks and insurance companies wanted to place too many restrictions on the company, and venture capitalists demanded too much control. So Charter opted for high yield securities, and since 1978, the company has raised $346 million in nine high yield issues. Since 1971, the company has also raised $61 million in common stock offerings.

During our study period from 1980 through 1986, the company raised $246 million in six high yield bond issues. The proceeds were used primarily for general corporate purposes, to refinance restrictive bank debt, and to refinance acquisition debt. Some of the funds were used to renovate and expand existing hospitals, some were applied to the construction of new facilities. Other funds were used to refinance debt originally incurred to acquire individual hospitals and hospital groups.

The use of high yield bonds has facilitated the company's internal growth and acquisition program, allowing Charter to build a national network of facilities while keeping debt service low relative to other funding alternatives. By identifying a niche market for health care delivery and consolidating its management and operations, Charter raised its operating profit margin from 12.86 percent in 1980 to 20.46 percent in 1986. This level of efficiency has helped Charter expand at the pace required in an industry that is undergoing dramatic and far-reaching changes. In September of 1988, the company went private in a transaction valued at approximately $2 billion.

Forum Group, Inc.

A new market is emerging across the United States. People are reaching retirement age with considerable wealth, both from home ownership and from the assets built up by working women. As they slow down physically, retirees may need someone to look after their housekeeping, transportation, security, social, and recreational needs. But they have no desire to leave the metropolitan areas where they have spent practically all of their lives. Forum Group is responding to the needs of this select group of retirees, by building luxury retirement communities all across the nation.

Forum began as an operator of long-term nursing facilities, but redefined its corporate strategy as it became aware of the dynamics of this emerging market. Forum entered the retirement living business in 1981 with the acquisition of Retirement Living, Inc., a successful Delaware-based chain of luxury units founded in the mid-1960s. In March 1985, Forum sold its hospital management division for over $200 million, which strengthened its balance sheet and allowed management to focus its attention on retirement communities for the affluent elderly.

Forum's staff was strengthened by the addition of over 100 specialists in retirement living marketing, development, and facilities management. The company has identified 150 geographical market areas in the United States with enough age- and income-qualified households to support luxury communities of the type Forum operates. The company is concentrating on the top thirty of these markets.

In 1987, Forum operated fourteen retirement communities, eighteen nursing homes, and five homes for the developmentally disabled. Each of Forum's retirement communities contains a full-service nursing component, providing additional service and convenience for residents. This arrangement helps couples and families stay closer together, even when one member requires nursing home care.

Forum believes the services of its affiliated construction company have reduced and will continue to reduce its construction time and costs. The company has also reduced the "empty time" of new projects with preopening marketing campaigns that have frequently resulted in waiting lists prior to the opening of Forum's facilities. Forum's rental policy is also attractive. The normal industry practice is to charge a nonrefundable endowment of as much as $150,000 to $200,000, which ties residents to a project for life. Forum, however, rents or leases units on an annual basis.

The company's rapid expansion required a source of financing free from restrictive covenants. High yield financing was the answer. In 1983, Forum raised $25 million in senior subordinated notes and $40 million in convertible subordinated debentures. The funds were used to refinance the more expensive and restrictive acquisition debt that had been assumed for the purchase of additional health care facilities. In 1986, the company raised another $105 million in high yield bonds. Of that amount, approximately $20 million was used to repay the balance on an outstanding revolving credit loan, approximately $50 million was used to repay Forum's outstanding commercial paper, $15 million was added to the company's cash reserves, and the remainder was used for working capital and the development and acquisition of additional luxury retirement living centers and other long-term health care facilities.

High yield debt became even more important after the Tax Reform Act of 1986, which substantially altered the risk/reward profile of the limited partnerships Forum had previously used as financing vehicles. Through acquisitions and internal growth, Forum's employment increased from 2,316 in 1981 to 5,159 in 1984. Employment was lowered by the sale of the hospital management business to 3,200 in 1985, but it began to rise again to approximately 3,700 in March 1987.

The Education Industry

Kinder-Care, Inc.

Kinder-Care's success combines two classic strategies: seizing an opportunity created by fundamental changes in society, and providing high-quality, standardized services to an otherwise fragmented industry. From its founding in 1970 to early 1988, Kinder-Care opened or acquired some 1,150 child care centers in forty states and two Canadian provinces, and the company continues to expand at a rapid rate. Kinder-Care is the largest company in the daycare industry; in 1988 it had licensed capacity to provide daycare services to over 130,000 children, from infants to twelve-year-olds. The company also owns Sylvan Learning Corp., which franchises centers for diagnostic testing and prescriptive instruction that serve more than 40,000 children and adults in forty-one states.

To expand on the services the company provides to the two-earner family, Kinder-Care has branched into other areas. Armed with nearly $275 million of capital raised in several common stock offerings, high yield bond issues, and convertible debt offerings between 1980 and 1986, the company has acquired an insurance company, two savings and loan institutions, a school portraits firm, a small chain of discount department stores, and a chain of off-price shoe stores. In January 1988, the company raised another $150 million in high yield bonds.

By 1988, the company was also examining opportunities in related areas. To supplement its two daycare centers in Canada, Kinder-Care considered further expansion abroad. It also saw a need for daycare facilities in convention centers and office complexes.

The company has kept costs down by spreading overhead over a large number of units. That includes everything from employee benefits to central purchasing. Employment nearly doubled between 1980 and 1986, rising from 8,000 to 14,300 people. In March 1988, the company had 19,000 employees.

The need for daycare services is obvious. In 1988, there were 10.5 million children under the age of six with working mothers. The care these children receive must be of the highest quality. As an owner-operator rather than a franchiser, Kinder-Care emphasizes quality control. Both its hiring policies and its physical plant are designed to minimize all risks to the children and provide the highest quality service to the youngsters in its care.

National Education Corporation

At the time we conducted our study, National Education Corporation was the world's largest and most diversified training company. It had benefited from strong internal growth and an acquisition program partially funded by high yield bonds. In 1988, the company offered a wide range of educational and training products and services to individuals, companies, and government agencies.

Through its many vocational and technical schools, National Education provides training solutions to meet the needs of individuals, schools, and corporations. The company's course offerings range from electronic engineering to avionics, from fashion merchandising to basic math and reading. To ensure that the training pays off for the students, job-placement specialists are located in each training center.

National Education is an aggressive innovator in both content and delivery of education materials. Its cutting-edge technology was dramatically illustrated in January 1987, when the company used the latest satellite technology to deliver training programs to customers in locations in North America and Europe. The company's modern delivery methods include interactive videodisks, computers, and specially designed printed materials.

Deltak Training Corp. is a subsidiary that offers courses to industries and governments through multimedia delivery systems, including print, videotape, interactive videodisks, and both computer-based and instructor-led training. Some 130,000 students take Deltak's correspondence courses. Once, correspondence courses meant sitting down with notebooks. Today, National Education's courses are just as likely to come on videotapes.

In an industry that has suffered from image problems in the past, National Education maintains a quality profile and is widely regarded as one of the most reputable companies in vocational training. It trains students for productive employment and then works actively to place them in appropriate jobs. Many companies, government agencies, and even community colleges call on National Education Corporation for advice and consultation on the most effective teaching methods and materials.

The company is no stranger to innovative financing, having issued high yield securities as far back as 1980. A year earlier, the company had acquired Intext, Inc., a publisher of educational materials that also provided individual study and industrial training programs. In 1980, National Education Corporation issued $15 million of nonrated convertible subordinated debentures, and used $10.2 million to repay bank debt incurred in purchasing Intext. The balance was used for internal expansion and further acquisitions of companies and products that complemented National Education's growth strategy.

Using the debt and retained earnings, the company quickly grew from twenty-five to fifty-one schools, more than doubling its number by 1987. In 1986, National Education raised $57.5 million in below-investment-grade convertible bonds, using $48 million to partially repay a revolving credit loan the company had used to acquire Deltak (for $84 million), and (for $5 million) RSI, a producer of training materials. In April 1986, National Education acquired Coastal, a chain of vocational schools in Virginia and Maryland, for $7.5 million. In July 1987, the company acquired Motivational Systems, and in December 1987, it purchased Advance Systems Incorporated.

National Education's innovations have certainly paid off. Between 1980 and 1987, sales more than quadrupled, from $89.3 million to $378.9 million. Over the same period, net income grew more than fivefold, from $4.1 million to $24.0 million, and employment grew from 2,623 to 5,100.

Business and Professional Services

Comdisco, Inc.

Comdisco's services facilitate the distribution of technological resources throughout the economy. The company has created a market that allocates both new and used equipment among various corporations according to their needs. This gives companies the flexibility to upgrade their equipment, reconfigure, or change immediately to newer, faster technology. Comdisco's clients avoid becoming "locked in" to their equipment and avoid all the risks and burdens of ownership.

Some companies need the latest, fastest computers with the greatest data capacity and they can pay for them. But they would hesitate to continue moving to the cutting edge of technology if they had to purchase new equipment every time technology improved. By leasing equipment from Comdisco, these companies are freed from decisions about whether to dispose of old equipment or forgo the latest advances. If new technology comes along, they simply change the terms of their lease and install the new equipment. Comdisco then sells or leases the "older" equipment to another company that wants to upgrade but lacks the need, or perhaps the funding, for state-of-the-art equipment.

Everyone benefits, because Comdisco provides an efficient market between the computer companies, the cutting-edge corporations, and other users. While Comdisco describes itself as a conduit in the marketplace, it is really much more than that—It actually creates the market.

Like many new companies with a new approach, Comdisco saw an opportunity, but had to create and efficiently service its market. Lacking an investment grade rating, Comdisco had to raise high yield capital: $15 million in 1977, $50 million in 1981, and another $250 million in 1983. The proceeds from these issues helped the company in a number of ways: $48.6 million was used to refinance bank debt, $45 million went to retire other debt, $100 million was used for acquisitions, and about $115 million went for general corporate purposes, such as financing internal growth and expanding ownership of equipment under lease.

Comdisco also entered a new line of business known as disaster recovery, which provides backup computer support in the event of a failure in a company's primary computer operations. As dependence on data processing has become more widespread, the need for disaster recovery services has multiplied. In addition, Comdisco has developed an oil and gas business and a risk arbitrage operation.

The fact that Comdisco's management and employees own 30 percent of the stock provides a strong performance incentive, and may help to explain the company's outstanding success. Starting with a handful of employees and less than $1 million in assets in 1969, the company has grown to over 1,000 employees and $2 billion in assets. Today, Comdisco is among the select group of corporations whose ratings have advanced from high yield to investment grade.

In 1988, Comdisco was the largest independent computer and high tech leasing company in the world. In 1986, the company's sales were $869.0 million, or nearly four times the $247.5 million recorded in 1980. The company is helping reduce the U.S. trade deficit by applying its skills abroad. It is financing computer purchases, thereby increasing sales of U.S. computer equipment in Canada, Europe, Japan, and Central and South America.

Retail Trade

The Limited, Inc.

By focusing on one small niche at a time and becoming the dominant factor in each one, The Limited has built a giant retailing and catalog sales company. Some observers suspect that The Limited will become the major force in U.S. retailing.

The company began a quarter-century ago with a $5,000 investment. In 1986, sales reached $3.21 billion, about twenty times the figure for a decade earlier. With over 3,000 stores, The Limited is a big company. Yet it was also one of *Business Week*'s "leanest and meanest" U.S. companies in 1987.

In 1985, The Limited raised $125 million in the convertible bond market, using the proceeds to expand its distribution facilities in Columbus, Ohio, and Indianapolis, Indiana. The funds also allowed the company to reduce its revolving credit borrowings related to the acquisition of Lerner Stores, a chain of 798 budget-priced women's apparel specialty shops.

By creating extensive distribution facilities and expanding its retail network internally and through acquisition, The Limited has become the world's largest distributor of women's apparel and continues to grow rapidly. Its size tripled from 1982 to 1987, and The Limited expects to double its size again in the early 1990s. Capital expenditures increased from $12.9 million in 1980 to $196.5 million in 1986. Over the same period, employment showed more than an eightfold increase, from 5,000 to 43,000.

Like so many aggressively growing stores, The Limited identified and took advantage of an opportunity that other companies had missed. It targeted fashion-conscious teenagers, whose ranks were swelled by the baby boom. That took the company into the exploding demand for leisure wear. The company also capitalized on another significant demographic trend, the surge in women entering the work force. The Limited also caters to the needs of larger women for professional work clothes, accessories, and stylish everyday apparel.

The Limited has tried to align the goals of the company and its employees. In 1988, managers and employees owned about 50 percent of the stock. The company's payroll stock purchase plan covered more than 30 percent of its work force, which The Limited claimed was the highest rate of any public company.

To keep its costs as low as possible, The Limited looked to the Pacific Rim in the early 1970s. Today, the company purchases about half of its merchandise abroad. Working through Mast Industries, The Limited finances, builds, and operates apparel factories offshore in joint ventures. As the dollar declined, however, The Limited began to search for domestic sources and partners. In 1987, the company held a trade fair to court U.S. suppliers, and was said to be considering investing in manufacturing facilities in the United States.

The Limited continued to break new ground with men's leisure wear and upscale men's clothing. At the conclusion of our study period, it had announced its intention to acquire the retail store and catalog business of Abercrombie & Fitch Co. The Limited had already branched out from trendy teenage and moderate-priced women's clothing with the acquisition of Bendel's (designer fashion) and the Victoria's Secret chain of lingerie retail stores and direct-mail catalogue business.

Additional projects included The Limited superstores, clusters of specialty stores carrying the company's various merchandise lines at shopping malls. The company was also considering private credit cards and expansion of its catalog business. Niche merchandising has long been considered The Limited's strength and the linchpin of the company's revolutionary role in U.S. specialty apparel retailing.

Wholesale Trade

Tyler Corp.

How does a company in slow-growth industries generate growth while not straying too far from the type of work it knows best? For Tyler Corp., the answer was to buy other companies in similar straits. Tyler's strategy covers four stages. First, pay a low price for companies in cyclical or weak industries. Second, support them, but give them management autonomy. Third, take advantage of the slow times to make them more efficient, lower their cost structure, and expand their customer base. And finally, gain market share from other companies that have failed to remain competitive and are forced to contract.

Tyler was formerly Saturn Industries, a low-cost producer of cast iron pipes and fittings for various kinds of construction. Since it began its growth strategy, it has added three companies: Atlas Powder, a maker of explosives used in mining, construction, and seismic businesses; Hall-Mark Electronics, a distributor of electrical components; and Reliance Universal, which makes industrial coatings.

In 1988, only Reliance Universal was in an expanding market. Headquartered in Louisville, Kentucky, the company makes custom-blended industrial coatings. The coatings are also used in the production of shingles and kitchen cabinets, office equipment, canopies, and certain types of packaging. In addition, Reliance Universal is the world's largest manufacturer of factory-made wood coatings or veneers used in furniture. The company makes synthetic resins for its own markets and also sells them to other coatings producers.

Tyler Pipe Industries, Inc., with half the market share in cast iron drains, waste and vent pipes, and fittings, sells mainly to developers of high-rise buildings and hospitals. With a profitable plant in Pennsylvania, it has a shipping cost advantage in parts of the Northeast, where building had been strong. Shipping west of the Mississippi from its Texas plant, Tyler also has an edge over its mainly southeastern U.S. competitors.

Hall-Mark Electronics is one of the five largest nationwide distributors of electronic components. It markets to industrial firms specializing in technically oriented applications. Hall-Mark acquired Allied Electronics in 1986 to expand its catalogs and sales staff and prepare for the upturn that should come with manufacturing sector expansion.

Atlas Powder is the largest manufacturer of explosives, selling mainly to coal mines. It sees a market niche for itself in the mid-size coal producer market, which it can ably serve through a company-owned, independent distributorship network.

As a multi-industry company, Tyler is concentrated primarily in mature or highly competitive sectors. Nevertheless, the company has maintained relatively stable returns on investment, increased its capital expenditures, and stabilized its employment levels in spite of wide-scale unemployment in its mature industry sectors.

Tyler has utilized high yield securities as part of its overall corporate strategy. In 1982, the company issued units that included $100 million of subordinated notes and common stock warrants. Of the proceeds, $77 million was used to refinance variable rate bank debt incurred in the 1980 acquisition of Hall-Mark Electronics. Another $20 million was used for general corporate purposes.

The company has become the low-cost producer in explosives and piping products and is a market competitor in its coatings division. Through a series of strategic smaller acquisitions in each area, Tyler has improved its market positioning. Despite a severe recession in the markets for electronic components, commercial construction, and pipes and fittings, Tyler has experienced steady sales growth, except for a drop in 1985. From 1980 to 1986, sales almost tripled, from $323.7 million to $961.4 million.

7

Leveraged Buyouts, Corporate Restructuring, and Debt in the 1980s

In Chapter 2, we examined the rise of corporate leverage since 1977 and the changing role of debt in the corporate capital structure. Junk bonds played an important part in these economic trends, providing public corporations with funds that allowed them to outperform their industries in several key performance measures.

As corporate debt levels rose, many companies started to view leveraged buyouts (LBOs) as an attractive way to restructure their operations and improve their competitive positioning. While the term *leveraged buyout* is used in a variety of ways, it generally refers to an acquisition in which the acquiror uses substantial debt (both senior and subordinated) to take a business private or to finance a change of corporate control.

Over the years, leveraged buyouts have accounted for an increasingly large share of all ownership changes and have become an important part of the junk bond story. Some investment banks estimate that while junk bonds have accounted for only about 8 percent of all merger and acquisition financing, high yield securities may account for as much as 25 to 30 percent of leveraged buyout financing. Since leveraged buyouts generally take public corporations private or allow divisional spin-offs of existing firms, they are outside the group of companies we examined in our previous study of high yield bonds.

The following information is taken from research conducted in 1989. It outlines the growth of leveraged buyouts, their risks and rewards, and the operational performance of companies that engaged in the transactions. Since junk bonds are an essential part of most LBOs, our findings can add another important dimension to understanding these securities and their overall economic impact.

As U.S. competitiveness declined in the late 1970s, leveraged buyouts emerged as one of many evolutionary responses to a new global economic order. The capital markets readily adapted to these corporate restructurings by creating sources of funding and new channels of supply. With the help of debt financing, managers, employees, and third-party investors increased their ownership participation in corporations as they pursued strategies to recapture old markets and create new ones.

In the search for a simple and single explanation for U.S. competitive decline, however, leveraged buyouts have become a convenient target. Critics of these transactions have confounded them with a variety of business and social policy issues, including corporate debt, financial defaults, takeovers, layoffs, and shutdowns. Yet few critics have provided empirical evidence to support the relationships they suppose to exist between LBOs and these economic concerns.

The fact that leveraged buyouts have evoked such strong criticism is particularly ironic. The use of leverage to buy property and access to property rights (in education, housing, and other sectors) has been a popular tradition throughout U.S. economic history. In the absence of inherited wealth or the granting of seignorial rights to property, debt has been a central tool for acquiring productive assets. Together with operating skills, talent, and hard work, leverage has been a primary means of creating wealth and producing income in our economy.

In recent years, the market for corporate control through new ownership has been increasingly contested. Not surprisingly, this controversy has resulted from a major shift in the way corporations are dealing with the pressures of a highly competitive global economy. Deconcentration and deconglomeration have been the central tendencies of the latest wave of restructuring, in which leveraged buyouts have played an important, though not primary role.

In contrast, earlier waves of mergers and acquisitions led to increased levels of economic and industrial concentration. At the turn of the century, horizontal acquisitions led to the formation of the great trusts. In the 1920s, vertical integration built large, monolithic corporations. In the late 1960s and early 1970s, companies with only a few major lines of business diversified into sprawling conglomerates. Throughout the first seven and a half decades of this century, the nation's 500 largest firms steadily gained increasing concentration in employment, profits, sales, and productivity.

The back-to-basics approach that many leveraged buyouts have taken— by streamlining their operations, divesting unprofitable units, and concentrating on core businesses—has reflected a dramatic shift in overall corporate strategy. While strategy changes have always been a source of controversy, to properly understand and appreciate leveraged buyouts, we need to view them in the context of the fourth wave of mergers and acquisitions in U.S. history, and the rise of corporate debt.

LBOs in Context: The Fourth Wave of Merger and Acquisition Activity

This century's fourth merger wave began in 1981 and has been the longest and perhaps most controversial force moving the nation's businesses toward more competitive corporate and industrial reorganization. Unlike earlier eras of economic restructuring, the current merger and acquisition wave is occurring at a time when the relative position of U.S. firms in the world economy is declining. Heightened global competition, deregulation, and technological and demographic changes are forcing corporations to enhance efficiencies, streamline their operations, and develop cost-effective strategies.

In part these problems were the vestiges of earlier waves of merger and acquisition activity, each of which had resulted in greater industrial concentration. While increasing concentration may have been appropriate in the heyday of American industry, new economic and competitive forces called for a dramatic shift in corporate strategy. This fourth wave of merger and acquisition activity has been the longest and perhaps most controversial phase of corporate reorganization.

Restructuring includes tendencies toward deconglomerization, which means that divisional divestitures yield higher rates of marginal revenue for divested firms. It also includes vertical and horizontal integrations, product line extensions, and market extensions. Because of innovations in financial markets, the mechanisms for accomplishing the transactions are more diverse than ever before. New business combinations are part of the new strategies that are being crafted to successfully confront change and take advantage of the opportunities that change provides.

Generally, restructuring in the United States has consisted of recapitalizations of companies, largely through various forms of leverage through stock buybacks, various forms of LBOs, and ESOPs. Additionally, some acquisitions have consolidated excess capacity in various industries and have enabled a number of low-margin, low-market-share operations to consolidate into higher-margin, higher-market-share businesses. Finally, the selling or spin-off of unrelated businesses have been a part of this restructuring process, either at the point of recapitalization or buyout, or soon thereafter.

The emergence of leveraged buyouts as a financial structure for mergers and acquisitions is unique to this era. Increasing access to credit has been the fundamental basis of the leveraged buyout movement in the United States. But as corporate leverage has increased, so has the level of debate surrounding the transactions. The use of debt to fund asset purchases is by no means new. But in the last ten years, leverage has played an unprecedented role in shifting corporate ownership and allowing managers and employees to become significant equity participants in the companies where they work.

To fully understand the increase in leveraged buyouts, we need to consider them in the overall context of merger and acquisition activity. The number and size of going-private transactions has increased dramatically since the end of the previous decade, from sixteen transactions in 1979, with an aggregate value of $635 million, to forty-seven transactions in 1987, valued at over $22 billion.

While the rise in going-private transactions has been impressive, total merger and acquisition activity has increased by a larger amount and at a faster rate, as indicated in Figures 7-1 and 7-2. As a percentage of total merger and acquisition activity, going-private transactions rose steadily until 1984, peaking at 27.01 percent of total merger activity, and have since declined.

Leveraged buyouts are often viewed within the narrow framework of going-private transactions. But in a more inclusive sense, leveraged buyout activities can also include unit buyouts, spin-offs, and tender offers by public companies. Under the more expansive definition, leveraged buyout transactions increased fairly steadily from 1981 (99 transactions) to 1986 (331 transactions), then dropped in 1987 (259 transactions). As a percentage of all merger value, LBO values climbed from 3.8 percent in 1981 to 26.8 percent in 1986, then dropped to 21.7 percent in 1987. The average purchase price of the companies involved in leveraged buyouts increased from $31.31 million in 1981 to $137.45 million in 1987 (see Table 7-1).

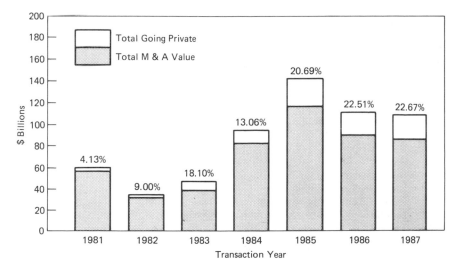

Figure 7–1. Going private transactions and merger and acquisitions activity— Aggregate activity, 1981–1987 (Mergerstat Review, W. T. Grimm & Co.).

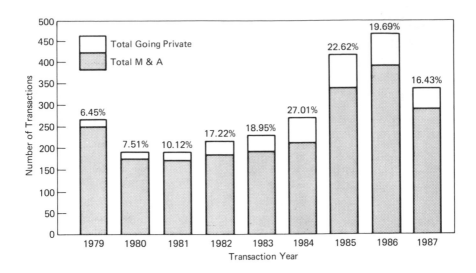

Figure 7-2. Going private transactions and merger and acquisitions activity, 1979-1987 (Mergerstat Review, W. T. Grimm & Co.).

Table 7-1. Number and Value of Leveraged Buyouts, 1981-1987 (dollar values in billions)

Year	Number of Trans.	Total $ Value	% Change in Total $ Value	Mean $ Value	% Change in Mean $ Value	LBO Value as a % of All Merger Value
1981	99	3.1	n.a.	.0313	n.a.	3.8%
1982	164	3.5	12.9%	.0213	-31.9%	6.5%
1983	230	4.5	28.6%	.0196	-8.0%	6.2%
1984	253	18.8	317.8%	.0743	279.1%	15.4%
1985	254	19.6	4.3%	.0772	3.9%	10.9%
1986	331	46.4	136.7%	.1402	81.6%	26.8%
1987	259	35.6	-23.3%	.1375	1.9%	21.7%
Total	**1,590**	**$131.5**				

Average value of LBOs 1981-1987: $82.7 million
Mean annual percent change in total dollar value: $79.5%
Source: Mergers from W.T. Grimm & Co., LBOs from *Mergers and Acquisitions* magazine.
Mergers information is based on announcements; total dollar value is based only on those deals where a dollar value was available. LBO information is based on completed transactions.

LBOs in Context: The Rise of Corporate Debt

Leveraged buyouts have been associated with the recent wave of merger and acquisition activity, but are clearly not the cause of it. The transactions have occurred in the context of overall debt creation and have followed the increased preference for debt in the corporate capital structure. Corporate debt has increased by 12 percent annually since 1983, or one third faster than it did in the 1970s.

The fact that debt is less expensive than other forms of capital has strongly influenced the amount and types of debt corporations have been willing to assume. In the typical LBO, debt replaces equity as the primary component of the capital structure. Frequently, LBO financing requires each owner to purchase strips of equity and tranches of debt. High yield financing promotes this structure and imposes a discipline on managers, who frequently become owners, by forcing them to pay out free cash flow that cannot be profitably invested in the business (Jensen, 1986).

Since increasing leverage lowers a company's overall cost of capital, leveraged buyouts have been a natural outgrowth of the search for more efficient capital allocation. As a financial and organizational response to changing markets, LBOs have enabled new owners to reposition their firms, reorganize factor costs, and achieve important competitive advantages.

Cost of capital differentials play an important role in determining the competitiveness of American companies. America's capital is some 2½ to 4 times as expensive as Japan's, for instance, in part because of the greater reliance on debt financing in that country.

Writing in the *New York Times* at the end of 1989, William Farley, chairman and chief executive of Farley Industries, illustrated the difference between the costs of debt and equity capital. Assuming the need for $5 million in start-up capital for a venture that you believe will be worth $100 million in 10 years, he said,

> If you can borrow the money from a commerical bank at 10 percent interest, over 10 years you will pay $5 million in interest. If you can sell high yield bonds at say 15 percent, you will pay $7.5 million in interest over 10 years. But if you had to give up a modest 25 percent in equity to get that $5 million—and if you pay no dividends—you will end up giving up $20 million in value. Even though this is a simplistic example, which does not account for inflation, it is clear that debt is much cheaper.

This is, of course, not always the case, as we shall see in Chapter 11. As market conditions change, the relative costs of debt to equity can become transposed. Under those circumstances, the case for de-leveraging balance sheets becomes stronger. The point, however, should always be to minimize captial costs through the appropriate mix of debt and equity in a corporation's financial structure.

Table 7-2. Leveraged Buyout Intensity, Productivity Change and Restructuring Intensity: Industrial Distribution of Activity.

Industry	LBO Intensity Measure	Change of Productivity Index	Restructuring Intensity Measure
Nonmanufacturing			
Mining & Natural Res. Extraction	0.3	33.95	5.8
Transportation	0.1	19.37	1.6
Communications	1.8	-34.78	0.9
Public Utilities	0.1	22.82	0.9
Retail Trade	2.3	4.29	0.4
Manufacturing			
Total Manufacturing	3.0	6.25	1.6
Durable Goods	2.8	8.55	1.5
Stone, Clay, and Glass	13.9	7.33	0.9
Primary Metals	1.7	11.06	1.5
Fabricated Metals	2.7	3.62	1.4
Nonelectrical Machinery	2.5	6.80	1.0
Electrical Machinery	3.0	8.43	1.6
Transportation Equipment	1.8	19.37	1.6
Instruments	1.7	8.27	2.8
Lumber	0.8	3.25	2.2
Furniture	1.1	3.00	0.4
Nondurable Goods	3.2	4.26	1.8
Food	5.1	6.04	3.8
Textiles	7.9	6.31	1.2
Paper	4.5	3.88	1.3
Chemicals	1.1	-0.13	2.2
Petroleum	0.0	25.33	0.4
Rubber	1.7	-13.08	0.8

Note: The LBO intensity measure is the industry dollar share of total completed transactions from 1978 through December 12, 1988, by the mean industry share of nominal gross national product over the period 1978 to 1987.

The change of productivity index is the difference of the industry's productivity (output per employee-hour, 1977 = 100) between 1983 and 1985.

The restructuring intensity measure is the ratio of the share of M & A activities accounted for by each industry relative to that same industry's share of U.S. output during 1980-1985.

Source: Drexel Burnham Lambert, COMPUSTAT, S&P, Survey of Current Business, DOC, Worldwide Economic Outlook, Morgan Stanley & Co., Inc., U.S. Department of Commerce, DOL.

Characteristics of LBOs

Industries That Have Used LBOs

As Waite and Fridson (1989) have shown, LBO activity has been concentrated in fewer industries than has merger and acquisition activity in general. Leveraged buyout activity has been much more predominant in manufacturing. Within manufacturing, the levels of LBO activity in stone, clay, and glass, apparel, textiles, food and paper have been substantially higher than the industries' relative shares of national output (see Table 7-2).

This pattern also remained true for the 169 leveraged buyouts from 1983 through 1988 in our study (Figure 7-3). Among these transactions, the concentration of LBOs was highest in durable and nondurable manufacturing. As a result of heightened global competition, these manufacturing industries, comprised largely of low-tech, mature sectors, have faced the greatest need to increase efficiency and productivity. They have also been industries with more stable demand and cash flow, both of which are necessary to pay back leveraged transactions.

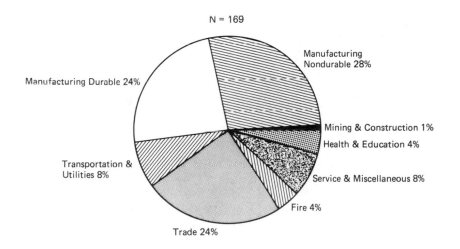

Figure 7–3. Leveraged buyouts by SIC code, 1983–1988 (*Investor's Digest Daily*, Drexel Burnham Lambert, Mergers and Acquisitions File, 1983–1988).

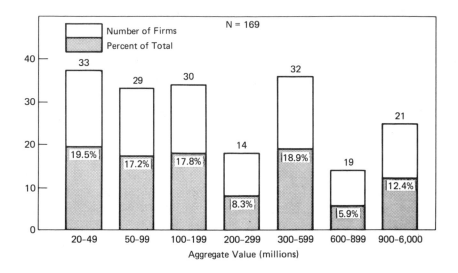

Figure 7–4. Size distribution of leveraged buyouts by aggregate value, 1983–1988 (*Investor's Digetst Daily,* **Drexel Burnham Lambert, Mergers and Acquisitions File, 1983–1988).**

Size and Distribution of Leveraged Buyouts

As Figure 7-4 indicates, over the period of our study, 54.5 percent of LBOs were concentrated among firms whose aggregate values were less than $200 million. But the average equity value of firms going private increased substantially, and so the average value of LBO transactions increased from $39.8 million in 1979 to $469.3 million in 1987.

As Lehn and Poulsen (1988) noted in an earlier study, the median equity values of LBO transactions increased by a lower amount, reflecting a handful of very large transactions (such as Beatrice and Safeway) during the latter part of the 1980s. According to the data we analyzed, median values increased to only $123.3 million by 1987, or just 26.3 percent of the average purchase value (see Table 7-3).

Types of Leveraged Buyouts

The analysis of leveraged buyouts is haunted by definitional problems. The financial structure of leveraged buyouts and the role of these transactions in general corporate strategy varies substantially from deal to deal. DeAngelo and DeAngelo (1987) used the term *leveraged buyout* to refer only to those going- private transactions with third-party equity investors. They found debt

Table 7-3. Mean and Median Values of Going Private Transactions, 1979-1987

LBO Cohort Year	No.	Total Paid (Millions)	Average Purchase Price (Millions)	Annual % Change	Median Purchase Price (Millions)	Annual % Change
1979	16	636.00	39.80		7.90	
1980	13	967.40	74.40	86.93	25.30	220.25
1981	17	2,338.50	137.70	85.08	41.10	62.45
1982	31	2,836.70	91.50	-33.55	29.60	-27.98
1983	36	7,145.40	198.50	116.94	77.80	162.84
1984	57	10,805.90	415.60	109.37	66.90	-14.01
1985	76	24,139.80	317.60	-23.58	72.60	8.52
1986	76	20,232.40	281.00	-11.52	24.50	16.39
1987	47	22,057.10	469.30	67.01	123.30	45.92
Total	**369**	**91,159.20**	**2,025.40**		**469.00**	
Average Values		**10,128.80**	**225.04**	**49.59**	**52.11**	**59.30**

Source: *Mergerstat Review,* W.T. Grimm & Co.

levels higher where a third-party financial sponsor was involved. Lowenstein (1985) refers to transactions where the management of a public company purchases the entire company and takes it private as *management buyouts*. Additionally, *tender offer buyouts* include leveraged buyouts where a tender offer is made. Finally, buyouts involving employee stock ownership plans (ESOPs) involve a wider range of equity participants than do management buyouts.

While these categories are not always mutually exclusive, they do provide us with a framework for an initial typology of leveraged transactions. In examining leveraged buyout transactions, it is important to consider:

* The amount of leverage
* The degree of management participation
* The role of third-party investors or financial sponsors
* The degree of employee participation.

Our LBO study established these categories:

Leveraged Buyout. An investor group, investor, or investment/LBO firm acquires a company, taking on a significant amount of debt (usually more than 70 percent of the total capitalization), with plans to repay the debt with funds generated from the acquired company's operations or from asset sales.

Management Buyout. A leveraged buyout in which the current management of the acquired corporation holds a significant equity stake in the company after the buyout is completed.

ESOP Buyout. A leveraged buyout in which an employee stock ownership plan of the acquired corporation holds a significant equity stake in the company after the buyout is completed.

Tender Offer Buyout. A leveraged buyout transaction completed through a tender offer rather than a merger.

Based on these definitions, as Figure 7-5 indicates, most transactions (48.5 percent) were financially sponsored by third-party equity investors that were also involved in the issuing of debt instruments. Tender-offer buyouts by financial sponsors (34.3 percent) and management buyouts (15.4 percent) were also significant. ESOP buyouts represent a relatively recent, but increasingly important part of the leveraged buyout market.

In examining leveraged buyouts, it is also important to distinguish between friendly and unfriendly transactions. Managers can respond in a variety of ways to transactions proposed by dissident shareholders, corporate acquirors, or LBO financial sponsors. The financing structure, offer size, and approach varies considerably among LBOs and can significantly affect how an offer is received.

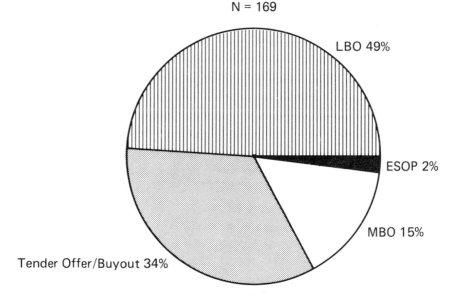

Figure 7-5. Leveraged buyouts by type of transaction, 1983–1988 (*Investor's Digest Daily,* Drexel Burnham Lambert, Mergers and Acquisitions File, 1983–1988).

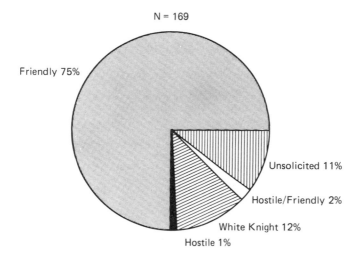

Figure 7-6. Leveraged buyouts by type of approach, 1983–1988 (*Investor's Digest Daily,* Drexel Burnham Lambert, Mergers and Acquisitions File, 1983–1988).

As Figure 7-6 indicates, contrary to the conventional wisdom about leveraged buyouts, the huge majority of LBOs from 1983 to 1988 were friendly. Of the 169 transactions during this period, 126 were friendly, accounting for 74.56 percent of the total. Only one transaction (0.59 percent) was deemed hostile, though eighteen (10.65 percent) resulted from unsolicited offers. Three of the buyouts (1.78 percent) began as hostile transactions but later became friendly, and twenty-one (12.43 percent) were white knight transactions that were most likely stimulated by takeover threats.

Leverage and Performance: Arguments and Evidence about Leveraged Buyouts

The Case Against Leveraged Buyouts

Leveraged buyouts have been the subject of intense criticism and public debate. The central argument against LBOs has been that the change in corporate financial structure can have a deleterious effect on competitive performance. Encumbered by inordinate levels of debt service, the argument continues, LBO firms will stumble and fail.

Some critics claim that all leveraged buyouts are characterized by lack of investment, declining competitiveness, poor financial performance, and job loss (Grant, 1988). The Congressional Research Service Report (1987) went so far as to suggest that leveraged buyouts are simply a way to put companies into play, acquire them for short-term profits through sell-offs, and generate earnings from speculative debt. According to the authors:

This has implications for the long term viability of companies, for the solvency of their investment advisors who are taking increasingly large equity positions in these deals, and for the stability of financial markets in general.

Certainly, selected highly publicized LBO failures (such as Revco, National Gypsum, and Owens Corning) fit the critics' description. Systematic evidence, however, indicates that LBO failure rates are lower than the failure rates for business in general. The evidence also shows that firms operating as leveraged buyouts, though varying in their types and success, tend to outperform other companies and reverse declining patterns evident under the firms' earlier organizational forms (see Table 7-4).

A closer look at the evidence provided by critics of leveraged buyouts can also be quite revealing. Lowenstein (1985) studied twenty-eight management buyout proposals from 1979 to 1984. The focus of the study was to determine whether or not the transactions added value and provided adequate shareholder protection. The study found that median and mean bids were at a high premium to current share prices and concluded that shareholders benefited from a competitive bidding atmosphere. Focusing exclusively on the Fred Meyer and Dan River buyouts, however, Lowenstein argued that management buyouts result in negative performance in sales, operating income, and firm growth. While these two examples supported his point, no systematic evidence was provided for his conclusion.

Additionally, Lowenstein and Herman (1986) examined fifty-six hostile tender offers initiated from 1975 to 1983. In twenty-one hostile transactions between 1975 and 1978 (prior to the rise of the contemporary leveraged buyout) that were financed mostly by cash offers from large public companies and bank debt, both bidders and targets experienced steadily rising returns on equity and profitability. In transactions initiated from 1981 to 1983, however, bidders in the sample experienced a deterioration in profitability that correlated to transaction size. The study concludes that the latter transactions were not undertaken by groups seeking entrepreneurial risk and contribution, but rather were speculative in nature. Unfortunately, the latter transactions were only followed for two years, leaving the long-term effects of larger transactions as a subject for further investigation.

Despite the suggestive findings and anecdotal evidence contained in these studies, none of them offers a systematic examination of the recent wave of leveraged buyouts or an in-depth look at the impact of the LBO debt structure on overall corporate performance.

Financial Returns

DeAngelo and DeAngelo (1984) examined the impact of going-private transactions on public stockholder wealth for seventy-two firms from 1973 through 1980. Within the sample, the average company's share price increased by 22.3 percent over the two days surrounding a proposal's announcement.

Table 7-4. Empirical Findings about the Impacts of Leverages Buyouts

Variables	*Studies* DeAngelo & DeAngelo (1984)	Lowenstein (1985)	Lowenstein & Herman (1986)	Jensen (1986)	Lewellen & Kracow (1987)	DeAngelo & DeAngelo (1987)	Kelso & Kelso (1987)	Congressional Research Service (1987)
Operational Performance								
Operating Income (post)								
Debt-to-Assets Ratio (pre-to-post)		+		+		+		+
Profitability			+ pre/-post			+		
Long-Term Debt	+	+	+	+		+	+	+
Return on Equity (ROE)		+	+					
Capital Expenditures (post)					+			
Total Firm Value (post)	+	+				+		+
Average Premium Earned	+56.3%	+56%	+80.2%	+50%		+		+31.9%
Average Price Increase at Buyout Announcement	+22.3%	+	+	+		+		
Ownership Structure								
Shareholder Effects	+30%	+				+	+	+
Bondholder Effects								
Prebuyout Share Management Ownership	+50.9%	+3.8%				+24.5%	+	
Postbuyout Share Management Ownership	+	+10.4%				+	+	+

Table 7-4 (continued)

Variables	*Studies:* Kaplan (1988)	Pound (1988)	Amihud (1988)	Kieschnick (1988)	Bureau of Labor Stats. (1988)	Jensen (1986)	Lehn & Poulsen (1988)	Lichtenberg & Siegel (1989)	KKR (1989)
Economic Gains (post)									
Receipt of Competing Bid (1980-1983)		+	+						
Receipt of Competing Bid (1984-1987)		+							
Management & Large Changes									
Employment Level Change (post)								+	
Layoff Events Attributed to Business Ownership Change									
Management Turnover (CEO or Chairman Exits)									
Operational Performance									
Operating Income (post)	+								
Debt-to-Assets Ratio (pre-to-post)		+				+			
Profitability									+
Long-Term Debt	+		+			+	+		
Return on Equity (ROE)									+

Table 7-4 (continued)

Capital Expenditures (post)									+ 1.9%
Total Firm Value (post)						+			
Average Premium Earned	+ 45.9%	+	+ 31%			+	+ 36.84%		+
Average Price Increase at Buyout Announcement			+ 20%				+ 16.34%		
Ownership Structure									
Shareholder Effects		+	+			+			+
Bondholder Effects			-1.15%				-1.21%		
Prebuyout Share Management Ownership	+ 9.3%						+ 24.7%		
Postbuyout Share Management Ownership	+ 30.99%								+
Management Ownership			+				+		
Economic Gains (post)	+	+							
Receipt of Competing Bid (1980-1983)							+ 28%		
Receipt of Competing Bid (1984-1987)							+ 48.6%		
Management & Large Changes									
Employment Level Change (post)	+ 3.34%						+	+ 4.2%	
Layoff Events Attributed to Business Ownership Change				+ 4.36%	+				
Management Turnover (CEO or Chairman Exits)	+ 25%				+				

After the adjustment for general market movements, the proposal price impact was on average a 30.4 percent rise over the price in prior months. Stockholder premiums at the transaction's closing were 56.3 percent above market value. These findings were largely corroborated in a follow-up article by the same authors updating the data through 1982 (DeAngelo and DeAngelo, 1987).

A study by Amihud (1988) of fifteen of the largest LBOs through 1987 found no significant difference between the share price premiums offered in buyouts led by management and the premiums in those led by outside investors (30.1 percent versus 28.6 percent).* Kieschnick (1988) found that in the year up to the quarter before the buyout, the stock return of firms that went private was lower than that of a control sample of public firms relative to the return on the S&P index during the same period. Stock performance was lower for firms in management-led buyouts than it was in buyouts led by outsiders.

Most of the financial research about LBO transactions has focused on whether or not economic value is created directly through enhanced operating efficiencies or various financial and tax factors. Leveraged buyout studies cite several possible ways that value may be created.

Tax advantages through interest deductions, increased depreciation from stepped-up asset valuations, and tax benefits associated with ESOPs are often cited as sources of value. Lowenstein (1985) and Marais, Schipper, and Smith (1988) found high correlations between premiums in going-private transactions and tax savings. There is no evidence, however, that tax savings cause leverage buyouts or are the primary motivation for initiating LBO transactions.

Wealth transfers from bondholders to the target firms has also been examined in going-private transactions where share premiums have been associated with significant reductions in outstanding bond values. Negative returns ranged from -3.51 percent to -1.21 percent (Travlos and Millon, 1987; Lehn and Poulsen, 1988) to findings of no significant change. In relation to the shareholder gains noted above, bondholder losses were minimal.

Inside information is also cited as a source of wealth enhancement through sell-offs of assets that managers know to be undervalued. Counterevidence, however, was found by Kaplan (1988), who showed that LBOs usually underperform their going-private projections in the years following the buyout.

---

*Interestingly, both values are lower than the average premium of 31 percent that Amihud reports for all fifteen transactions (Table 7-4). No explanation for the discrepancy is provided.

Reduced regulation is often seen as a source of cost savings, but has not been extensively studied.

Increased management ownership has been found to realign management incentives in ways that make the company run more profitably and efficiently. Kaplan (1988) and Bull (1988) found that profit rates increased significantly following going-private transactions.

Undistributed cash flow relative to equity values may indicate an ability to create value through an LBO, especially where managers own relatively little equity prior to the transaction (Jensen, 1986; Lehn and Poulsen, 1988).

Ownership Change and LBO Performance

In leveraged buyouts, debt is a primary means for accomplishing a change in corporate ownership. In most LBO transactions, management ownership increases, although the amount of increase is subject to considerable variation. In a study of transactions valued at over $100 million, Lowenstein (1985) found that management ownership increased from a median of 3.8 percent before the buyout to 10.4 percent afterward. Kaplan (1988) studied seventy transactions valued at over $50 million and found that management ownership increased from a prebuyout median of 3.5 percent to a postbuyout median of 22.63 percent.

The presence of significant leverage creates a powerful incentive to increase efficiency and profitability, reducing the risk of business failure or default. Whether the new owners are managers or third-party investors who carefully monitor the firm's development, ownership closely ties rewards to performance, creating a strong incentive to improve operating results.

As Pound (1989) and Jensen (1986) have shown, debt exerts a control that effectively induces management to meet or exceed performance standards. The debt instrument places managers under a contractual obligation to produce a certain level of cash flow or lose the company to the bondholders. In order to more closely examine the impact of ownership change through LBOs, we began our study by assembling a data set on leveraged buyout transactions valued at over $25 million. We examined 169 transactions from 1983 through 1988, but limited our study to those cases for which consistent pre- and postbuyout data were available. As a result, our final sample consisted of forty-three transactions from 1984 through 1986.

In order to measure performance before and after the buyouts, we organized our data into groups, or cohorts, by the years in which the leveraged buyouts took place. Of the forty-three transactions in our study, twelve were in the 1984 cohort, thirteen in the 1985 cohort, and eighteen in the 1986 cohort. This increase roughly parallels the overall increase in LBO activity during the study period. The forty-three transactions represented 65 percent of the total value of LBOs during our study period. Additional supporting data were analyzed for the years preceding and following the transactions, from 1983 through 1988.

We assembled data from a variety of sources. Building upon base data from *Investment Dealer's Digest,* we used the Drexel Burnham Lambert Mergers and Acquisitions Database to obtain a complete list of LBO transactions over $25 million. We examined Datext historical financial series to match LBO transaction dates and assemble before and after time series on income and balance sheet items. Derived variables were computed from this data. When gaps appeared, we examined SEC filings to establish a comprehensive data set on these transactions. Finally, using Trinet data, we were able to develop an annual employment series preceding and following the LBO transactions and examine a wider range of cases in our study of employment and sales performance.

We designed the study to examine a broad range of performance measures relevant to leveraged buyout transactions. Our variables included net sales, market productivity, labor productivity, and operating income, as well as working capital, interest coverage, capital expenditures, and the employment effects of LBOs. For each variable, we examined both changes in performance *within* the pre- and postbuyout periods and aggregate change *between* the pre- and postbuyout periods. The indicators we studied included:

- The average absolute level of performance between the pre- and postbuyout periods
- The average annualized differences between years during the periods before and after the buyout
- The mean percentage change between years during the periods before and after the buyout

Taken together, these variables allowed us to place leveraged buyouts in clearer focus, providing accurate empirical evidence on the role of debt in ownership change and industrial competitiveness in the 1980s. In Chapter 8, we will go beyond pre- and postbuyout performance to examine how buyout companies and plants outperformed their industry norms.

Net Sales

Net sales is an important indicator of overall volume growth and competitive performance. For each cohort, the years prior to the LBO were characterized by changes in sales ranging from a decrease of 6.66 percent for the 1984 cohort to an increase of 4.80 percent for the 1985 cohort. After the LBO, sales increased by a weighted average rate of 39.86 percent for all cohorts. As Figure 7-7 indicates, patterns of sales declines were consistently reversed, while low rates of growth were substantially increased. The growth in sales volume after a firm went private through an LBO was extensive.

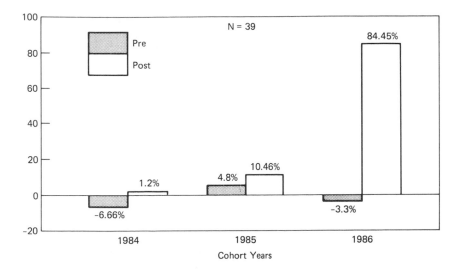

Figure 7–7. Sales in LBO firms—Mean percentage changes for cohorts, 1984, 1985, 1986 (*Investor's Digest Daily,* Drexel Burnham Lambert, Datext, Trinet).

Examining these changes in greater detail, we found that for the 1984 and 1986 cohorts, on an average annualized basis, sales declined significantly before the buyout and rose substantially thereafter. The postbuyout sales growth for the 1985 cohort was more than double the sales growth of the prebuyout period. The average absolute postbuyout gain for the 1985 cohort was more than two and a half times the prebuyout figure. The weighted average absolute sales change between the pre- and postbuyout periods for all cohorts was 8.14 percent.

In an examination of a broader range of sixty-one transactions, using Trinet data, these patterns of change held. Declining prebuyout sales patterns were reversed by the LBOs in the 1984 and 1986 cohorts. In the 1985 cohort, modest prebuyout sales growth of 1.44 percent increased almost eightfold in the postbuyout period to an average annual change of 11.33 percent (see Table 7-5).

Market Productivity: Sales Per Employee

Sales per employee is an important measure of productivity. In the prebuyout period, the cohorts had been experiencing slow growth in sales per employee, averaging 3.59 percent. In the postbuyout period, however, these rates increased to an average of 17.41 percent per year for all cohorts, or more than four and a half times the prebuyout average (see Figure 7-8).

In examining variations between cohorts before and after the buyout, we found that annual sales per employee before the buyout were increasing

Table 7-5. Sales Changes in Leveraged Buyout Firms ($000)

LBO Cohort Year	No.	Prebuyout				Postbuyout				Pre-Post Average Absolute % Change
		Average Absolute	Average Annualized Difference	Mean % Change		Average Absolute	Average Annualized Difference	Mean % Change		
1984	15	675,706.60	-16,095.50	-2.30		741,507.60	21,664.10	3.22		9.74
1985	19	836,019.00	11,772.36	1.44		982,684.20	101,057.80	11.33		17.54
1986	27	1,280,975.00	-61,918.40	-4.09		1,398,896.00	587,455.50	72.40		9.21
Weighted Average Cohort Values	61	993,545.66	27,115.40	-1.93		1,107,603.40	296,825.54	36.37		11.48

Source: Drexel Burnham Lambert, Mergers & Acquisitions Transaction Database, Datext, 1980-1987

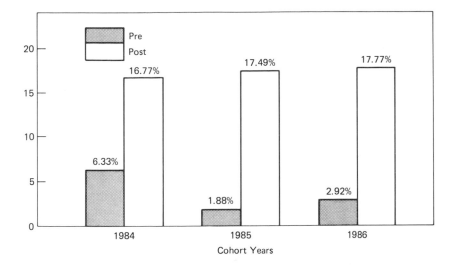

Figure 7-8. Sales per employee in LBO firms—Mean percentage changes for cohorts, 1984, 1985, 1986 (*Investor's Digest Daily,* Drexel Burnham Lambert, Datext, Trinet).

modestly for the 1984 cohort (6.3 percent), the 1985 cohort (1.9 percent), and the 1986 cohort (2.92 percent). During the postbuyout period the mean percentage changes in sales per employee were 16.8 percent, 17.5 percent, and 17.8 percent respectively. Overall, the weighted average absolute level of sales per employee increased by 35 percent between the pre- and postbuyout periods.

Labor Productivity: LBO Intensity and Productivity Change

Another way of examining the impact of leveraged buyouts on productivity is to examine labor productivity, measured as output per employee = hour. Data on individual firms are not available for this variable during our study period. The U.S. Department of Labor, however, does trace labor productivity on an aggregate basis for a wide range of industries. Utilizing this data at the 2-digit standard industrial classification level, we were able to construct a productivity index that measured differences in the productivity of various industries from 1983 to 1985 in terms of output per employee-hour (1977 = 100).

We then compared this measure of labor productivity with the intensity of leveraged buyout activity in various industries to see if significant patterns emerged. We measured leveraged buyout intensity by the industry dollar share of total completed transactions relative to the mean industry share of gross national product, as indicated in Table 7-6.

Table 7-6. Labor Productivity Changes and Leveraged Buyout (LBO) Intensity, 1980-1987

| | | LBO Intensity¹ | | | | |
| Productivity Increases² | High | | | Low | | |
	Industry	LBO Intensity	Productivity Index	Industry	LBO Intensity	Productivity Index
High	Retail Trade	2.3	4.29		0.8	3.25
	Manufacturing	3.0	6.25	Lumber		
	Durable Goods	2.8	8.55	Petroleum	0.0	25.33
	Stone, Clay, & Glass	13.9	7.33			
	Primary Metals	1.7	11.06	Mining & Natural Resource Extraction	0.3	33.95
	Fabricated Metals	2.7	3.62			
	Nonelectrical Machinery	2.5	6.80			
	Electrical Machinery	3.0	8.43	Transportation	0.1	19.37
	Transportation Equipment	1.8	19.37	Public Utilities	0.1	22.82
	Instruments	1.7	8.27			
	Furniture	1.1	3.00			
	Nondurable Goods	3.2	4.26			
	Food	5.1	6.04			
	Textiles	7.9	6.31			
	Paper	4.5	3.88			
Low	Communications	1.8	-34.78		NA	
	Chemicals	1.1	-0.13			
	Rubber	1.7	-13.08			

¹LBO intensity is measured by the industry dollar share of total completed LBO transactions divided by the mean industry share of nominal gross national product, 1978-1987.

²Productivity change is measured by the difference of the industry's productivity as measured by output per employee-hour, 1977 = 100.

Sources: Bureau of Labor Statistics, U.S. Department of Labor; Survey of Current Business, U.S. Department of Commerce; Drexel Burnham Lambert, Inc., Merger and Acquisitions Transaction Database; World Economic Outlook, Morgan Stanley & Co., Inc.

Table 7-6 shows that in both durable and nondurable goods manufacturing, where the majority of LBO activity has been concentrated, productivity increases have been significant. Eleven of the fifteen manufacturing industries studied showed a positive correlation between LBO intensity and rising productivity. Outside of manufacturing, a similar pattern held for retail trade. While productivity increased in lumber, petroleum, mining and natural resource extraction, transportation, and public utilities, the increases were not associated with intensive leveraged buyout activity. LBO intensity was associated with productivity declines in communications, chemicals, and rubber production. Still, in the lion's share of industrial sectors, the association between intensive leveraged buyout activity and productivity increases was strong.

Operating Income

Operating income (Figure 7-9) is probably the key operational performance indicator of a corporation's ability to generate cash flow. For the 1984 cohort, in the prebuyout period, firms showed a decline in operating income at an average rate of 15.05 percent. For the 1985 and 1986 cohorts, firms showed modest increases of 2.03 percent and 1.96 percent respectively.

Ownership change through an LBO dramatically improved operating income performance. Average percentage changes during the postbuyout period ranged from 25.95 percent (1985) to 39.92 percent (1986). The weighted average absolute change from the pre- to postbuyout periods was also impressive, at just under 30 percent for all cohorts.

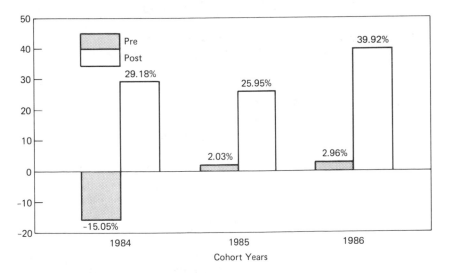

Figure 7–9. Operating income in LBO firms—Mean percentage changes for cohorts, 1984, 1985, 1986 (*Investor's Digest Daily*, Drexel Burnham Lambert, Datext).

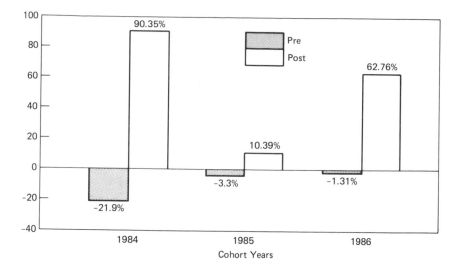

Figure 7-10. Working capital in LBO firms—Mean percentage changes for cohorts, 1984, 1985, 1986 (*Investor's Digest Daily,* Drexel Burnham Lambert, Datext).

Working Capital Changes

Working capital declined on a mean percentage basis for all LBO cohorts prior to the buyout. Declines ranged from 21.9 percent for the 1984 cohort to a more modest 1.31 percent for the 1986 cohort. After the buyout, all cohorts reversed this declining trend with substantial increases in working capital, as indicated in Figure 7-10. The weighted mean average annual increase in working capital for all cohorts was a remarkable 60.76 percent in the postbuyout period.

The turnover of working capital also reflects the efficiency of the use of funds raised through the new financial structure. Working capital turnover rates of -29.02 percent and -10.29 percent for the 1984 and 1985 cohorts were reversed, and working capital turnover improved by a mean annual rate of 80.73 percent and 38.02 percent for those same cohorts. The decline in working capital turnover for the 1986 cohort is consistent with the observation that buyout improvements tend to emerge after adjustments in the initial years following consolidation (see Figure 7-11).

Interest Coverage

Interest coverage, or the ratio of income to interest expense, is a key indicator of a company's viability and is of particular interest when a corporation takes on substantial leverage. In our study, interest coverage declined substantially under the LBO financial structure, dropping at a rate of 81.6 percent on

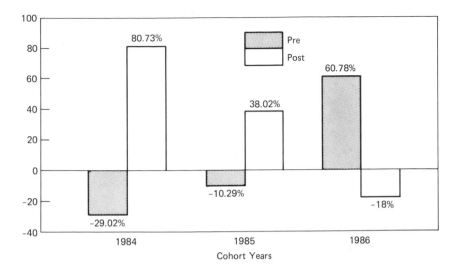

Figure 7–11. Working capital turnover in LBO firms—Mean percentage changes for cohorts, 1984, 1985, 1986 (*Investor's Digest Daily,* Drexel Burnham Lambert, Datext).

a weighted average absolute basis. It is important to note, however, that interest coverage was declining rapidly (by 25.8 percent and 6.12 percent annually) for both the 1984 and 1986 cohorts *prior* to the leveraged buyout.

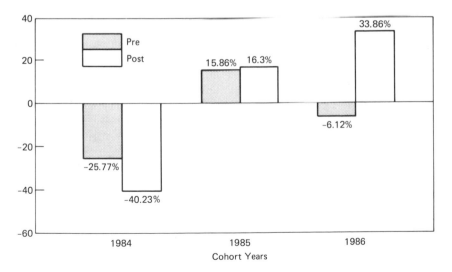

Figure 7–12. Interest coverage in LBO firms—Mean percentage changes for cohorts, 1984, 1985, 1986 (*Investor's Digest Daily,* Drexel Burnham Lambert, Datext).

During the years after the buyout, average interest coverage for all cohorts increased by a weighted mean average rate of 8.12 percent annually. Interest coverage ratios declined in the postbuyout period for the 1984 cohort, increased marginally for the 1985 cohort, and improved significantly for the 1986 cohort (see Figure 7-12).

Capital Expenditures

Investment in new plant, property, and equipment represents an important indicator of long-term planning and strategy. Prior to their leveraged buyouts, firms showed either relatively small increases in capital expenditures (1984 cohort firms) or modest decreases in such spending (1985 and 1986 cohort firms). (See Figure 7-13.) The 1986 cohort in particular experienced disinvestment, largely as the result of store consolidations by Safeway, Macy's, and Nutri/System, Inc.®

During the prebuyout period, the firms of the 1984 cohort increased their annual investment by $2.65 million. After the buyout, that rate increased to $22.08 million, or over eight times as much. The 1985 cohort reversed a prebuyout pattern of investment decline of $4.87 million annually, experiencing an average annual increase of $1.4 million in the postbuyout period. The 1986 cohort experienced substantial disinvestment before the buyout, with an average decline of $14.43 million annually. That trend accelerated to an average annual decline of $36.13 million, reflecting asset sales in the years following the buyout. Overall, however, the weighted average absolute change in capital spending between the pre- and postbuyout periods was positive, increasing by 3.76 percent.

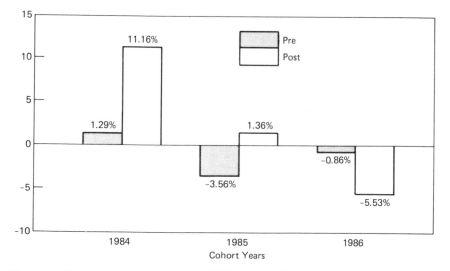

Figure 7-13. Capital expenditures in LBO firms—Mean percentage changes for cohorts, 1984, 1985, 1986 (*Investor's Digest Daily,* Drexel Burnham Lambert, Datext).

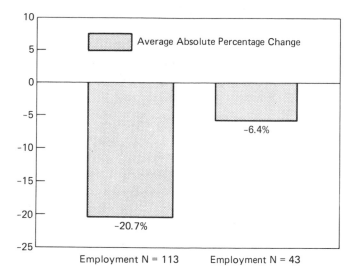

Figure 7-14. Employment performance—Prebuyout to postbuyout (Datext, Trinet, 1980-1987)

During the period after the buyout, firms in the 1984 and 1985 cohorts showed patterns of rising capital expenditures, while the 1986 cohort showed a mean change of -5.53 percent. Our findings are consistent with other research in this area, which shows that after a buyout, companies usually experience an initial sell-off of unproductive assets, then engage in new capital expenditures.

Employment Effects

Employment has become a central theme in the policy debate over leveraged buyouts, yet it remains the most difficult factor to evaluate. Employment disclosure is not required of those firms that continue to file 10-K reports with the SEC after going private. Nor, for that matter, is it required of public companies. Nevertheless, using Trinet data, we were able to track employment for 113 leveraged buyouts, as well as for our primary study sample of forty-three transactions (see Figures 7-14 and 7-15).

The association of layoffs with LBOs is spurious. For the most part, the absolute changes in employment that occur following a buyout appear to be the result of spin-offs from the surviving unit. In fact, consistent with earlier findings about mergers and acquisitions generally (Yago and Stevenson, 1989), on an average mean basis, LBO firms in both the larger and smaller samples reversed patterns of job loss prior to ownership change and increased employment after their buyouts. (See Figure 7-16.)

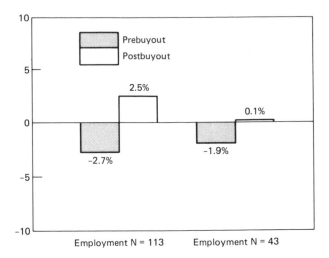

Figure 7–15. Employment performance—Mean percentage changes (Datext, Trinet, 1980–1987).

These findings are consistent with a recent study by Lichtenberg and Siegel (1989) of the relationship between employment and ownership. In addition, the Bureau of Labor Statistics (1988) recently studied 2,020 mass layoffs and plant closings in twenty-nine states. While the total employment effects were substantial, only 4.36 percent of these events, representing 6.6 percent of the total jobs lost, resulted from changes in business ownership.

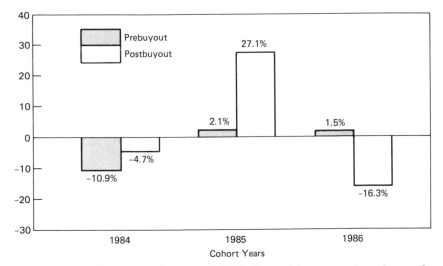

Figure 7–16. Employment performance in LBO firms—Mean percentage changes for cohorts (Datext, Trinet, 1980–1987).

In our cohort analysis, we found that LBO firms reduced their rate of job loss prior to ownership change in the 1984 cohort and improved their rate of employment growth by nearly thirteen times in the 1985 cohort. In the 1986 cohort, employment increased modestly prior to the buyout, but declined at a rate of 16.3 percent in the postbuyout period, where the effects of the Beatrice spin-offs and other divestitures were felt (Figure 7-16). Since most divestitures occur in the period immediately following the buyout, the impact of the restructuring on employment becomes more salutary as companies move farther away from that period. This holds true for the 1984 and 1985 cohorts, where a greater number of postbuyout years could be measured.

In short, during the initial years after the buyout, business fundamentals are restored as the firm restructures to concentrate on its core activities. The competitive position of the LBO firm is enhanced, as indicated by the other market and productivity measures discussed earlier. After an initial reduction in employment from spin-offs of ancillary business units, total employment recovers, and even rises as the employees who remain with the company are joined by others who are newly hired.

A thorough examination of the evidence indicates that leveraged buyouts have a positive effect on employment:

- On average, LBO firms tend to reverse declining employment trends and increase employment after their transactions are completed.
- While employment may initially drop at the company level, due to spin-offs and divestitures, this does not imply that layoffs, plant closings, or increased unemployment will occur. In many cases, the employees of divested units continue their work under new management or ownership arrangements.
- Only 6.6 percent of jobs lost through plant closings and layoffs can be attributed to changes in ownership, and LBOs represent only a fraction of ownership changes.

Operating Performance Summary

The findings in our study and earlier research demonstrate that leveraged buyouts can be a positive way for corporations to restructure and build value. While there have been enormous shifts in the size and content of the LBO market and wide variations in the performance of specific deals, this new capital structure tends to result in favorable fundamental changes in corporate organization, behavior, and performance.

The leveraged buyouts in our study substantially improved their sales performance and market productivity between the pre- and postbuyout periods. In the majority of industries, there was a strong correlation between intensive leveraged buyout activity and enhanced labor productivity. Operating income and working capital showed dramatic increases following the buyouts, and working capital turnover improved in two of the three cohorts we examined.

With the addition of substantial leverage, overall interest coverage declined under the LBO structure. After the buyouts, however, average interest coverage steadily increased. Capital spending rates rose significantly in the postbuyout period in two of the three cohorts we studied, and on average, capital spending increased. Employment trends varied between cohorts, but were also generally favorable. On average, the forty-three companies and 113 LBOs studied reversed prebuyout employment losses by increasing employment in the postbuyout period.

8

LBO Companies

Our statistical analysis in the last chapter provides a sound empirical basis for understanding the overall economic impact of leveraged buyout transactions. However, while market trends and aggregate data are highly instructive, they provide little insight into the specific effects of leveraged buyouts on individual companies.

To place LBOs in their proper perspective, we need to remember that each transaction takes place in a specific company. While our data may reveal general patterns, the trends that emerge are the result of individual management decisions, specific corporate strategies, and competitive pressures felt at the firm level.

To investigate these factors in greater detail, we gathered information on ten specific leveraged buyout companies. These studies gave us an inside look at the many factors that can lead to leveraged buyouts and the various ways companies respond to their new financial and ownership structure. We used data from Trinet, Datext, and a variety of other sources, and since our data sources were not always in agreement, we sometimes used independent calculations or other tests to resolve discrepancies. Although mathematical precision was not always possible under these circumstances, we utilized the most accurate data available, and we believe our figures provide a highly reliable guide to general performance trends.

As in our histories of high yield firms, many of the leveraged buyout companies we studied are subject to rapid and dramatic change. We completed our data collection in mid-1989, and references to the companies' "current" operations, holdings, competition, or business plans should be understood in this general time context.

For purposes of discussion, we divided our company histories into two convenient categories:

Strategic Buyouts. In these cases, firms sought to restructure financially in order to expand their markets, diversify their products, improve their operations, or achieve other strategic objectives. The firms studied included Harte-Hanks Communications, Nutri/System, MacAndrews & Forbes, Color Tile, Beatrice, and Macy's.

Defensive Buyouts. In these cases, companies were faced with possible acquisitions by other companies or financial groups and used restructuring as a means to maintain control of the company. The defensive buyouts we considered were Safeway, Conwood, Levitz Furniture, and Fruehauf.

We will also discuss divisional spin-offs later in the chapter.

Strategic Buyouts

Harte-Hanks Communications, Inc.

Prebuyout Position. Harte-Hanks Communications, Inc., grew out of a newspaper business started in Texas in the 1920s by Houston Harte and Bernard Hanks. By the 1980s, the company had acquired a variety of interests in three principal business areas. Newspapers remained a mainstay of the company's business mix, representing 46 percent of operating revenues in 1983. The company also provided consumer direct marketing, including market research and direct mail services. In addition, it maintained a broadcasting, entertainment, and cable division consisting of television and radio stations, entertainment production activities, cable systems, and a cable TV shopper's channel.

Harte-Hanks's strategy was designed to satisfy the interests of the company and its shareholders, communities, and employees through strategic positioning, operational improvements, and above-average growth in profitability. With competition from newspapers, magazines, radio, television, and other media, the company faced several challenges. It needed to remain on the leading edge of technology and cope with shifting economic, demographic, and regulatory trends. To maintain consistent growth, Harte-Hanks had to deal effectively with rising programming costs, expanding network commercial inventory, and the growth of barter syndication.

In 1983, the company established a comprehensive strategic initiative that focused on managing people and assets more effectively. It was also designed to improve productivity, generate revenues, control expenses, and redirect or eliminate marginal operations, products, and systems. As a result, the company sold several newspapers and radio stations in 1983 and early 1984, while concurrently building, expanding, and acquiring facilities for cable TV systems.

The Buyout. For a variety of reasons, analysts speculated that Harte-Hanks would be a likely leveraged buyout candidate. As it happens, management felt the stock was undervalued and that the company could be better run as a private entity. Harte-Hanks believed an LBO would provide the freedom to take advantage of investment opportunities without pressure for the consistent and predictable quarterly earnings growth expected of publicly held companies. In particular, Harte-Hanks planned investments of over $100 million in cable television and consumer direct marketing. But with a debt-to-equity ratio already at 58 percent, management was concerned about shareholder reactions to additional acquisitions.

In the summer of 1984, an investor group consisting of officers, directors, and members of the Harte and Shelton families offered to pay $445 million for the company. Goldman Sachs & Co. acted as financial adviser for the investment group, and Salomon Brothers Inc. was retained to review the proposal. Although two shareholders sued, alleging that the original proposal was unfair, a settlement was reached when the offer was sweetened to $457 million in cash, equity, and high yield debt securities. As a result of the buyout, Harte-Hanks Communications, Inc., became the wholly owned subsidiary of H. H. Holding, Inc., a corporation formed by members of Harte-Hanks management and the Harte and Hanks-Shelton families.

Postbuyout Performance. In every performance measure we studied, Harte-Hanks showed dramatic improvements following its leveraged buyout. Net sales, which stood at $164.6 million prior to the buyout in 1984, jumped to $551 million in 1985, then rose to $576.4 million in 1986. Sales per employee also soared from a prebuyout $15,500 to postbuyout figures of $54,300 in 1985 and $183,400 in 1986.

The prebuyout operating income for 1984 was $58.7 million. After the buyout, the figure jumped to $185.7 million in 1985 and continued to increase annually, reaching $333.3 million in 1987. Capital expenditures for new plant, property, and equipment rose from prebuyout levels of $261.2 million to $276.9 million in 1985 and then dropped back to $267.5 million in 1986. At year-end 1983, Harte-Hanks employed 10,021 persons. That figure dropped to 4,220 in 1984 as a result of the company's cost-containment programs and asset sales. In postbuyout 1985, the figure increased to 11,069, then slid to 9,750 in 1986, and 9,488 in 1987. Despite the decline, employment remained more than twice as high as it was in the buyout year.

Nutri/System, Inc.

Prebuyout Position. Nutri/System, Inc., was founded by Harold Katz in 1972 on the premise that individuals seeking significant weight loss would like to visit centers offering an individualized program of food products, dietary guidelines, mild exercise, and counseling services. The company experienced substantial revenue and income growth in each fiscal year, from the introduction of Nutri/System food products in 1978, to going public in 1981, to franchise expansion in 1982.

In that year, the company began a diversification program that proved unsuccessful, and two of the new businesses—cosmetics and figure salons—were quickly abandoned. Nevertheless, Nutri/System, Inc. was a high flyer on Wall Street until its customer base eroded and many unhappy franchises sued the company.

In 1985, there were 680 company-owned and franchised Nutri/System weight loss centers in operation throughout the United States and Canada. Most of the 45,000 active clients of these centers were middle- and upper-income women over thirty seeking substantial weight loss. In addition to paying fees for behavior education, diets, and maintenance programs, customers could purchase a proprietary line of food products called Nu-System Cuisine. The company provided service guarantees and incentives to promote its food products and help its customers reach and maintain their weight loss objectives.

Early in 1985, Nutri/System hired a new president, Donald McCulloch, to build a new senior management team and improve the service and financial performance of the weight loss centers. The company's strategy focused on developing new products and markets, maximizing the expertise and effectiveness of the franchises, establishing research relationships at major universities, and negotiating better prices with food suppliers.

The company's prime competition came from other health professionals and weight control products and programs. The company also faced challenges from litigation by franchise owners in 1982 and 1985, which affected company morale and employee turnover.

The Buyout. A Massachusetts investor group offered $87.5 million in 1986 for Nutri/System, Inc., but withdrew when it faced financing difficulties and realized the company was not worth the price. A Nutri/System senior management group led by Donald McCulloch then proposed a management buyout valued at $59.59 million in cash and securities. The members of the investor group each contributed at least $10,000 to the capital of the Holding Company, and it was arranged for the current managers and directors to remain in place.

Funding for the buyout included a $35 million offering of senior debt securities through Merrill Lynch Capital Markets, with the balance provided from bank loans and internal funds. Harold Katz, who owned 58 percent of the company's stock, gave the management group an irrevocable proxy to vote his shares in favor of the merger. The Philadelphia office of the Connecticut National Bank was retained for a fairness opinion and unanimously supported the transaction, which was approved on August 6, 1986.

Postbuyout Performance. Prior to the buyout, net sales had dropped from $124.9 million in 1984 to $101.3 million in 1985. In 1986, the year of the buyout, net sales continued to slide to $95.9 million. But in the following year, they rose to $118.3 million. In the prebuyout period, sales per employee had increased from $65,600 in 1984 to $77,300 in 1985. After the buyout, sales per employee declined, from $62,000 in 1986 to $48,100 in 1987.

Operating income showed a decreasing trend before the buyout, dropping from $30 million in 1984 to $14.6 million in 1985. After the buyout, the pattern was reversed, with operating income increasing from $10.1 million in 1986 to more than twice that figure, or $21.4 million, in 1987. Capital expenditures showed a continuing decline through the pre- and postbuyout periods, dropping from $29.6 million in 1984 to $3.1 million in 1987. Employment dropped from 1,905 in 1984 to 1,310 in 1985, then increased to 1,548 in 1986, continuing to rise to 2,457 in 1987. Nutri-System's product and service offered little room for new capital expenditures after the establishment of the company's distribution system. Operating efficiencies after the buyout increased income and employment.

MacAndrews & Forbes Group, Incorporated

Prebuyout Position. The predecessor of MacAndrews & Forbes Group, Inc., had been primarily engaged in the wholesale and retail jewelry business until 1980, when it acquired MacAndrews & Forbes Company. A public company traded on the AMEX, MacAndrews & Forbes has been engaged in a wide range of business activities.

The company is the only U.S. manufacturer of licorice extract and possibly the world's largest manufacturer of this popular flavoring. Through a subsidiary, Wilbur Chocolate Co., Inc., MacAndrews & Forbes is a leading manufacturer of high-quality chocolate- and cocoa-related products, which are sold to confectioners, bakeries, dairies, and food processors.

In December 1982, MacAndrews & Forbes acquired 82 percent of Technicolor, Inc., which later became a wholly owned subsidiary. Technicolor, Inc., offers worldwide film processing for professional photographers and consumers, videocassette duplicating for the home-video market, and support services for various government agencies.

In July 1984, MacAndrews & Forbes acquired approximately 80 percent of the common stock of Consolidated Cigar Corporation; in July 1986, the company exercised an option to purchase the remaining shares. The unit has over a 45 percent market share in the little cigar category and is the largest cigar company by dollar sales in the United States.

In July 1987, Revlon Group became an indirect, wholly owned subsidiary of MacAndrews & Forbes, placing the company at the center of the market for cosmetics, fragrances, and beauty products. In addition, MacAndrews & Forbes is a leading distributor of Timex and Citizen watches, Speidel watch bands, and Parker pens through its distribution division, A. Cohen & Sons.

The company faces a variety of domestic and international challenges in the many markets in which it operates. Licorice competes with other flavorings and moistening agents in the tobacco industry and in the manufacture of drugs, confections, and sweeteners. The industrial chocolate industry is highly competitive, as are watches, beauty products, and cigars.

The company's film processing and videotape operations are subject to worldwide labor, economic, and import restrictions, and fluctuations in international currency values. After an intensive review by management of Technicolor's businesses, the division was restructured, with proceeds from sales and liquidations used to reduce outstanding debt.

The Buyout. On May 16, 1983, MacAndrews & Forbes's chairman and CEO, Ron Perelman, announced a proposal to purchase all equity held by other stockholders for between $45 and $48 per share. On September 23 of the same year, MacAndrews & Forbes Holdings, Inc., a Delaware corporation with Mr. Perelman as its sole stockholder, submitted an offer at $50 per share in cash and securities. A special committee of nonmanagement directors rejected the offer as inadequate and suggested that any revised offer should be made on an all cash basis.

Mr. Perelman next offered $56 in cash for each share. The offer was deemed fair to shareholders and was accepted in March 1984. Despite the special committee's fairness opinion, however, at least nine lawsuits were filed by shareholders, alleging that the proposal was unfair and only enhanced the interests of Mr. Perelman.

Postbuyout Performance. Prior to the buyout, sales had increased from $163.4 million in 1982 to $273.4 million in 1984. Following the buyout, the positive trend continued, with sales reaching $422.6 million in 1985, dropping to $341 million in 1986, then soaring to $2.1 billion in 1987 with the Revlon acquisition. Sales per employee also continued an upward trend. Before the buyout, sales per employee had increased from $46,700 in 1982 to $86,500 in 1984. After the buyout, sales per employee rose to $187,800 in 1985 and $230,300 in 1986.

Capital expenditures had risen from $55.4 million in 1982 to $69.6 million in 1984, the year of the buyout. They continued to rise in 1985, reaching $72.6 million, then slowed to $56.6 million in 1986, and increased to $57.5 million in 1987. The employment pattern was erratic in the prebuyout period, dropping from 3,494 employees in 1982 to 2,620 in 1983, then rising to 3,410 in 1984. Employment increased in 1985 to 4,200, then declined to 3,410 in 1986. In 1987, employment exploded to 28,843 with the acquisition of Revlon.

Color Tile, Inc.

Prebuyout Position. From its base in Fort Worth, Texas, Color Tile Inc. sells home improvement products through 823 specialty retail stores in the United States and Canada. Do-it-yourself and commercial customers come to Color Tile for nationally advertised brands and private label products under the Color Tile, Color Your World, and Ultima names.

In the United States, 665 Color Tile Supermart stores market ceramic, mosaic, quarry, and wood parquet tiles, resilient flooring, wallpaper, paint, tools, and installation materials. There are 136 Color Your World stores in Canada and twenty-two in the United States, selling primarily paint and wallpaper. In addition, Color Tile has three manufacturing plants in the United States and three in Canada, which produce about a third of the products sold. The company also has five warehousing and distribution centers in the United States and two in Canada.

Color Tile competes with general merchandise stores, discount houses, home improvement centers, and other specialty retailers. The company's competitive position depends on more than just product selection. Consumers want detailed product information and often require in-store installation instructions from trained personnel. Color Tile's fortunes have steadily risen through the company's careful attention to customer service, and increasing consumer interest in home renovation.

The Buyout. On August 15, 1986, a group of Color Tile managers and shareholders who jointly owned 25 percent of the company's stock announced an LBO proposal by Merrill Lynch Capital Partners, Inc., to acquire the company at $26.25 per share in cash. On August 22, 1986, Marshall Cogan, Chairman of General Felt Industries Inc. (GFI) outlined a competing proposal to acquire the company at $30 per share in cash.

Color Tile referred the buyout proposal to a committee of independent directors, which retained Salomon Brothers Inc. as its financial advisor. Drexel Burnham was retained as the placement agent for the purchases and as the dealer manager in the offer. The management group led by Merrill Lynch was prepared to go higher than $30 per share, but when GFI sweetened its offer to $31.50 per share, or about $300 million, the management group dropped out of the bidding. Color Tile agreed to merge with General Felt, an established name in the home products industry, and the LBO was approved in September of 1986.

Postbuyout Performance. After the leveraged buyout, Marshall Cogan was named Chairman and CEO of Color Tile. Under his direction, the company showed positive results in most of the performance measures we tracked.

Prior to the buyout, Color Tile's net sales had risen from $282.8 million in 1984 to $347.3 million in 1985 and $387.1 million in 1986. In postbuyout 1987, net sales continued to increase to $487.6 million. Sales per employee had dropped slightly from $78,708 in 1984 to $78,592 in 1985. In the buyout year of 1986, sales per employee increased to $84,152 and continued to rise in 1987 to $95,551.

Prior to the buyout, operating income had increased from $153.8 million in 1984 to $214.6 million in 1985. In the buyout year, operating income dropped to $45 million, but in postbuyout 1987, it surged to $251.5 million. Capital expenditures showed a steady increase, from $153.8 million in 1984, to $159.5 million in 1985, to $165.1 million in 1986, and continued to rise in 1987 to $169.6 million. The employment trend was also positive, going from 3,593 employees in 1984, to 4,419 in 1985, to 4,600 in 1986, and reaching 5,103 in postbuyout 1987.

Beatrice Companies, Inc.

Prebuyout Position. Beatrice Companies was founded in Beatrice, Nebraska, in 1894 and succeeded by a Delaware corporation in 1924. Prior to its buyout, Beatrice was believed to be the largest packaged foods and consumer products company in the United States, measured by sales. From its headquarters in Chicago, the company produced, marketed, and sold a wide variety of food and nonfood products to consumer, commercial, and industrial markets.

Beatrice had three primary business segments prior to the buyout: U.S. food, consumer products, and international food. Certain other operations, including Avis (car rental), Jensen (high fidelity equipment), and Danskin and Pennaco (knitwear) were slated for divestment and classified as discontinued operations before the company entered into its LBO agreement.

U.S. Food was the largest of Beatrice's operations, selling and distributing more than 150 brands in 90 product categories. There were eight divisions within the U.S. Food segment, including grocery, meats, dairy, cheese, fruit juices, soft drinks, bottled water, and warehousing. These divisions sold such familiar brands as La Choy, Wesson, Hunt's, Peter Pan, Swiss Miss, Orville Redenbacher, Swift Premium, Butterball, Sizzlelean, Louis Sherry, Hotel Bar, Tropicana, and Great Bear.

The Consumer Products segment had two divisions: personal products and consumer durables. They sold home products, water treatment, luggage, intimate apparel, family products, cosmetics, and fragrances under such popular brand names as Stiffel, Samsonite, Vogel-Peterson, Culligan, Playtex, Max Factor, Almay, and Halston.

The International Food division had operations in more than thirty countries, and sold well-recognized brand-name products from six primary categories: food distribution, dairy and ice cream, snacks and baked goods, confectionary, beverages and fruit juices, and processed meats.

In June 1984, in an attempt to focus its assets in the food and consumer products businesses, Beatrice acquired Esmark. Esmark's national brands complemented Beatrice's regional brands. Esmark also gave Beatrice a strong sales force, a leading research and development team, and one of the most efficient distribution networks in the food industry.

Most of Beatrice's product lines faced stiff competition from large and small firms in the United States and abroad. The company competed with generic products and private label brands of retailers, wholesalers, and cooperatives on the basis of quality, consumer loyalty, and price.

The Buyout. Despite Beatrice's size and strong brand franchises, the company suffered from a big-for-bigness'-sake mentality, an older management team, and huge corporate overhead. Bureaucratic, morale, and corporate identity problems took their toll, with resignations, firings, and productivity problems. With so much focus on buying and selling businesses, long-term planning had all but ceased in many parts of the company.

In August 1985, Beatrice's board ousted the chairman and CEO, James Dutt, replacing him with the former vice-chairman, William Granger. The investment banking firm of Kohlberg Kravis Roberts & Co. (KKR) and the former Esmark management team, headed by Donald P. Kelly, saw this as an opportunity to provide new management direction, decentralize operations, and eliminate excessive corporate spending. In mid-October 1985, KKR, advised by Drexel Burnham and Kidder, Peabody, offered $40 in cash and $5 in preferred stock for each share of Beatrice, in a deal valued at $4.91 billion.

Beatrice rejected the offer and considered a restructuring in which it would sell assets and spin off the proceeds to shareholders. The company engaged Lazard Freres and Salomon Brothers to seek out other bidders, but no white knights appeared. In late October, KKR sweetened its bid to $40 in cash and $7 in preferred stock. On January 8, 1986, KKR modified its offer to $40 in cash and 10/25 of a share of preferred stock in BCI Holdings, with annual dividends of 14 percent per year, payable for six years either in cash or in additional shares of exchangeable preferred stock.

The board of directors unanimously approved the modified offer on February 2, 1986. The buyout would provide the company with three advantages. It would free Beatrice from dividend payments, which amounted to $170 million in 1984; under private ownership, acquisitions and divestitures would be much easier to accomplish; and the buyout would put a new management team in place, with the performance incentives that come with a 12- to 15-percent equity stake in the company.

Financing for the transaction included $3.5 billion of term and revolving credit loans through Bankers Trust, Citibank, and Manufacturers Hanover. Drexel Burnham underwrote a public offering of $2.5 billion in high yield debt securities, and various limited partnerships agreed to purchase approximately $407 million of BCI Holdings common stock and $10 million in warrants.

The buyout was approved on April 11, 1986, at $50 per share, including $40 in cash and $10 face value of BCI preferred. At $6.2 billion, the transaction was the largest deal on record at the time. After the buyout, five limited partnerships with partners from BCI and KKR owned approximately 98.3 percent of the common stock in BCI Holdings.

Like most buyouts, the transaction engendered a good deal of litigation. Twelve class action suits were initiated in Delaware against Beatrice, its directors, and KKR, seeking damages and injunctive relief. The final buyout proposal was modified to settle complaints about "golden parachutes" for top executives and bonus/severance payments to middle managers.

Postbuyout Performance. Following the buyout, KKR appointed Mr. Kelly as the new chairman and CEO of BCI Holdings. KKR and Mr. Kelly called the buyout the "deal of the century," when they realized that through asset sales, they could generate a windfall profit of $3.8 billion. In April 1986, Mr. Kelly set out on a selling spree that grossed more than $5 billion in less than a year.

The remainder of the company, however, has been something of a white elephant. Over fifty companies have passed on opportunities to purchase businesses like Wesson Oil and Hunt's. A major sticking point is $1.9 billion in balance sheet intangible assets, or goodwill, which acts as a drag on earnings. At the current rate of depreciation, Beatrice won't fully amortize its goodwill for forty-seven years. KKR hopes to sell the remaining assets in a block to maximize profits and avoid the tax complications of successive sales.

BCI has already sold Avis Inc. to Wesray for $250 million. In June 1986, the company sold its Coca-Cola bottling operations in Los Angeles and mid-America to Coca-Cola Company for about $1 billion. Playtex was spun off in a management buyout for $1.25 billion in August 1986. In November, managers and investors bought Americold cold store warehouses for $480 million. In December, Webcraft Technologies was sold to managers and an investment group for $280 million.

BCI sold its dairy operations to Borden for $315 million. TLC Group L.P. purchased the International Food units in August 1987 in a leveraged buyout valued at $985 million. And in March 1988, Seagram Co. bought Tropicana for $1.2 billion.

Just a year and a half after taking the company private, KKR planned a public offering for the remainder of BCI. Through rapid debt repayment, the company was quickly approaching its prebuyout debt level of $2 billion. The smaller, food-focused, low-debt company would have made an attractive public offering, but the October 1987 market crash intervened and the plan was discarded. The investors who took Beatrice private are now talking about borrowing again to pay themselves a dividend of as much as $800 million.

In the prebuyout period, Beatrice's net sales increased from $9.33 billion in 1983 to $12.60 billion in 1984, then dropped to $11.40 billion in 1985. In 1986, sales remained at $11.40 billion, but dropped to $8.93 billion in 1987 as the company sold off assets. Sales per employee declined in the prebuyout period, from $125,950 in 1984 to $113,960 in 1985. After the buyout, however, sales per employee showed substantial improvement, climbing to $142,450 in 1986 and to $143,368 in 1987.

Employment at Beatrice increased from 72,000 in 1984 to 100,000 in 1985, but dropped rapidly after the buyout as a result of restructuring and asset sales. In 1986, employment declined to 80,000, then fell to 62,000 in 1987.

On a purely financial basis, the Beatrice buyout has been one of the most successful transactions in history. While the reshuffling of assets may be unsavory to some, most of the units that have been sold have continued to be productive and profitable under new management and ownership.

R. H. Macy & Co., Inc.

Prebuyout Position. R. H. Macy was founded in 1858 and incorporated in New York in 1919. By 1985, Macy's was the nation's tenth largest retail department store business, operating ninety-five stores in fourteen states, including twenty-three stores under the Bamberger's name. Macy's sells a wide assortment of merchandise in the medium to higher price range. Ready-to-wear apparel and accessories for women, men, and children account for 68 percent of total sales. Furniture, home furnishings, housewares, and electronics account for another 30 percent of sales, with other categories making up the remainder.

Macy's conducts business through four regional store groups in major cities and suburban areas: Macy's New York, Bamberger's, Macy's California, and Macy's Atlanta. The company's largest store, located at Herald Square in New York City, is billed as the world's largest department store. The company and its subsidiaries operate stores and have equity interests in shopping centers in various locations throughout the country. Prior to the buyout, Macy's planned aggressive expansion and store improvements throughout the sun belt.

Over 75 percent of the company's stores are located in major shopping enters, and each store is operated by local management under policies set by the firm's corporate officers. Each store does its own buying, and the company's 700 buyers have a domestic buying office in New York and foreign buying offices in nineteen major markets from London, Paris, and Frankfurt to Shanghai, Singapore, and Sri Lanka. The company also has representatives in ten other countries.

All of the stores do business on a cash and credit basis, with credit purchases accounting for 61 percent of total sales. Macy Credit Corp. funds the customers' credit purchases with long- and short-term borrowings.

Macy's stores compete directly with department stores and other retail outlets in the areas where they operate. Since retail trade is highly competitive, Macy's constantly strives to improve the efficiency and effectiveness of its operations through expansion, modernization, and improvements in customer service.

The Buyout. In May 1985, Macy's chairman and CEO, Edward S. Finkelstein, and Goldman Sachs & Co. began discussing the feasibility of a management buyout. In June, Mr. Finkelstein advised the board that such a transaction could help retain key managers and motivate them to keep Macy's on the leading edge of the retail market. The plan would also be timely in light of anticipated sales and earnings trends that could negatively impact the market value of the company's stock.

In July 1985, a special committee of eleven directors was formed to consider the buyout concept, and Macy's later retained James D. Wolfensohn, Inc., as its financial advisor. In October, Mr. Finkelstein and other directors and members of senior management announced a buyout proposal at $68 per share. The committee rejected the offer, but consented to review an offer at $70 per share, or $3.58 billion, to be submitted by December 1, 1985.

While management and Goldman Sachs tried to arrange financing at the higher price, the special committee directed Wolfensohn to seek out other offers. Unfortunately, neither of these efforts was successful. Wolfensohn contacted several other parties, five requested information, two met with management, but no offers were received. Meanwhile, Goldman Sachs was unable to obtain financing commitments at $70 per share, so on December 11, it submitted a new proposal at $68 in cash per share, or $3.5 billion, backed by commitments from Citibank, Manufacturers Hanover Trust, and General Electric Credit Corporation. Under the proposal, the management group would also pay $107.50 per share, or $16 million, for outstanding shares of cumulative preferred stock.

The transaction prompted two class action suits when the buyout proposal was initially announced, and two more when the bid dropped from $70 to $68 per share. All four suits alleged unfairness to shareholders and violation of fiduciary responsibilities. Despite these complications, the board unanimously approved the buyout proposal at a special meeting on June 19, 1986. Financing for the transaction totaled nearly $3.707 billion, including bank debt, common and preferred stock, senior and high yield subordinated debt securities, and notes secured by mortgages on Macy's real estate and leasehold interests.

Postbuyout Performance. In the prebuyout period, Macy's net sales showed an upward trend, rising from $4.07 billion in 1984 to $4.37 billion in 1985. This trend continued in the postbuyout period, with net sales of $4.79 billion in 1986 and $5.21 billion in 1987. Sales per employee also showed a steady increase, from $75,280 in 1984, to $76,638 in 1985, to $84,841 in postbuyout 1986 and $93,043 in 1987.

Operating income also improved in both the pre- and postbuyout periods, from $1.32 billion in 1984 to $1.41 billion in 1985, to $1.58 billion in 1986 and $1.74 billion in 1987. Macy's also showed a steady increase in capital spending. In the prebuyout period, capital expenditures rose from $1.41 billion in 1984 to $1.60 billion in 1985. After the buyout, the figure shot up to $2.26 billion in 1986 and rose to $2.46 billion in 1987. Employment increased from 52,000 in 1984 to 57,000 in 1985. In 1986, the year of the buyout, employment dropped to 55,000, then recovered to 56,000 in 1987.

Defensive Buyouts

Safeway Stores, Incorporated

Prebuyout Position. Safeway Stores, Incorporated, a California-based company, is the nation's largest supermarket chain and the largest food retailer in the world by sales volume. At year-end 1985, the company owned 2,365 supermarkets, including Liquor Barn discount liquor stores, Food Barn warehouse food stores, and superwarehouse stores in the United States, Canada, and the United Kingdom. The company also operates extensive manufacturing, processing, and distribution facilities.

Safeway's supermarkets offer competitively priced nationally advertised and private label brands, and unbranded merchandise usually sold by retail food stores. In addition to food items, Safeway sells everything from cigarettes, soaps, and cosmetics to auto accessories, appliances, cameras, hardware, and toys. The supermarkets also feature a variety of services, either directly or through third-party concessionaires, including check cashing, automated teller machines, appliance rentals, and film developing, and cooperate with local recycling programs and community clothing collection drives.

In 1985, Safeway sold operations in Australia, Germany, and Toronto, Canada. The Australian operations were sold to acquire a 20 percent interest in Woolworth's Limited of Australia, that country's largest food retailer and second largest retailer overall. Safeway also owns 49 percent of Casa Ley, S. A., a Mexican retailer and wholesale outlet company. In every country where Safeway does business, it faces strong competition on the basis of price, service, and the quality and mix of its products.

The Buyout. In June 1986, Safeway had several suitors interested in purchasing the company through an LBO. After acquiring enough shares to require filing a Schedule 13D, the Dart Group Corp., led by Herbert H. Haft, offered $58 per share or $3.6 billion for the remaining shares of Safeway. Concerned about a possible management shakeout and Dart's reputation in retail management, Safeway rejected the offer, filed suit, and instituted a poison pill to force Dart to retreat. Although Dart sweetened its offer to $64 per share, the high cost of the proposed transaction led Standard & Poor's to place both Dart and Safeway on CreditWatch, and Moody's Investor Service also began a review of both companies.

In July 1986, Safeway announced an agreement to sell the company to a group of investors headed by Kohlberg Kravis Roberts & Co. (KKR) and Safeway's top managers. The first 45 million outstanding shares would be sold for $69 a share in cash. Each of the remaining 16 million shares would be exchanged for $61.68 in bonds plus a warrant valued at $7.40, which would allow shareholders to buy stock in SSI Holdings, a corporation formed as part of the deal.

Safeway retained its current management, and certain managers were offered the right to buy 10 percent of the new company. Six holding companies were organized by KKR to effect the acquisition of Safeway. KKR also reached an agreement that would allow Dart to walk away from the transaction without the appearance of greenmail.

Financing was provided by a $3 billion short-term loan arranged by Bankers Trust Company through a syndicate. The loan was refinanced a few months later with high yield securities, some of which were sold by KKR's financial advisor, Morgan Stanley & Company. Although the buyout was legally contested by a union representing Safeway employees, the company settled all claims in shareholder suits against the acquisition.

Postbuyout Performance. Before the buyout, Safeway's net sales decreased from $19.6 billion in 1985 to $6.6 billion in 1986. After the buyout, net sales recovered to $18.3 billion in 1987. Sales per employee were also declining in the prebuyout period, from $119,500 in 1985 to $38,400 in 1986. In 1987, following the buyout, the figure jumped to $139,800.

Operating income followed a downward trend in the prebuyout period, dropping from $4.8 billion in 1985 to $1.6 billion in 1986. After the buyout, the trend was reversed, and operating income climbed to $4.5 billion in 1987. Capital expenditures declined both before and after the buyout, going from $4.5 billion in 1985 to $3.85 billion in 1986, then sliding to $2.3 billion in postbuyout 1987. Employment increased prior to the buyout, rising from 164,385 in 1985 to 172,412 in 1986. In 1987, that figure declined to 130,992 employees, reflecting asset sales in the postbuyout period.

Conwood Corporation

Prebuyout Position. From its headquarters in Memphis, Tennessee, Conwood Corporation is engaged two primary lines of business. The company is a major factor in the smokeless tobacco industry, marketing thirty-six brands of snuff and chewing tobacco to food and tobacco wholesalers. The company also operates a popcorn and concession supply unit, that processes and sells popcorn to grocery outlets, theaters, and concession operators. Conwood has its own manufacturing and warehousing facilities, through which it distributes bulk popcorn, concession equipment, and supplies. A third business unit, which produced household insecticides, was sold in the mid-1980s.

Conwood Corporation distributes its products nationally, principally in the South, and in some foreign markets. The company has no foreign operations and its export sales are less than 10 percent of total sales. The smokeless tobacco industry is highly competitive, with several major companies aggressively seeking market share. The popcorn and concession supply unit faces competition from a number of regional and national companies.

The Buyout. As cigarette sales declined, the smokeless tobacco industry experienced strong growth, particularly in the South. This led to speculation that Conwood would become a takeover target. In September 1983, Conwood retained Resource Holdings, Ltd., a financial consulting firm, to seek out potential merger partners.

In November of that year, Gulf Broadcasting Co. expressed interest in the company at $33.50 per share, or $373 million. Conwood met with Gulf Broadcasting, but could not reach a definitive agreement, and negotiations ended in April 1984. A month later, the Dalfort Corporation expressed an interest in Conwood, but discussions ended in August 1984.

Talks resumed in April 1985, and the Pritzker family of Chicago bid $36 per share, or $400 million, for Conwood in a leveraged buyout that would merge Conwood with a subsidiary of the Dalfort Corporation. Jay Pritzker, Dalfort's Chairman, expected Conwood's current management to remain in place, and a family spokesman said the LBO would be "mutually beneficial" for Dalfort and Conwood.

Goldman Sachs was retained as financial advisor for the merger and decided that the offer price was fair to shareholders. The transaction called for $350 million of funding. This came from an initial capitalization of $20 million, $210 million borrowed from Citibank, and a $120 million high yield subordinated loan from Hyatt Corporation, a limited partner of the purchasing group and an affiliate of the Dalfort Corporation. The balance of the purchase price was obtained from Conwood's cash reserves. The merger agreement was approved in June and became effective on September 30, 1985.

Postbuyout Performance. Conwood improved its operating performance in several areas after the buyout. In the prebuyout period, net sales plummeted from $198.5 million in 1984 to $61 million in 1985. After the buyout, net sales steadily recovered, to $179.1 million in 1987. Sales per employee also declined in the prebuyout period, from $140,800 in 1984 to $125,500 in 1985, but increased to $127,900 in postbuyout 1986.

Conwood's buyout also reversed a declining trend in operating income. From 1984 to 1985, operating income dropped from $98.8 million to $31.9 million. In the postbuyout period, that figure increased to $104.9 million in 1987. Capital expenditures rose from $2.2 million in prebuyout 1984 to over fifteen times that amount, or $33.2 million, in postbuyout 1986, dropping slightly to $30.7 million in 1987. Conwood also increased employment from a relatively constant 1,350 in the prebuyout period to 1,400 in the postbuyout years.

Levitz Furniture Company

Prebuyout Position. The Levitz Furniture Company started as a Pennsylvania corporation in February 1965, succeeding a business partnership commenced in 1936. The company and its subsidiaries sell a wide variety of brand name furniture and home furnishings, as well as furniture carrying the Levitz label. Showroom merchandise is usually displayed in model room settings throughout the chain, which at year-end 1984 had eighty-five retail facilities, including sixty-nine warehouse-showrooms in twenty-five states.

Each of the company's warehouse-showrooms incorporates a warehouse and showroom in a single facility. Unlike most other furniture retailers, Levitz maintains large inventories and purchases in rail-carload and truckload lots. This allows the company to offer lower prices than conventional furniture stores and to provide rapid delivery on about 90 percent of the merchandise it sells. Levitz controls inventory levels with data processing equipment at its administrative offices and at each retail location.

The retail furniture business is highly competitive and includes individual, chain, department, and discount stores. Most retailers carry minimal inventories and only purchase merchandise when they receive a sales order. As a result, their customers may have to wait weeks or months for delivery. The Levitz warehousing concept cuts delivery time to just a few days, offering its stores a distinct competitive advantage. Levitz is also price competitive in most of its markets, though the Miami warehouse-showroom features higher priced furniture and accessories.

The Buyout. In the spring of 1984, Levitz received an offer from the Dalfort Corporation valued at $34 per share, including $20 in cash and $14 in securities. In April, Dalfort made a second offer to acquire Levitz at $33.50 per share, increasing the cash portion to $23 per share and reducing the securities portion to $10.50 per share.

In June, Levitz appointed an ad hoc committee to review the offer and other offers that might be received. The ad hoc committee retained Sachnoff Weaver & Rubenstein, Ltd., as legal counsel, and Drexel Burnham Lambert as its financial advisor. Shortly thereafter, both Dalfort offers were rejected.

Meanwhile, the company was receiving other inquiries. Kelso & Co., Inc., wanted to structure a management leveraged buyout using an employee stock ownership plan. In August of 1984, Levitz received an offer from Alger Associates, Inc., to purchase all outstanding shares for about $37 per share in cash and securities, or $303.4 million. Jefferies & Co. supported the Alger Associates offer with a purchase commitment. But the Alger/Jefferies offer was also rejected as unfair to shareholders.

In November, the ad hoc committee engaged Dean Witter Reynolds Inc. as its financial advisor when a group consisting of Citicorp Capital Investors Group Ltd., Drexel Burnham Lambert, and certain members of management, headed by Levitz chairman and CEO, Robert Elliott, proposed a leveraged buyout at $39 per share in cash, or about $318 million.

Levitz had received financing commitments of about $350 million from Manufacturers Hanover Trust Company and six other banks and financial institutions. Approximately $50 million of the transaction funding came from the sale of Levitz common stock and cumulative preferred stock by the buying group, up to $120 million was provided by certain banks, and $180 million was provided from the sale of high yield debt securities to the institutional investors. The buyout was unanimously approved by the Levitz board in December 1984, and by shareholders in April 1985.

Postbuyout Performance. Levitz experienced some readjustment during the buyout year, followed by positive results in most of the performance areas we examined. Net sales dropped from prebuyout 1984 levels of $761.8 million to $730.1 million in 1985, then shot up to $835.8 million in postbuyout 1986. Sales per employee showed a modest increase, from $134,745 in 1985 to $134,805 in postbuyout 1986, continuing to rise to $141,178 in 1987.

The prebuyout operating income was $414.9 million in 1984, which dropped to $341.1 million in the year of the buyout, then recovered to $390.6 million in 1986. Capital expenditures also declined, from $335 million in 1984 to $324.3 million in 1985, then surpassed the prebuyout levels, in 1986, at $339.5 million.

Since Trinet employment data were not consistent with the sales and sales per employee figures reported above, we separately calculated employment at 5,656 in 1984 and 5,418 in 1985. In the postbuyout period, our calculations showed employment of 6,200 in 1986, which dropped to 5,645 in 1987. The main data discrepancy occurred in 1986, where Trinet showed a relatively steady employment increase, but Datext sales and sales per employee figures implied a sudden but temporary rise.

Fruehauf Corporation

Fruehauf Corporation is a good example of a flawed LBO strategy. The application of this strategy was to entrench management further. Without changes in corporate strategy, the new financial structure simply sank the company.

Prebuyout Position. Fruehauf was started in a Detroit blacksmith shop by August Fruehauf, a farmboy who turned into a successful entrepreneur, incorporating his company in Michigan in 1918. From its headquarters in Detroit, Fruehauf corporation is engaged in manufacturing, financing, leasing, service, and sales of truck trailers, automotive parts, maritime equipment, and aerospace products.

As the world's largest manufacturer of truck trailers, Fruehauf benefited from the one-stop shopping concept. The company would accept a trade-in, finance a new trailer in a sale or lease arrangement, and provide service through some 140 company-owned branches strategically located on commercial transportation routes in the United States and Canada.

The Trailer Operations division manufactures truck trailers under the Fruehauf and Hobbs trademarks for various body and chassis designs and load capacities, including vans, and refrigerated, platform, tank, and dump trucks, as well as chassis and interchangeable containers for transporting cargo by truck, rail, or ship. The division sells axles, suspensions, and other components and subassemblies to original equipment manufacturers, and it fabricates used truck trailers accepted as trade-ins or repossessed by the company. In addition, the company offers long-term and short-term leases under the RenTco servicemark, and has an international sales division that is active in major markets around the globe.

The Automative Operations division manufactures wheels and brake components for passenger cars, trucks, truck trailers, and truck tractors. Kelsey-Hayes Co., acquired in 1973, is the largest independent producer of steel and aluminum passenger-car wheels, and a leading manufacturer of disc brakes, rotors, and related equipment for cars and trucks in the United States. Kelsey-Hayes also manufactures industrial equipment, specialty and agricultural vehicles, and has wheel and brake manufacturing interests in France, Italy, and Spain.

The Maritime Operations division engages in ship repair, and the manufacturing of cargo handling equipment, barges, gates, and hoists for dams. The Aerospace Operations division produces helicopter transmissions, hydraulic components for military aircraft, blades for jet engines and turbines, and fabricated assemblies for jet engines.

Fruehauf faces stiff competition in each of its markets. There are hundreds of producers of truck trailers and bodies, all competing on the basis of performance, service, warranty, and delivery. The automotive parts and aerospace products markets are also highly competitive in both the United States and Canada. On the East Coast, Fruehauf is a major factor in the ship repair market and a minor factor in the market for heavy cranes and new ship construction.

The Buyout. In 1985, Fruehauf faced pressure from deregulation of trucking rates, and Robert Rowan, the company's chairman and CEO, fired the head of trailer operations after a series of clashes over marketing strategy. At the time, analysts speculated that Fruehauf's undervalued stock, rich assets, and sleepy management would make the company attractive to corporate raiders.

In March 1986, Asher B. Edelman, a New York investor and chairman of Datapoint Inc., approached Fruehauf with a friendly buyout offer of $41 per share, or $783.1 million. Fruehauf rejected the offer and a later attempt by Mr. Edelman to take control of the board through a proxy fight. In May 1986, Edelman offered to buy the company at $42 per share, but was again rejected. In June, he launched a tender offer at $44 per share, with E. F. Hutton as his financial advisor.

Fruehauf's board rejected the Edelman offer on June 25, 1986, and announced their own buyout proposal at $48.50 per share, in which Merrill Lynch & Co. and seventy Fruehauf executives would purchase a controlling interest in the company. Kidder, Peabody and Salomon Brothers acted as financial advisors to Fruehauf. Mr. Edelman indicated his willingness to offer as much as $49.50 per share for the company, but Fruehauf again rejected his offer, accepting the $48.50 bid from Merrill Lynch and management.

A federal district court judge, however, blocked Fruehauf from completing the deal, ruling that the company first had to negotiate in good faith with the Edelman group. The court cited a breach of fiduciary duty to shareholders and gave Fruehauf one week to disclose all relevant financial data about the value of the company. In response to the court order, Fruehauf's board agreed to accept the higher of two sealed bids, one from Edelman, and one from the management group.

On August 18, 1986, the bids were opened. Initially, it appeared that Mr. Edelman had won. But during negotiations, the Merrill Lynch/management group matched Edelman's offer of $49.50 per share in cash and securities, offering a higher percentage of cash, and a securities package that brought the total value of their bid slightly higher than the Edelman offer.

The Merrill Lynch/management group agreed to purchase up to 14,575,000 shares of common stock at $49.50 per share, and also to buy Mr. Edelman's 2.1 million shares for $49 each, giving him a $30 million profit. Fruehauf also reimbursed Mr. Edelman for $21 million in expenses incurred during the takeover battle.

The complicated structure of the buyout totaled $1.2 billion, and included financing through preferred stock, common stock, high yield debt, and working capital. In addition, the investor group assumed a sizeable amount of existing debt. All litigation between Fruehauf, the acquisition corporation, and the Edelman group was settled, and the Merrill Lynch/management group acquired 78 percent of the outstanding Fruehauf shares.

The Merrill Lynch group said it intended to dispose of Fruehauf's heavy-duty automotive, aerospace, leasing, and finance operations to pay down the debt and focus on core businesses in truck trailers and automotive parts. Analysts said the recapitalization of Fruehauf would put substantial pressure on the company to improve operating margins. Unfortunately, the needed improvements never occurred.

Postbuyout Performance. Merrill Lynch and Fruehauf management predicted that the trailer business would grow by 24 percent between 1987 and 1990. Instead, Fruehauf's trailer business went into a tailspin, with 1988 revenues 45 percent below projections, or a loss twenty times larger than the company expected. Despite substantial reductions in LBO debt, Fruehauf reported a $41.5 million deficit in 1987 and expected to continue to be hampered by large preferred stock dividend and interest requirements.

In 1988, the company began a comprehensive restructuring of unprofitable trailer operations. Some factories and regional sales centers were closed, and consultants ordered engineering and marketing departments closed to cut costs. While competition and excessive trade-in inventories contributed to the losses, the real problem was the crushing debt Fruehauf incurred in the LBO. At the time, the company was losing $1 million a week.

The company received two offers from Varity Corp., a farm and industrial equipment maker in Toronto, but no action was taken. In January of 1989, Fruehauf told the SEC it might run out of cash during the year, and in late March, the company announced plans to dismember the company. The announcement makes Fruehauf the largest LBO failure on record.

The trailer and maritime operations have been sold to Terex Corp. for $232.5 million, or $100 million less than book value. The profitable Kelsey-Hayes division will probably also be sold to complete the dismantling of the company.

Datext data show a prebuyout decline in Fruehauf's net sales from $2.84 million in 1984 to $2.62 million in 1985. The decline continued during and after the buyout, with net sales of $2.23 million in 1986 and $1.84 million in 1987. Using these sales figures and available employment data, we calculated sales per employee at $106,194 in 1984, $98,800 in 1985, $85,495 in 1986, and $115,754 in 1987.

Unfortunately, the data available on Fruehauf contained several anomalies. Datext data on sales per employee followed the general pattern outlined above, with the exception of a much higher figure in 1986. Trinet suggested a sales decline in 1985, followed by slow but steady growth. Based on their sales and employment figures, sales per employee would dip in 1985 then increase rapidly as employment declined.

Operating income declined steadily before and after the buyout, from $597,087 in 1984 to $546,248 in 1985, dropping to $425,859 in 1986, then falling to $305,469 in postbuyout 1987. Capital expenditures rose prior to the buyout, from $1.28 million in 1984 to $1.38 million in 1985. After dipping to $526,692 in the buyout year, capital spending increased to $894,519 in 1987. Employment at Fruehauf steadily declined from 26,700 in 1984 to 26,500 in 1985, to 26,100 in 1986. In postbuyout 1987, employment dropped by more than 38 percent to 15,936.

A third transaction category, divisional spin-offs, deserves special comment. Although we did not review detailed information in this category, a May 9, 1988, article in *Business Week* highlighted a number of divestitures and spin-offs that followed Kohlberg Kravis Roberts & Co.'s $6.2 billion leveraged buyout of Beatrice Companies, Inc.

Headlining the article was Playtex International, which went private in its own management buyout shortly after the Beatrice transaction. Under the leadership of Joel Smilow, Playtex sold Max Factor & Co. cosmetics to Revlon Inc. to repay debt, and focused its attention primarily on the apparel business. The company pared inventories, reduced new product rollouts, altered its advertising strategy, and improved margins for retailers. According to *Business Week,* "Operating profits in 1987 show increases up 33 percent to $46.4 million, even though sales dropped 4 percent, to $310.4 million. And after two years of decline, Playtex held its market share steady at 18.3 percent in the first quarter of 1988."

According to the article, despite the increased debt incurred in their divestitures or spin-offs, most of the former Beatrice subsidiaries have had gains in sales, profits, or market share. Avis, which was sold to Wesray in 1986, has subsequently gone private in an ESOP leveraged buyout. While public figures are not available, the company's chairman, Joseph Vittoria, says Avis earned $61 million before taxes in 1987, or 44 percent more than during its first year under Wesray. The company has kept operating costs down, repaid substantial debt, and appears to be closing the gap with Hertz, the leader in the car rental industry.

While it is difficult to generalize from isolated cases, the results at Playtex and Avis suggest that the widespread concern over postbuyout divestitures and spin-offs is largely misguided. While performance varies from case to case, divested units and spin-offs seldom go out of business or disappear from the economy. Instead, they continue as productive companies or divisions, often with enhanced performance under their new management or ownership structure.

Observations on the Company Studies

If our studies show nothing else, they certainly indicate that leveraged buyouts can occur in a wide range of companies for a wide range of reasons. Our sample companies spanned several product and service sectors, from communications and media, weight control, consumer products, and retailing to food, furniture, and trucking. The transactions had outcomes ranging from total success to total failure, though the vast majority of the buyouts were successful.

Some companies pursued leveraged buyouts because they felt their stock was undervalued. Others sought freedom from the constraints imposed by public shareholders. Still others saw going private as a means of increasing productivity and profits by giving managers the incentives that come with equity ownership. In some cases, companies sought merger partners to avoid management displacement. In others, managers bought the company themselves, to avoid outside interference and more aggressively pursue opportunities in their primary markets.

Our case studies confirmed what Lowenstein (1985) had earlier observed, that bidding contests tend to drive prices higher. In the Levitz buyout, competitive bidding raised the price from $33.50 to $39 per share, an increase of over 16 percent. The Safeway contest brought a final price almost 19 percent higher than the original offer. And at Color Tile, shareholders earned 20 percent more than the first offer through competitive bidding and affirmative negotiations.

The case studies also showed that financial advisors and independent directors can have a strong influence on the bidding process. In their fiduciary role, advisors and independent directors are not afraid to turn down inadequate offers or make suggestions regarding the types of bids that will receive favorable consideration.

Of course, the fact that a financial advisor or independent committee feels that an offer is fair is no guarantee that shareholders, employees, and other stakeholders in the company will agree. In most of the buyouts we examined, there were a number of legal suits claiming that the transactions were inadequately priced or otherwise unfair to shareholders. In some cases, these legal claims helped boost the premiums that shareholders received. But with the exception of the Fruehauf transaction, litigation played only a secondary role in the final outcome of the buyouts we examined.

Many of the transactions we studied had complex structures involving several holding companies. Financing arrangements were also complex, often calling for syndicated bank loans and the sale of several types of securities. In some cases, initial borrowings were later refinanced with high yield bonds.

In other respects, the transactions were highly individual. Even where two companies had similar products or services, the differences in the companies, their strategies, and their markets served to underscore the unique nature of each LBO. While both MacAndrews & Forbes and Conwood had tobacco interests, cigars and chewing tobacco are separate products subject to entirely different market forces. While Color Tile, Levitz, Safeway, and Macy's were all engaged in retailing, their buyouts were as different as the markets for flooring, furniture, food, and full-service department store merchandise.

While performance varied from case to case, most of the buyouts we examined showed positive results, often with some adjustments made in the buyout year. The employment declines that Safeway and Beatrice experienced after their buyouts reflected asset sales, and should not be taken as an indication of massive layoffs or job losses. While the Fruehauf buyout proved unsuccessful, the company's brands did not disappear, but will continue to survive under their new ownership. If one views the Fruehauf failure in light of overall trends in the LBO market, the transaction has been more than amply balanced by successes like Beatrice, which have generated windfall profits and tremendous gains to pre- and postbuyout investors.

As a socioeconomic phenomenon, the LBO movement sounds several themes of inquiry at once. It raises important questions about the impact of ownership change, the economic enfranchisement of managers and employees, shifting patterns of productivity, and the role of capital in international competitiveness. This study has focused primarily on the descriptive and empirical issues that can shed light on these questions and help us better understand the recent changes in corporate structure and financial strategy.

While critics may characterize leveraged buyouts as "paper shuffling," "shell games," or "Ponzi schemes," systematic empirical research shows that these transactions can provide beneficial contributions to corporations and the economy. By relying on factual data instead of rhetoric, we can demystify LBOs and focus our attention on the significant variations among them. In so doing, we can help identify those factors of financial management structure in leveraged buyouts that optimize their social and economic impact.

9

Leveraged Buyouts and Industrial Competitiveness

So far, we have seen that junk bonds have been associated with positive improvements in operating performance among public companies and those going private through leveraged buyouts. Since operating performance is a primary indicator of industrial competitiveness, it would seem logical to conclude that high yield securities have had a positive influence on corporate competition.

Unfortunately, as we have already seen, logic is not the only variable in the debate about high yield securities. Rhetoric, prejudice, and self-interest have led many to claim that junk bonds have had a negative impact on critical variables affecting industrial competitiveness. It is commonly assumed that the debt incurred in leveraged buyouts will be a drain on productivity and cause reductions in R & D spending. The idea that junk bond takeovers cause layoffs and plant closings is so well entrenched in popular thinking that empirical evidence to the contrary is often ignored.

To get at the truth, I joined Frank Lichtenberg of the Columbia University Graduate School of Business and Donald Siegel of the National Bureau of Economic Research and SUNY-Stony Brook to examine the effects of LBOs on three factors influencing industrial competitiveness: productivity, employment, and research and development. In most cases of an LBO or MBO, high yield bonds were instrumental in financing the change in ownership.

Leveraged Buyouts and Productivity

Productivity is among the most important factors in determining industrial competitiveness. It directly affects prices, wages, and a company's ability to maintain and increase its market share. Since 1973, U.S. industry has experienced a prolonged slowdown in the rate of productivity growth, which is often cited as a primary cause of our nation's competitive decline.

One might naturally expect leveraged buyouts to result in relative increases in productivity, since the compensation of senior managers, and indeed the very survival of the firm, is much more strongly related to performance after the buyout than before. Jensen (1989) states that the average CEO in a sample of LBOs receives at least $64 per $1000 change in shareholder wealth from his typical 6.4 percent equity interest, whereas the average CEO in a Forbes 1000 firm experiences a total wealth change of about $2 per $1000 change in stockholder value. While this provides a strong incentive to improve shareholder wealth, the leverage itself provides an even stronger incentive to avoid default. Thus, changes in both the risks and rewards facing LBO managers are believed to result in productivity improvements.

As we saw in Chapter 7, such improvements do in fact occur. Firms involved in leveraged buyouts from 1984 through 1986 showed dramatic increases in sales per employee between the pre- and postbuyout periods, with average absolute improvement of over 35 percent.

Other research has shown that productivity increases are not limited to leveraged buyouts, but are characteristic of mergers and acquisitions in general. Lichtenberg and Siegel (1987) examined the relationship between productivity and changes in ownership of U.S. manufacturing plants in the 1970s. They found that the least productive plants in an industry were the most likely to change owners, and that following ownership change, the plants tended to experience above-average improvements in productivity.

A more recent study by Lichtenberg and Siegel (1989) indicated that changes in ownership are associated with substantial reductions in administrative overhead, measured by the ratio of central office employees to plant employees, and that this is a major source of acquisition-related productivity gains.

Total-Factor Productivity

A primary objective of our study was to analyze the relationship between leveraged buyouts and total-factor productivity (TFP), or output per unit of total input. Total-factor productivity is perhaps the single best measure of technical efficiency and is a highly reliable indicator of industrial competitiveness. In his pioneering studies in the 1950s, Robert Solow (1957) established that most of the long-run increases in economic welfare, or output per capita, experienced by the United States and other industrialized countries were due to increases in total-factor productivity.

Total-factor productivity measures production outputs as a function of inputs, including labor, capital, and raw materials. For our purposes, production output consists of the value of shipments, adjusted for changes in finished goods and work-in-progress inventory. Labor input consists of "production-worker-equivalent" employee-hours; capital input consists of the "perpetual inventory" estimate of the net stock of plant and equipment; and materials input consists of materials purchased, adjusted for changes in raw materials inventories.

Using data from the U.S. Bureau of Census, we were able to estimate total-factor productivity for LBO plants relative to their respective industries. We then determined the percentage deviation of the LBO plants from the average productivity of all establishments in the same industry and year.

From 1981 through 1986, the cumulative productivity growth of plants involved in LBOs was 2.8 percentage points higher than that of plants not involved in LBOs. The difference in growth rates is highly statistically significant. For plants involved in MBOs, the difference in growth rates was even higher, at 3.9 percentage points.

Data from the Bureau of Labor Statistics (BLS) on total-factor productivity growth for manufacturing as a whole provide a convenient benchmark against which to measure these productivity growth differentials. According to the BLS, total-factor productivity in the manufacturing sector increased by 19.9 percent from 1981 to 1986. This figure may be considered a weighted average of the productivity growth rates of LBO and non-LBO plants, with weights roughly equal to the fraction of employees in the plants in each group.

With the help of plant and employment data, we were able to calculate productivity growth rates for LBO and non-LBO plants at .226 and .198 respectively. The productivity growth rate of LBO plants was therefore about 14 percent higher than that of other plants. Using similar calculations, we found that the productivity growth rate of MBO plants was about 20 percent higher than that of plants not involved in MBOs.

In an earlier study, Lichtenberg and Siegel (1987) found that the productivity growth rate of plants that changed owners was about 9 percent higher than that of plants that did not undergo ownership change. As special cases of ownership change, then, LBOs and MBOs appear to have significantly higher rates of productivity growth. Moreover, subsequent refinements in the understanding of ownership change suggest that the differences outlined above may understate the true productivity growth differentials for plants engaged in LBOs and MBOs (Lichtenberg and Siegel, 1989).

Total-Factor Productivity over Time

Having seen that LBO and MBO plants have significantly higher rates of productivity growth than plants not engaged in these transactions, we next wanted to determine when these productivity improvements occurred relative to the buyout. To find out, we calculated the average level of productivity

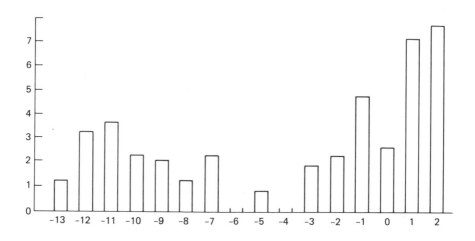

Figure 9-1. Relative productivity of MBO plants over time (author generated).

for LBO and non-LBO plants for each year, from thirteen years prior to the buyout to two years after the transaction. We also performed similar calculations for MBO and non-MBO plants.

The average productivity differences of LBO and non-LBO plants by year relative to the year of the LBO are reported in Table 9-1 and plotted in Figure 9-1.

The results indicate that plants involved in LBOs in any year t tended to have above-average productivity in every year from t - 13 to t + 2. But the relative productivity of LBO plants appears to have declined in the years prior to the LBO, and then increased sharply beginning at the time of the buyout. The average value of the difference in three periods is as follows:

	Period	Average difference in productivity between LBO and non-LBO plants
I:	(t - 13) to (t - 7)	2.0
II:	(t - 6) to (t - 1)	1.2
III:	t to (t ⁵ 2)	2.7

In year t + 1, the productivity difference was larger and more significant than it was in any previous year, although it declined and was only marginally significant in year t + 2. The average productivity difference increased from 1.2 in the two years before the LBO to 2.9 in the two years after the transaction.

Table 9-1. Differences Between Buyout Plants and Nonbuyout Plants in Mean Productivity Residual, by Year Relative to Year of Buyout (t-statistics in parentheses)

Year	$\overline{e}$ LBO	$\overline{-e}$ Non-LBO	$\overline{e}$ LBO	$\overline{-e}$ non-MBO
-13	1.6 (1.3)		1.2 (0.6)	
-12	2.9 (2.6)		3.2 (1.8)	
-11	2.6 (3.0)		3.6 (2.3)	
-10	1.9 (2.4)		2.2 (1.7)	
-9	1.8 (2.4)		2.0 (1.6)	
-8	1.4 (2.1)		1.3 (1.1)	
-7	2.0 (2.9)		2.3 (1.9)	
-6	1.2 (1.6)		-0.1 (0.1)	
-5	1.1 (2.1)		0.7 (0.8)	
-4	1.2 (1.9)		-0.0 (0.1)	
-3	1.3 (2.2)		1.9 (1.6)	
-2	1.3 (1.7)		2.2 (2.0)	
-1	1.1 (1.4)		4.9 (3.1)	
0	2.2 (2.5)		2.7 (1.7)	
1	3.5 (3.1)		7.2 (3.2)	
2	2.3 (1.7)		7.7 (3.0)	

The productivity differences for MBO and non-MBO plants are reported in Table 9-1 and plotted in Figure 9-1. The pattern is similar to the pattern for LBOs, but more pronounced:

	Period	Average difference in productivity between MBO and non-MBO plants
I:	$(t - 13)$ to $(t - 7)$	2.3
II:	$(t - 6)$ to $(t - 1)$	1.2
III:	t to $(t + 2)$	5.9

The relative productivity of MBO plants was as high as 3.6 in $t - 11$, but dropped below the level of non-MBO plants in the sixth year prior to the buyout and was essentially zero in the fourth year before the transaction. The relative productivity of MBO plants began to increase three years before the buyout, and reached a prebuyout peak of 4.9 in year $t - 1$. Despite this, the average productivity more than doubled, from 3.6 in the two years before the buyout to 7.5 in the two years after the MBO. The difference between the productivity increases associated with LBOs and MBOs using annual measures was even greater than that suggested by the five-year growth-rate results.

Relative Changes in Output and Input

We have shown that LBO plants, especially those involved in management buyouts, experience higher rates of productivity growth than do other plants in the same industry. By definition, differences in productivity growth rates are due to differences in output growth rates, differences in input growth rates, or both. An increase in productivity occurs either when output increases relative to input or when input decreases relative to output. By comparing data on output and input, we can further pinpoint the sources of the productivity advantages enjoyed by LBO and MBO plants.

Table 9-2. Differences Between Buyout and Nonbuyout Plants in Mean Cumulative 1981-1986 Growth Rates of Output and Inputs (t-statistics in parentheses)

Output	Capital	Labor	Materials
0.7	-6.4	-3.2	0.2
(0.4)	(3.9)	(1.8)	(0.1)
2.5	-2.9	-1.4	-0.5
(0.7)	(1.1)	(0.5)	(0.1)

Each of the estimates reported above is an estimate of the coefficient 1 in a regression of the form.

$$n \, Z86_i = {}_0 + {}_1 \, B08186_i + {}_2 \, n \, Z81_i + {}_j + V_i$$

where Z86 and Z81 denote output, capital, labor, or materials in 1986 and 1981, respectively; B08186 equals 1 if the plant was ever involved in an LBO (or MBO) during 1981-1986, and otherwise equals zero; j represents a complete set of industry dummies; and the subscript i is the plant index.

The first column of Table 9-2 indicates that LBO plants had a higher rate of growth of output from 1981 through 1986 than did non-LBO plants. MBO plants had an even higher output growth rate relative to non-MBO plants, but neither figure was statistically significant. Thus, it appears that both LBO and MBO plants maintained a relatively constant market share during our study period.

Given these output data, the superior productivity performance of LBO and MBO plants must have resulted from lower growth rates of total input. Our data on capital, labor, and materials confirmed this hypothesis. The cumulative growth rates of labor and capital (but not of materials) were significantly lower among LBO plants than among non-LBO plants. Among MBO plants, the differences in all three input growth rates were negative, but none was significant.

Output and Input Data over Time

While five-year growth-rate differences offer a high level of precision, they provide little information about the changes in inputs and outputs over time. To shed light on this question, Table 9-3 presents differences between LBO plants and non-LBO plants in annual growth rates of output and inputs from two years before to two years after the buyout.

While the differences in output growth were positive before the buyout and negative afterward, the change was not significant. The differences in capital and labor growth were negative in every year, but significant only in the years before the buyout. In the case of all three inputs, the average difference in growth rates was lower, or more negative, in the three years before the buyout than it was in the two years after. In other words, input use was declining prior to the buyout and at a faster rate than in the postbuyout period.

Since the largest and most significant productivity increases occurred after the buyout, one might expect to find lower and more significant input differences in the postbuyout years. Due to the relatively small number of LBOs in any given year, however, the standard errors on the differences are fairly large, reducing the relative accuracy of such year-by-year comparisons. In addition, overall productivity data include adjustments for mean reversion, while the yearly data on output and inputs do not. Finally, capital, labor, and materials are assigned different relative weights in our productivity calculations, weights that are not reflected in the output and input data in Table 9-3. Together, these factors help reduce the significance of what might otherwise appear to be an anomalous result.

Other Labor-Related Variables

The Census establishment data enabled us to examine the behavior of labor-related variables other than total input. Table 9-4 reports differences between LBO plants and non-LBO plants in the growth rates of the wage bill (B),

Table 9-3. Differences Between LBO Plants and Non-LBO Plants in Mean Growth Rates (in percent) of Output and Inputs, by Year Relative to Year of LBO

Year	Output	Capital	Labor	Materials
-2	0.5	-0.9**	-1.9	1.2
	(0.4)	(2.4)	(1.1)	(.06)
-1	0.3	-0.4	-2.9**	-0.8
	(0.2)	(1.0)	(2.4)	(0.4)
0	-0.0	-0.8*	-0.9	-1.3
	(0.0)	(1.8)	(0.8)	(0.7)
1	-0.7	-0.1	-1.3	2.5
	(0.5)	(0.3)	(0.9)	(1.0)
2	-0.2	-0.9	-1.0	-0.5
	(0.1)	(1.4)	(0.6)	(0.2)
Averages				
-2, -1, 0 (Before)	0.3	-0.7	-1.9	-0.3
1, 2 (After)	-0.5	-0.5	-1.2	1.0

t-statistics in parentheses
*significantly different from zero at .05 level (one-tailed test)
**significantly different from zero at .01 level (one-tailed test)

Year 0 is the year in which the LBO occurs (is completed). The growth rates refer to changes from the previous year (e.g., the growth rate for year -2 is the change from year -3 to year -2).

employment (E), and the annual wage rate ($WA = B/E$), separately for non-production and production workers, by year relative to the year of the LBO. Nonproduction workers account for about 30 percent of total employment in manufacturing establishments.

Table 9-4 also reports differences in growth rates of the hourly wage rate (WH) and of annual hours of work per employee (H) for production workers only. Hours for nonproduction workers are not reported in the survey.

The first column of the table shows that in the three years before the LBO, the wage bill of nonproduction workers grew at about the same rate in LBO and non-LBO plants, but in the two years after the LBO, this wage bill grew much more slowly in LBO plants. The average annual rate of relative decline

Table 9-4. Differences Between LBO Plants and Non-LBO Plants in Mean Growth Rates (in percent) of Labor Variables, by Year Relative to Year of LBO (*t*-statistics in parentheses)

Year	Wage Bill			Employment			Annual Wage Rate			Hourly Wage Rate	Annual Hours
	N	P	N-P	N	P	N-P	N	P	N-P	P	P
-2	3.5	-0.6	4.1	1.3	-0.0	1.3	2.2	-0.6	2.8	-0.0	-1.6
	(1.2)	(0.0)					(2.1)		(2.3)	(0.0)	(1.4)
-1	-2.6	-0.3	-2.3	-2.7	0.1	-2.8	0.1	-0.4	0.5	0.6	-2.7
	(2.4)	(0.1)					(0.8)		(0.4)	(0.8)	(2.2)
0	-3.1	-0.4	-2.7	-3.1	-0.3	-2.8	-0.0	-0.1	0.1	0.0	-0.8
	(2.7)	(0.4)					(0.0)		(0.1)	(0.1)	(0.7)
1	-3.4	0.8	-4.2	-3.3	-1.4	-1.9	-0.1	2.2	-2.3	1.7	-1.7
	(2.4)	(1.3)					(0.1)		(1.5)	(1.9)	(1.1)
2	-7.2	1.2	-8.4	-2.1	-0.3	-1.8	-5.1	1.5	-6.6	0.6	1.2
	(1.3)	(0.3)					(3.6)		(3.8)	(0.6)	(0.7)

Averages

	Wage Bill			Employment			Annual Wage Rate			Hourly Wage Rate	Annual Hours
Before (-2,-1, 0)	-0.7	-0.4	-0.3	-5.1	-0.1	-1.4	0.8	-0.4	1.2	0.2	-1.7
After (1, 2)	-5.3	1.0	-6.3	-2.7	-0.9	-1.8	-2.6	1.9	-4.5	1.2	-0.3
After-Before	-4.6	1.4	-6.0	-1.2	-0.8	-0.4	-3.4	2.3	-5.7	1.0	1.45

Note: *N* denotes nonproduction workers.
    P denotes production workers.

in the postbuyout period was 5.3 percent. The decline was particularly pronounced (7.2 percent) in the second year after the buyout. In contrast, the wage bill of production workers increased slightly in relative terms after the LBO, so the difference in growth rates between the nonproduction and production portions of the total wage bill dropped sharply after the buyout.

The postbuyout decline in the nonproduction wage bill was due to almost equal reductions in nonproduction employment and in annual wages (2.7 percent and 2.6 percent, respectively). Nonproduction employment declined faster than did production employment after the buyout, and annual wage rates for nonproduction workers declined while annual wage rates for production workers increased. This suggests that LBOs reduce the need for nonproduction workers (i.e., layers of management) relative to the need for production workers. Since the annual wages of nonproduction employees tend to be about 53 percent higher than those of production employees, the decline in their relative wage rates would appear to reduce inequality of wages within LBO plants.

The growth in the annual wage rate of production workers was significantly higher in LBO plants than in other plants in the same industry in the two years following the LBO. About two thirds of this difference was attributable to hourly wage rates, and one third to annual hours. After the LBO, total hours of production workers declined, but at a slower rate than before the LBO. The differences both before and after the LBO were small and insignificant.

To summarize the preceding observations:

1. Total hours worked by production employees declined more slowly after the LBO than before the transaction.
2. Hourly and (especially) annual wage rates of production workers increased after leveraged buyouts.
3. Both employment and annual wages of nonproduction workers declined sharply after leveraged buyouts.

It is interesting to consider the increase in production-worker wages and the decrease in relative employment of nonproduction workers in post-LBO plants from the perspective of efficiency wage theory. A premise of that theory is that the firm has two alternative means of inducing production workers to expend effort. It can use the carrot of high wages, by paying a wage premium, or the stick of intensive supervision, by maintaining a high ratio of nonproduction to production workers. Our evidence suggests that in the course of the pre- to post-LBO transition, managers increase the size of the carrot and reduce the use of the stick.

Plant Closings

The differences between buyout and nonbuyout plants in productivity, output, and inputs reported above were all based on the group of "surviving" plants, or those plants present in our extract from the LRD in 1981 that had not closed by some subsequent year. Calculations for any particular year from 1981 through 1986 were based on all plants ever in the sample that had not closed prior to that year.

Since plants that close are likely to be a nonrandom sample of all plants (in terms of their productivity, for example), estimates based on the "censored" sample of surviving establishments may be biased. However, correcting for nonrandom observations over time poses extremely difficult methodological problems. To accommodate these factors in our discussion of plant closings, we limited our objectives to documenting the extent of plant failure and assessing the *direction* of bias in our comparisons of buyout and nonbuyout plants.

To better understand the relationship between productivity and plant closing, we began by examining the average productivity residual in each year from 1972 to 1981 for plants that closed in 1981 and plants that did not. As Table 9-5 shows, the productivity of plants that closed in 1981 was significantly lower than that of other plants in each of the ten years prior to closing. This productivity gap steadily widened as the closing date approached.

Table 9-5. Plants Closing in 1981: Mean Deviation from Respective Industry Means of Productivity Levels, Output Growth, and Employment Growth, 1972-1981 (standard errors in parentheses)

	Productivity Level	Output Growth	Employment Growth
1972	-0.27 (.013)		
1973	-0.30 (.011)	-.009 (.018)	-.016 (.016)
1974	-.041 (.012)	-.058 (.017)	-.021 (.012)
1975	-.042 (.013)	-.000 (.018)	-.026 (.011)
1976	-.048 (.013)	-.015 (.018)	-.016 (.012)
1977	-.049 (.010)	-.029 (.015)	-.031 (.012)
1978	-.066 (.012)	-.071 (.015)	-.037 (.011)
1979	-.074 (.013)	-.078 (.020)	-.066 (.013)
1980	-.086 (.013)	-.136 (.023)	-.132 (.015)
1981	-.184 (.023)	-.839 (.043)	-.759 (.038)

Note: 482 plants closed in 1981; 18,768 plants remained open.

We also examined data on output and employment for plants that closed and plants that remained open in 1981. Plants destined to close had negative relative rates of output and employment growth in the ten years prior to closing. Following the productivity trend, these output and employment gaps tended to widen as the closing date approached.

Combined with our earlier findings, these results are highly suggestive. Table 9-6 shows that the probability of plant closing is inversely related to productivity, and Table 9-6 reveals that LBO plants, and MBO plants in particular, exhibit above-average productivity around the date of the buyout and shortly thereafter. In the absence of other evidence, one would expect to find a lower incidence of plant closings among LBO (and especially MBO) plants than among nonbuyout plants.

To test this hypothesis, we compared the closing rates of cohorts of LBO and MBO plants with the closing rates of all other plants in our extract of the LRD in each year from 1981 to 1986. For obvious reasons, our yearly samples were conditioned to include only plants that had not closed prior to the year in question.

Table 9-6. Conditional Rates of Plant Closing (in percent) for LBO or MBO Plants, by Cohort, and for All Sample Plants, 1981-1986

Year	All Sample Plants	1981 LBO Plants	1982 LBO Plants	1983 LBO Plants	1984 LBO Plants	1985 LBO Plants	1986 LBO Plants
1981	2.3	1.2					
1982	2.9	7.0	2.5				
1983	2.6	4.7	0.8	1.9			
1984	1.6	2.3	0.8	0.6	1.9		
1985	2.0	0.0	1.7	1.3	3.0	1.9	
1986	1.9	3.5	3.4	3.2	3.0	4.3	1.2

Year	All Sample Plants	1981 MBO Plants	1982 MBO Plants	1983 MBO Plants	1984 MBO Plants	1985 MBO Plants	1986 MBO Plants
1981	2.3	0.0					
1982	2.9	16.7	0.0				
1983	2.6	0.0	0.0	2.6			
1984	1.6	0.0	0.0	0.9	0.0		
1985	2.0	0.0	0.0	1.8	5.0	1.8	
1986	1.9	0.0	6.3	2.6	1.7	1.8	1.4

The top panel of Table 9-6 shows closing rates among plants involved in all LBOs. There are a total of twenty-one year-specific closing rates for the six LBO cohorts, eleven of these are smaller, and ten are larger than the closing rates for all sample plants in the corresponding year. These data suggest that plants previously involved in LBOs are neither more nor less likely to close than other plants.

The lack of a difference in closing rates may be due to the fact that while LBO plants are more productive than non-LBO plants, they are also somewhat smaller. On average, LBO plants tend to have 17 percent to 25 percent fewer employees than non-LBO plants, and Dunne, Roberts, and Samuelson (1987) have shown that large plants are less likely to close. Thus our findings about plant closings appear to be consistent with our productivity results, as long as employment levels are taken into account.

The second panel of Table 9-6 compares closing rates for the MBO cohorts to closing rates for all plants in our sample. Only five of the twenty-one closing rates for the MBO cohorts equal or exceed the closing rates for all sample plants in the corresponding year. The preponderance of zeros for the 1981 and 1982 MBO cohorts may partly reflect the small number of MBO plants in those cohorts, each of which contained sixteen or fewer establishments. But even among the last four cohorts, whose minimum initial size was fifty-seven plants, only three out of ten closing rates for MBO plants equalled or exceeded the closing rate for all sample plants in the corresponding year. Thus, MBO plants appear to be appreciably less likely to close than plants not involved in MBOs.

Our finding a difference for these plants but not for LBO plants in general may be due not only to the markedly higher productivity of MBO plants, but also to their greater size. On average, MBO plants are only 1 to 13 percent smaller than plants not involved in buyouts. Apparently, the motivation to remain open and stick out hard economic adjustments is greater among those management buyout plants.

The lower closure rates among plants involved in management buyouts suggest that estimates of differences between MBO and non-MBO plants based on our censored sample may hide an even greater difference. Table 9-1 may underestimate the productivity increase associated with management buyouts, and the actual differences in output and input growth of MBO plants may be greater than the estimates in Table 9-4.

Investment in Research and Development

In an earlier section, we examined the relationship between LBOs and the growth of the capital stock, which is closely related to the rate of net investment in plant and equipment. In this section, we investigate the relationship between LBOs and investment in research and development. There is considerable evidence that R&D investment has a significant positive impact on long-term productivity growth.*

In our discussion of total-factor productivity, data were only available for two years following the buyout, which limited our analysis to the *short-term* effects of buyouts on productivity. Analysis of the link between buyouts and R & D investment may provide at least indirect evidence concerning the implications of buyouts for *long-term* productivity growth.

The LRD file does not contain any information about investment in research and development in manufacturing establishments. And even if it did, such information would not be very meaningful. Lichtenberg and Siegel (1989) reported that 47 percent of personnel engaged in R & D are employed in auxiliary establishments, including central administrative offices and R & D laboratories, rather than in manufacturing establishments.

Research and development is a relatively centralized function within companies, and R & D output is largely a "public good" that is easily diffused across a company's establishments. As a result, it is the amount of R & D conducted in the entire company, rather than in specific establishments, that determines the contribution of R & D to productivity at both the plant and firm levels. No doubt, this is why the government's official survey of industrial R & D activity, the NSF/Census RD-1 survey, is a firm-level survey.

We used data from the RD-1 survey from 1978 to 1986 to assess the impact of LBOs on investment in research and development. We compared the average R & D intensity of firms involved in LBOs to that of all firms, using two intensity measures: the ratio of R & D expenditures to sales, and the ratio of full-time equivalent R & D scientists and engineers to total company employment.

Since the RD-1 data are at the firm level, we limited our sample of leveraged buyouts to those involving entire firms. Recall that there were eighty major LBOs of entire firms observed in the Census data from 1981 through 1986, and that these accounted for about 70 percent of the aggregate value of LBOs. Of these, forty-three were included in the sample of RD-1 survey firms in each of the years 1978 through 1986. We therefore used these 43 companies as our set of LBO firms.

Table 9-7 presents the average values of R & D intensity in the years 1978 through 1986 both for LBO firms and for all RD-1 survey respondents. The top panel shows the intensity values for R & D spending. The bottom panel shows intensity values for R & D employment. For LBO firms, the average values of both these measures tended to increase over the nine-year period and were never higher than they were in the last year, when all the buyouts were completed.

---

*See Lichtenberg and Siegel (1989) for an econometric analysis of this impact based on Census microdata.

Table 9-7. Mean R & D Intensity: LBO Firms vs. All R & D Performers, 1978-1986

Year	(1) Mean R & D Intensity of LBO Firms (90)	(2) Mean R & D Intensity of All R & D Performers (90)	(1)/(2)
A. R & D Expenditure Sales			
1978	1.2	2.9	.41
1979	1.2	2.9	.41
1980	1.4	3.0	.47
1981	1.4	3.4	.41
1982	1.6	3.5	.46
1983	1.7	3.7	.46
1984	1.5	3.6	.42
1985	1.5	3.7	.41
1986	1.8	3.4	.53
B. R & D Scientists & Engineers/Total Employment			
1978	1.4	3.1	.45
1979	1.4	3.3	.42
1980	1.5	3.2	.47
1981	1.5	3.3	.45
1982	1.5	3.8	.39
1983	1.5	3.9	.38
1984	1.5	3.8	.39
1985	1.7	4.0	.43
1986	1.7	3.6	.47

Among LBO firms, the intensity of R & D spending rose by 50 percent from 1978 to 1986. Among all survey respondents, the intensity of R & D spending also increased, but by less than 28 percent, even in the years when R & D spending was most intensive.

LBO firms increased their intensity of R & D employment by 21 percent over the nine-year period. The intensity of R & D employment also increased for all survey respondents, and by a higher percentage in 1982 through 1985, the years when overall R & D employment was most intensive.

Since overall R & D intensity was increasing, the *relative* R & D intensity of LBO firms, shown in the last column of Table 9-7 increased less than did the absolute R & D intensity. Nevertheless, the relative intensity did increase, particularly in the last three years, when most of the LBOs occurred.

Table 9-8. Proportions of (Current or Previous) LBO Firms and of All Firms Increasing R & D Intensity from Previous Year

Year	Firms Involved in LBOs in Current or Previous Years (90)	All R & D Performing Firms (90)
1981	50	20
1982	75	55
1983	41	30
1984	29	29
1985	48	38
1986	37	31

The data in Table 9-7 cast doubt on the hypothesis that LBOs are associated with reductions in the propensity to perform R & D. Another way of examining the data, one that accounts more closely for the *timing* of the LBOs, also yields results inconsistent with this hypothesis. For each year from 1981 through 1986, we identified the set of firms that were involved in an LBO either in that year or in a previous year. For both these firms and for all survey respondents, we then calculated the proportion of firms that had increased their R & D intensity since the previous year. The results are presented in Table 9-8.

The proportion for firms involved in current or past LBOs was never lower than the proportion for all firms, and was equal in only one year. This suggests that firms that have undergone leveraged buyouts are generally more likely than other firms to increase their R & D intensity in any given year.

There have been at least two large-scale studies of the effect of changes in ownership in general on R & D investment: Hall (1988), and Lichtenberg and Siegel (1989). Both found essentially no difference in the growth of R & D between firms involved and those not involved in ownership change.

We are aware of only one other very limited attempt to assess the effect of LBOs in particular on R & D. It is described in a February 1, 1989, memorandum by the National Science Foundation (NSF), prepared in response to a request from the Subcommittee on Telecommunications and Finance of the House Committee on Energy and Commerce. NSF identified eight companies among the top 200 R & D performers involved in "LBOs or other restructurings," and determined that these companies reduced their R & D expenditures by 12.8 percent from 1986 to 1987. In contrast, top-200 companies not involved in mergers, LBOs, or other restructurings, increased their R & D spending by 5.4 percent.

The National Science Foundation (NSF) granted us access to their list of eight companies involved in "LBOs or other restructurings." Only one of these companies appeared on our presumably comprehensive list of major LBOs. The rest of the companies were evidently involved in "other restructurings" such as stock repurchases. There are at least three reasons, therefore, why the figures calculated by the NSF might be regarded as a highly unreliable estimate of the effects of LBOs per se on R & D investment:

1. Only one of the eight companies was actually involved in a major LBO.
2. NSF calculated the change in R & D spending in only a single year.
3. They evaluated the change in the level of R & D spending rather than the change in R & D intensity, which can be misleading if companies are divesting divisions, as they frequently do when restructuring.

Despite the NSF findings, therefore, concerns about sharp reductions in R & D investment following LBOs appear to be unwarranted. On the whole, LBO firms tend to increase the intensity of their R & D spending and employment over time, and are at least as likely as other firms to increase their R & D intensity in any given year.

Commentary on LBOs and Industrial Competitiveness

Our examination of the performance of leveraged buyout firms in productivity, employment, and research and development indicates that these transactions have a positive effect on industrial competitiveness. LBO plants had rates of total-factor productivity growth that were about 14 percent higher than those of other plants in the same industry. The productivity impact of LBOs was much larger than would have been predicted by previous estimates of the productivity impact of mergers and acquisitions in general. Among plants involved in management buyouts, the productivity growth differential was even greater, at about 20 percent.

Plants engaged in LBOs showed above-average productivity growth before and after their buyouts, with substantial improvements during and after the buyout year. MBO plants showed a similar trend, with productivity improvements beginning before the buyout and increasing dramatically afterward. These relative productivity increases were the result of lower input growth, perhaps reflecting management's incentive to carefully monitor costs among LBO plants, rather than higher output. While critics may claim that high leverage will result in productivity declines, our examination of the empirical evidence suggested just the opposite.

About 12 percent of the plants present in 1981 are known to have closed within the next five years, during which time the closure rates among LBO plants were about the same as the closure rates for all sample plants. MBO plants, however, were less likely to close than other plants, as one would expect given their higher relative productivity and the inverse relationship between productivity and plant closing. These findings directly contradict the popular belief that plants are more likely to shut down following leveraged transactions.

Our findings also contradicted the popular notion that LBOs are less likely than other firms to engage in R & D spending and employment. On the contrary, we found that from 1978 to 1986, the R & D intensity of forty-three LBO firms increased more than the R & D intensity of firms in general. Moreover, firms that had completed LBOs were generally more likely than other firms to increase their R & D intensity in any given year.

While critics may speculate that leveraged buyouts are bad for companies and the economy, our empirical research showed just the opposite. Using data at the plant and firm level, we consistently found that leveraged buyouts and management buyouts are associated with positive performance in productivity, employment, and research and development—three critical indicators of industrial competitiveness.

10

Public Policy Responses to High Yield Bonds

"Policy," according to former Federal Reserve Governor Henry Wallich, "is the name we give to our future mistakes." In light of what we have learned about high yield bonds and leveraged buyouts, these words may prove to be a profound understatement.

The evidence shows that high yield companies outperform their industries in employment, sales, productivity, capital investment, and capital spending. Leveraged buyouts show dramatic improvements in a wide range of performance measures, and tend to outperform other companies in productivity, employment, and R & D intensity. With all these benefits flowing out of the use of junk bonds, you would naturally expect public policy to favor them. Instead, Congressional leaders and state legislators have rushed to regulate, restrict, or reject high yield bonds and the transactions they make possible.

"We don't want to necessarily stop junk bonds or LBOs," one senator told me. "Things are just moving too fast, and we need to slow them down." Other, less moderate voices have been heard on Capitol Hill, using words like "scourge," "plague," and "greedmongers" to describe the practitioners in this new wave of corporate finance and business strategy. Borrowing language and arguments from a lobbying organization backed by the Business Roundtable, the *Congressional Record* has periodically been filled with long speeches about stopping the "raid on America." And despite the growing empirical evidence noted in earlier chapters that leveraged buyouts create value for shareholders, corporations, and the economy, legislators continue to view them as "paper shuffling" and "shell games."

What could result from political resistance to high yield bonds? The efficient access to capital that funded the current wave of corporate restructuring could simply disappear, making it increasingly difficult for small and medium-sized companies to build new plants, develop new products, or respond to changing markets and technologies. Without access to high yield debt, companies would inevitably face the restrictive covenants associated with bank debt and private placements, or be forced to rely on expensive equity offerings in markets that are at best unpredictable.

Corporations would not be the only ones affected. Fixed income investors would lose an important way to increase their risk-adjusted returns, and equity investors would find acquisition premiums, that is, higher returns resulting from ownership change or the threat of ownership change, considerably harder to obtain. Political resistance to junk bonds and restructurings could reverse decades of credit liberalization that has provided attractive investment outlets for institutions and a cost-efficient source of funds for capital formation.

In the early days of the junk bond market, skepticism was more prevalent than resistance. In fact, opposition to structural changes through increased leverage didn't emerge until the fight against Big Oil, which was initially led by Boone Pickens and Mesa Petroleum in 1985. While many have tried to liken Pickens and other corporate raiders to the robber barons of the past, such comparisons miss the point. The more appropriate historical reference for Pickens is Huey Long, whose populist attacks against big oil companies and utilities defined a generation of economic reform legislation in state houses and Washington. Indeed, for forty years since the New Deal, efforts at business reform remained largely in the legislative arena. Over that period of time, however, corporate power continued to concentrate through waves of business combination and conglomeration unhindered by political regulation.

By the 1970s, the burgeoning consumer and environmental movements refocused attention on problems of industrial organization. Representative of those concerns were extensive deliberations by the Anti-Trust Subcommittee of the U.S. Senate led by the late Senator Phillip Hart (D-Michigan). Senator Hart's hearings for an Industrial Reorganization Act focused upon problems of "shared monopolies" in large automobile and oil companies that engaged in administered pricing and other anti-competitive market practices. Proposed solutions focused on government intervention and regulation leading to divestiture of various operations.

Beyond additional symbolic regulations, however, the legislated divestitures recommended in the Industrial Reorganization Act never occurred. Later antitrust regulations (e.g., Hart-Scott-Rodino), which required review of acquisitions in similar industries, had the unanticipated consequence of encouraging the types of unproductive horizontal diversifications and conglomeration that were negatively affecting corporate performance by the late 1970s. In short, public policy initiatives identified inappropriate solutions (government intervention) to a correctly perceived problem (conglomeration and concentrated corporate power leading to economic inefficiences).

Instead of government intervention, competitive market pressures began to restructure American corporations. By the 1980s, concern over the power of large oil companies shifted from the public forum to individual firms, when Texaco, Phillips, and Unocal took turns in the spotlight as the focus of economic and political attention.

Ironically, these market pressures, which culminated in the intensive merger and acquisition activity of the mid- to late 1980s, accomplished the reforms that Congress had been unable even to conceive correctly, much less implement.

Pickens recalls learning how large corporations had begun to organize to stop contests for corporate control.

> First, they put pressure on our banks. Either directly, through the board positions they held, and later by inserting provisions requiring immediate debt repayment in case of change of control. If you lay down the membership of the Conference Board, the Business Roundtable, the American Petroleum Institute, and the national Petroleum Council, you will find big oil companies prominent in each one. In 1985, the Roundtable called a meeting and one of the CEOs who refused to participate called and told me about it. I think it was Roger Smith that asked for $50,000 from each member. I understand they raised $9 million for a PR and lobbying campaign to get Boone Pickens to stop takeovers. (Interview with T. Boone Pickens, Jr., May 14, 1989)

As Drexel Burnham's vice chairman and CEO, Frederick Joseph recounts about that time,

> I tend to be nonparanoid, but a lot of people whose judgment I respect have told me that there really are significant elements of social revolution vendetta in some of the legislative proposals, press coverage, responses by Wall Street competitors, and maybe in the enthusiasm of the prosecutors because we are a politically attractive target. (Interview with Mr. Frederick Joseph, November, 1988)

According to Joseph, the first real rash of antitakeover, antijunk rhetoric and legislation came in 1985, and was led by Nicholas Brady and Howard Baker, men Joseph says he likes. Both of these advocates were hired by Unocal in the private sector and worked overtly to assist the company in its fight against Boone Pickens.

As Pickens recalls:

> In the Unocal deal, we got a call from the Bank of Montreal indicating that Volker (of the Federal Reserve) had called them and not approved of the bank making loans to guys like Boone Pickens. They dropped us....

> Brady got up in front of the Senate and told about all the abuses that
> were going to go on if our takeover succeeded. He was being paid $5-20
> million by Unocal and that was not revealed. I thought this was unusual
> and so I followed him on the next panel and I said, "I think we need
> to get this record straight, that Nick Brady is working for UNOCAL.
> (May 14, 1989 interview)

At the time, raiders were going after companies that were sitting on vast
assets that could have been better utilized, either for internal growth or to
increase investor returns. The resulting takeover battles focused the public's
attention on capital laws. As Frederick Joseph recalls:

> That caused thirty-one bills to be introduced in a single year, including
> the Junk Bond Control Act of 1985 by Pete Dominici. I went to see him
> and said, "Do you know what a junk bond is?" He said, "Nope, but
> I bet you I am going to learn now." (Author and interview, November
> 1988)

Legislative bills were promoted not only by well-connected oil companies,
but also by financial firms that faced increasing competition as a result of
the massive restructuring caused by deregulation. Older, established financial institutions sought new protective legislation to insulate themselves from
the threat of more competitive firms that were making full use of the junk
bond market. According to Joseph,

> At the same time, some of the legislation introduced into the thrift in-
> dustry against junk bonds was the direct result of the big, old thrifts at
> the core of the political power in the industry finding it very difficult
> to compete with some more aggressive thrifts that were buying high yield
> bonds and getting very high returns, which put them in a position to pay
> higher rates or roll faster and expand aggressively. (November 1988)

Big thrifts were not the only financial institutions affected by the junk bond
revolution. As we noted earlier, junk bonds provided a flexible, fixed-rate
alternative to bank loans, causing corporate bonds to gain market share at
the expense of bank financing. Insurance companies were also under pressure
to earn competitive returns. Those who were unwilling or unable to invest
in junk bonds suddenly found themselves at a competitive disadvantage, and
attempted to artificially alter the rules to suit their investment policies. As
Joseph notes,

> Equitable led the fight in New York to restrict high yield bonds. Their
> problems were directly related to competing with insurance companies
> that were getting 300 to 400 basis points or more in their portfolio by
> buying high yield bonds. The political reaction was a response by people
> who either didn't want to or couldn't compete on the investment side
> with the high yield bond investors. (Interview, Fredrick Joseph, November
> 1988)

During the hostile takeover battle between Mesa Petroleum and Unocal, Unocal petitioned the Federal Reserve Board in May 1985, requesting that margin requirements in Regulation G be applied to debt securities issued by a shell corporation involved in a tender offer. The Fed did apply Regulation G to certain types of transactions, and a Senate bill was later introduced to further amend margin requirements used in acquisitions. The net effect of the legislation was to restrict the amount of junk bonds that could be used to finance acquisitions by shell corporations.

As a person active in the junk bond market recalls looking over the landscape of Corporate America in the mid-1980s and noting,

> Everywhere you looked, entrenched managers were pursuing negative present value projects. Gulf Oil was continuing to drill wells as the barrel price fell off a cliff, because that's what they'd always done. Thrifts kept putting out thirty-year fixed-rate mortgages, even though deregulation had made other mortgage products more popular.

As Milken pointed out, these managers insisted on resisting change and defining their business by the past until somebody stopped them. "Not surprisingly," he said, "competitive forces started to stop them through new strategies and takeovers."

Boone Pickens recollects the following about that period:

> If you go back to the late 70s and early 80s where the oil industry was clearly overcapitalized, you will find they were doing unusual things because there was no accountability to stop them. Nobody really paid any attention to these things other than a few academics examining the cash flow of the large oil companies who discovered they were opening the window and throwing money out.

Whatever the economic impact of high yield securities, the public policy response has been an overwhelming reaction to regulate the market's success. Let us review the dimensions of public policy responses at the federal and state level to the rapid expansion of the market for high yield securities. Both federal and state legislations have been proposed or enacted in a number of public policy areas (see Table 10-1).

Federal and State Policies Regulating High Yield Securities

As numerous measures were introduced to further police cheating in the securities markets, high yield securities became a target of concern over fair market practices. As part of regulations of tender offers, revisions were proposed in the Securities Exchange Act to restrict the issuing of securities that would cause a reduction in the national bond rating of an existing security. A moratorium on hostile takeovers financed by junk securities was also proposed (leaving hostile takeovers financed conventionally by cash-laden large corporations and foreign investors unhindered), along with the prohibition

Table 10-1. Existing and Proposed Regulations of High Yield Securities and Restructuring

Federal	Federal and State			State		
Securities	Federal Reserve	Banking	Tax	Savings & Loans/ Commercial Banks	Insurance	Pension Funds
S.634—Bill to amend Securities Exchange Act and restrict new securities that would cause a reduction in bond rating.	Regulation G margin requirements application to debt securities issued by a shell corporation in takeovers.	S.1653—Junk Bond Limitation Act of 1987. Limit junk securities held by federally insured institutions (current cap is 11%).	Interest—Deductibility of debt.	Restrictions on investments in high yield securities by state chartered banks and savings and loans—California, Texas, Florida	Restrictions on investments in high yield securities—Maryland, Texas, New York.	Restrictions on investments by pension funds in LBOs.
HR.687—Moratorium on hostile takeovers financed by junk securities and prohibition of junk security holdings by federally insured institutions.	S.1847—Bill to amend margin requirements for financial instruments used in acquisitions.	Thrifts—divestment of high yield bonds by savings and loans by 1994.	Reclassification of high yield securities regarding qualification for interest exclusion.			

of junk security holdings by federally insured institutions. As of this writing, the high yield market has been subjected to considerable legislative distortion. On July 27, 1989, the House and Senate adopted a provision that would bar savings and loans from owning high yield bonds. Thrifts must divest currently held bonds over a five-year period. The evidentiary record of this study and other academic research were discounted by Congress. Further reports by the General Accounting Office and Data Resources, Inc. (on the impact of a recession on high yield bonds) and Wharton Econometric Forecasting (on high yield bonds compared to other Savings and Loan investments in the past) were also neglected in deliberations. Other measures on interest deductibility and merger and acquisition regulation are still under deliberation.*

Federal Reserve Policy

During the hostile takeover battle between Mesa Petroleum and Unocal, Unocal petitioned the Federal Reserve Board in May 1985, requesting that margin requirements in Regulation G be applied to debt securities issued by a shell corporation involved in a tender offer. The Fed did apply Regulation G to certain types of transactions and a Senate bill was later introduced to further amend margin requirements used in acquisitions.

Federal bank regulators have recently taken steps to extend the limitations that had already been imposed on the ability of financial institutions under their supervision to acquire and hold low-rated bonds. New legislative proposals have focused primarily on the use of proceeds from the bonds to finance restructuring, especially hostile takeovers and LBOs. This issue has been of particular interest to state supervisors of insurance companies and Federal officials charged with guaranteeing the safety of corporate pension fund benefits.

---

*Diversification into limited activities not directly related to housing was intended in the Garn-St Germain Act (1982) to strengthen the ability of savings institutions and thereby better play their primary housing finance role.

In enacting the Garn-St Germain Act legislation, Congress noted that the benefits of such broader investment powers were essential to the development of a healthy S & L industry and outweighed the risks of expanded investment authority.

The exercise of the commercial lending and investment powers authorized by the Garn-St Germain Act enabled S & Ls to diversify their portfolios, increase their overall yield on assets, and operate profitably. Profitable operations increased an S & L's net worth, which, in turn, lessened the exposure of the Federal Savings and Loan Insurance Corporation insurance fund. Thus, the power to invest in commercial loans and corporate debt obligations, including high yield corporate bonds, had proven to be a vital tool in restoring the net worth of many S & Ls.

By the end of the decade, however, thrift investment in high yield bonds was under attack despite all the evidence in favor of such investment. Indeed, the General Accounting Office had determined that high yield bonds had been the second-best investment that thrifts had had over the past decade, second only to credit cards.

Barriers to High Yield Financing and Investing Banking Policy

Commercial banks chartered or insured by the Federal government have always faced limitations on the debt securities they can hold. National banks are restricted to investing in bonds that are investment grade and not "speculative" in nature. The Senate and House Banking Committee and the Comptroller of the Currency authorize national banks to invest in corporate debt securities according to a risk-based capital reserve requirement that currently prevents banks from investing more than 10 percent of their capital and surplus in corporate issues.

Curiously, while low-rated bonds are considered speculative, unrated issues are not. Unrated securities may not exceed 5 percent of the bank's capital and surplus, and are subject to the prudent banking judgment rule, which says that the issuer must be able to meet its obligations and the bank must be able to sell the security with reasonable promptness at a price corresponding to fair market value. Despite the fact that noninvestment grade companies often have stronger credit characteristics than unrated issuers, securities that are rated noninvestment grade and bonds issued to finance a corporate takeover cannot be purchased by national banks.

Member banks of the Federal Reserve System are subject to similarly restrictive guidelines. Federal Reserve examiners have recently been directed to scrutinize commercial bank loans provided to finance leveraged buyouts. Though no quantitative guidelines have yet been issued, banks have been informally encouraged to exercise restraint in senior and subordinated debt lending for leveraged buyouts. Federal Reserve officials have suggested that they would be unhappy about seeing a doubling of the current 10-percent ratio of money-center-bank commercial loans granted for LBOs.

State law authorizes investment by state chartered banks according to rules of "prudence" and permits investment in corporate debt obligations subject to the same limits imposed on national banks. Insofar as state banks become members of the Federal Reserve System and obtain FDIC insurance, they are subject to federal rules and the scrutiny of FDIC examiners. Thus, state banks face the same limitations applicable to national banks. Recently, the FDIC reiterated advice to avoid high yield securities and instructed examiners to review bank loan portfolios for high yield investments and LBO loans.

Thrift Policy

Many thrift institutions, including Federal savings and loans and certain savings banks, are chartered and regulated by the Federal Home Loan Bank Board. Other thrifts are subject to state regulation or controls imposed by the FDIC or FSLIC. Under Federal Home Loan Bank Board guidelines, thrifts can put up to 1.0 percent of their total assets in debt securities and 10 percent in commercial loans. As a result, a maximum of 11 percent of their assets can be invested in high yield securities. Some states have more lenient guidelines. In California, Texas, and Florida, for example, thrifts can invest up to 40 percent of their assets in high yield securities, while other states have adopted the Federal cap of 11 percent. Some states are considering measures to further limit investments in high yield securities.

The Federal Home Loan Bank reported that 161 of the 3,025 FSLIC-insured thrifts in the country held such bonds in their portfolios. These figures indicate that only 5.3 percent of the thrifts hold such investments. In 1988, the total book value of the high yield securities owned by these institutions was $13.2 billion—less than 5.0 percent of their total assets and roughly 1.0 percent of the assets held by all S&Ls in the nation. Eleven of the institutions, however, held $9.1 billion of the high yield bonds in September of that year, amounting to 10.3 percent of their total assets and 69 percent of the high yield securities held by all FSLIC-insured S&Ls.

The Federal Home Loan Bank Board has recently issued guidelines for credit analysis, loan loss reserves, and asset diversification that would restrict high yield investment. In 1989, even more stringent policies were considered, which would completely eliminate the ability of thrifts to invest in high yield bonds.

Since there is no evidence that high yield securities have caused any of the S&L losses in recent years, the new restrictions and proposals are particularly ironic. Under the guise of protecting thrifts from undue risk, they would effectively reduce the institutions' earning potential by limiting the returns they are allowed to receive.

High yield securities remain the functional equivalents of commercial loans and, if depository institutions have the right to extend such credit in the traditional borrower-lender manner, they should have the right to extend funds via securities investment as well. As a practical matter, it is only by recognizing that loans and high yield bonds are simply two forms of the same credit extension process that will permit smaller depository institutions to access any wide range of corporate customers. Furthermore, the underwriting process and prospectus disclosure under the securities laws do provide a reasonable basis for credit extension by a prudent lending institution which does its own "due diligence" analysis from that documentation. The high yield bond market enables credit to be extended in the capital markets across the entire corporate creditworthiness spectrum, just as direct bank lending has always been available, at a price, to corporate borrowers.

Insurance Companies

Insurance companies currently account for over 30 percent of all high yield bond investments. State laws and regulations generally govern investment in securities by companies in the life insurance industry. Most states do not impose constraints on investment in high yield bonds. But in New York, Maryland, Florida, and Texas, broad limits have been proposed to restrict the percentage of assets life insurance companies can invest in high yield securities. While Maryland withdrew its proposal, the New York State Insurance Commission adopted a 20 percent limit on publicly traded high yield bond investments issued to finance LBOs and bonds issued in the form of large denomination private placements. Arizona and Texas have similar provisions, and California is considering them. New York also restricts property and casualty insurance companies, specifying a minimum amount of the company's capital that is not eligible for investment in high yield bonds.

The National Association of Insurance Commissioners estimated that noninvestment grade bonds represented 3.5 percent of insurance company assets, and only 0.9 percent of the total assets of property and casualty insurance companies. Only 35 of the 4,400 insurance companies monitored by the association had more than 20 percent of their assets in noninvestment grade bonds. Nevertheless, high yield bonds remain an important source of income for insurance companies, and their trading activity supports the high yield market by increasing liquidity and demand.

Tax Legislation

In 1987, the Senate Finance Committee and House Ways and Means Committee considered a provision to limit the tax deductibility of interest on acquisition-related debt. A recent study by the Securities and Exchange Commission (Netter and Mitchell, 1988) showed that the announcement of this provision helped precipitate the sliding share values that became the October Crash of 1987.

Nevertheless, resistance to tax increases and the need to reduce the federal deficit may make interest deductibility a convenient target, with serious implications for businesses and the capital markets on which they depend. A proposal has been adopted to reduce the intercorporate dividends receiving deductions from 70 to 50 percent. In both 1988 and 1989, Congress also considered provisions to limit interest deductions on acquisition debt and to tax the market discount on bonds.

States have also considered measures to limit the interest deductibility of acquisition-related debt. Though California's Tax and Revenue Subcommittee dismissed one such proposal on "equitylike" debt and "excessive leverage," in April 1989, New York passed such a proposal without hearings during the final days of a budget debate.

Additionally, Congress recently mandated the Treasury Department to revise Subchapter C of the federal tax code. While the outcome is not yet clear, the Treasury could recommend that certain high yield securities be reclassified from debt to equity, thereby eliminating them from the interest exclusion associated with debt.

Antitakeover Legislation

One of the more significant moves to restrict restructuring activity has come in the form of antitakeover legislation designed to protect existing managers of public companies. From 1985 to 1989, antitakeover sentiments swept through state legislatures as part of the regulatory wave against junk bonds, buyouts, and changes in corporate control. In all, some thirty-six states now offer statutory protection from takeovers. No shareholder vote is required for in-state companies to be protected under these statutes.

In every state, local corporations threatened by ownership change sponsored and promoted antitakeover legislation. In 1985, CBS faced a takeover attempt by Ted Turner and Grumman Aerospace was confronted by various suitors. Both companies offered testimony in the New York State legislature and prepared briefing documents to help lawmakers swiftly pass takeover protection measures in the summer of that year.

In December 1985, James Baker, the chairman of Arvin Industries, an Indiana auto parts company, received a takeover threat from the Belzberg family of Canada. Baker called on his long-time friend, Robert Garton, then president of the Indiana senate, to save his company and community from the ravages of a takeover battle. Within four weeks, an antitakeover bill was drafted, passed, and signed into law. Two months later, the state revised its corporate code by adopting an additional antitakeover statute.

When G. Heileman Brewing Co. of La Crosse, Wisconsin, faced an unsolicited bid from Australian Alan Bond, the state quickly passed legislation that supported the use of "poison pills" and prevented a raider from selling off target assets for up to three years to pay for a takeover. In light of the evidence that takeovers do not generally promote layoffs or plant closures, it is interesting that the local press cited protecting jobs as one of the main advantages of the legislation.

In Arizona, Greyhound sought protective legislation to thwart a takeover attempt by Irwin Jacobs. The bill passed, although according to the Scottsdale press, "several House members branded it as anti-free enterprise." In Ohio, Sir James Goldsmith's bid for Goodyear led to prompt legislative action. And in Connecticut, Champion International spearheaded a move to establish more protective laws after Uniroyal and Scovil had been acquired and dismantled, and Singer had moved to New Jersey to seek a safer haven.

In Washington state, Boeing anticipated an unsolicited bid from Boone Pickens and sought modifications in the state's antitakeover laws. A special legislative session was called, and protective action was taken. But the new law, which covered only corporations with more than 20,000 employees, was clearly designed just to protect Boeing, the state's largest employer.

At the hearings, a concerned shareholder asked, "Where is our free-enterprise system going when it caters to the interests of thirteen board members to the detriment of 70,000 stockholders?" Boone Pickens also accused the state of protecting the interests of company managers at the shareholders' expense. "In each of the states passing takeover legislation, a powerful company treated the state legislature like it was their own banana republic," Pickens said.

Even disinterested parties have questioned the propriety of laws designed to protect incumbent managers and prevent shareholders from earning acquisition premiums. In March 1987, the Federal Trade Commission released a study showing that the market value of ninety-four New York companies declined slightly when the state announced its 1985 antitakeover legislation. The drop represented nearly $1.2 billion in immediate capital losses to shareholders, which could be far less than the acquisition premiums shareholders will have to forgo as a result of the new law. The FTC concluded that "this very strong statute does not protect shareholders," and a researcher for the Investor Responsibility Research Center commented that "rather, the law protects managers at the expense of shareholders."

A study by the Securities and Exchange Commission showed similar results among thirty-six Ohio companies. Antitakeover laws in that state depressed stock values by an average of 2 percent, causing shareholder losses of up to $1.45 billion. And another study by two U.S. government economists estimated that Indiana's antitakeover law cost shareholders $2.65 billion, or more than 6 percent of the value of the nineteen companies examined.

The debate over antitakeover legislation centers on key concerns about the market for corporate control. If incumbent managers are not fully utilizing a company's assets to enhance growth or improve shareholder returns, why should outsiders be prevented from doing so? Furthermore, if managers are pursuing negative value projects, or using perks, bonuses, or other means to appropriate profits that rightfully belong to shareholders, how can antitakeover laws be justified?

Unfortunately, as we noted in Chapter 1, state legislators have more on their agenda than the welfare of shareholders. They are concerned about keeping large corporations and their tax revenues in their state. They are busy courting campaign contributions and bargaining for support on other issues that affect the business and economic climate in their communities. Most important, they want to avoid any association with protakeover votes that could seriously affect their plans for re-election. Together, these pressures have led to an unprecedented wave of antitakeover legislation, with protective laws falling into four basic types:

- Some laws limit the voting rights of a shareholder who acquires a certain amount of stock, making further share purchases useless without the approval of the remaining shareholders.
- Other laws may delay business combinations for a certain number of years or place a moratorium on the sale of assets to pay for the acquisition.
- Still other laws impose fair price criteria coupled with supermajority voting requirements.
- Another type of antitakeover legislation allows minority shareholders to cashout their holdings at the expense of the acquiring shareholder.

Often, these takeover protections come in a package. In other cases, they may have unusual consequences. In some states, moratorium provisions may take precedence over shareholder votes. In New York, for instance, an acquiror who seeks control of shares without board approval would have to wait two to five years to pursue any sort of merger, even if the business combination had been approved by the shareholders.

Under control share acquisition laws in twenty-one states, an acquiror of a certain percentage of a company's shares must win the approval of a majority of outstanding shares and a majority of disinterested outstanding shares before exercising control. Thus, buying a controlling number of shares in the corporation does not necessarily ensure voting control.

The fair price and supermajority laws that exist in twenty-two states stipulate that any two-tier takeover must be recommended by the board of directors of the target company and approved by 80 percent of the outstanding shares and two thirds of the shares not held by the interested shareholder.

Freeze-out laws exist in nineteen states. These laws discourage acquirors from consummating the merger or gaining access to the target's assets. They bar any business combination between a 20 percent shareholder and the target company for a period of five years, or they may require board approval for the merger to take place.

Eleven states have enacted measures that endorse the use of "poison pills", which dilute corporate stock and make takeovers too expensive to be economically viable. Thirteen states have given directors a broader range of considerations they may apply in exercising their business judgment. Thus, instead of simply asking whether a transaction will benefit their shareholders, they can ask how their suppliers or communities might be affected by a takeover attempt.

Perhaps the most stringent antitakeover provisions impose a direct cap on voting rights after a potential acquiror purchases 20 percent of a company's shares. Additional shares provide only 10 percent of the voting rights those shares normally would carry. Under such a provision, an acquiror who purchased 70 percent of a company's stock would only have 25 percent of the voting power, and could still be outvoted by the remaining shareholders, whose shares would each count for a full vote.

In Delaware, the rush to provide protective regulation was the scene of the most clear-cut exercise of established corporate power. More than 50 percent of the companies in the Fortune 500, or nearly half of those listed on the New York Stock Exchange, are incorporated in Delaware. Many new companies have reincorporated there to take advantage of the state's wide range of takeover defenses. After testifying against the Delaware legislation, Pickens recalls his conversation with that state's governor.

> "You ought to veto it," I told him. "Well, I've had a lot of pressure put on me. Basically, I agree with you, this is against shareholder rights."
> I said, "Where did you get pressure from?" He said, "General Motors, Boeing, Texaco, and DuPont."

As Romano (1989) has noted, Delaware depends heavily on corporate franchise fees. In 1987, some 184,000 corporations paid Delaware state franchise fees totalling $170 million, or seventeen percent of the state's total revenue. Many states have attempted to copy Delaware's antitakeover provisions to attract incorporations and income.*

Public Policy and Private Power

Rather than focus on making capital more readily available, the course of public policy has been to restrict high yield securities and restructuring activity. Most of the measures we have seen have discriminated in favor of large, well-established companies with higher credit ratings. The burden of increasing regulation and restriction must be borne by smaller, emerging firms and older companies in transition or distress.

While restricting capital access to these companies may make it easier for blue-chip corporations to compete, we need to ask how the benefits of this policy compare with the disadvantages. For example, if we limit the access to capital of smaller firms that could use it to create jobs, larger firms might show a relative improvement in their rate of job creation. But since the overall rate of job growth would decline, what value would such a relative improvement be to our economy or our competitive position in world markets?

If we take steps that will slow the sales growth of America's fastest-growing firms, what advantage will we have achieved? And if we make it impossible to replace ineffective managers with others who focus on profits and productivity, what good will we have done?

To use a simple analogy, a tourniquet is an excellent way to stop your arm from bleeding. But if there is nothing wrong with your arm, applying a tourniquet can be very dangerous. It can stop the flow of blood and eventually cause gangrene. Capital is the lifeblood of any business. And restricting capital access is very much like applying a tourniquet. If a business is literally dying, restricting its capital access may be a good way to prevent massive losses and defaults. But if the business is small, healthy, and growing, or simply needs capital to restructure and recover, restricting capital access could be a serious or death-dealing blow.

In addition to affecting individual companies, restrictions on who can issue or hold high yield securities have affected the viability of the junk bond

---

*In April 1989 Pennsylvania enacted the nation's most far-reaching antitakeover law. The Pennsylvania statute would not only prevent hostile takeovers of companies headquartered in that state, but it would also make it more difficult for dissatisfied shareholders to change management through proxy fights. The turmoil and uncertainty in the capital markets from late 1989 through early 1990 had led to an increased use of proxy fights, rather than hostile takover bids, to fight entrenched managers. The Pennsylvania law effectively made it nearly impossible for shareholders to replace the management of a company.

market. While the market remained relatively stable until 1989 despite interest rate volatility, legislative pressures, and the stock market crash, continued efforts to inhibit issuance and investment in high yield securities have had a negative impact on pricing, liquidity, and investor confidence.

Still, the urge to regulate junk bonds, takeovers, and LBOs appears to be a fundamental impulse in government, fueled largely by ignorance and misunderstanding of the empirical evidence in favor of these securities and the transactions they make possible. No other financial instrument in the debt or equity markets has undergone as much investigation, and none has met with as much political controversy or legislative scrutiny. Nevertheless, the resounding success of the high yield market as a source of capital for internal growth and industrial restructuring has largely been ignored.

The frequent initiatives to regulate a seemingly effective and expanding market are worthy of considerable reflection. While the text of the policy discourse is primarily economic, the driving force behind it is political. And when the case against high yield securities is finally written, we would do well to ask ourselves why double standards were applied for noninvestment grade and investment grade securities and why selective prosecution and investigation were undertaken.

The Policy Discourse

As we have seen, the gap between political perception and economic reality about high yield securities is considerable. Junk bonds have been confounded with an assortment of factors to which they bear little if any relation:

- High yield bonds are assumed to be the cause of takeovers.
- High yield bonds are associated with insider trading scandals, greenmail, and plant closings.
- Junk securities are blamed for bad loan portfolios of failing thrifts, banks, and pension funds.

While junk bonds may be used in takeover finance, we have already seen that they neither cause nor are they the primary financing vehicle for hostile transactions. Moreover, the fact that a deal is called "hostile" does not mean that it is bad. In at least some instances, unsolicited takeovers have provided shareholders with handsome premiums and have brought new life and vitality to target companies. In other cases, thwarted takeover attempts have given entrenched managers the incentives they needed to enhance shareholder values and run their companies more profitably and productively.

Insider trading and greenmail are indeed deplorable practices. But trying to stop them by regulating the use of junk bonds is like trying to stop bank robberies by closing all the banks. We cannot solve insider trading by closing down the capital markets. But we can prevent it with more careful monitoring of compliance procedures and trading profits. We cannot prevent greenmail by attacking a class of securities that account for only a small portion of acquisition financing. Instead, we need to look at who proposes premium repurchases, why they propose them, and whose interests are served or harmed. Only then can we frame legislation that will specifically address this critical concern.

While junk bonds are associated with plant closings and job loss, all the empirical evidence shows that such an impression is entirely unfounded. High yield companies are producing jobs four and a half times faster than their respective industries. Leveraged buyouts are no more nor less prone to close their plants than are other companies, and among management buyouts, the rate of plant closing is significantly lower than the rate among plants in general.

The problems of failed banks and thrifts have resulted from bad real estate, energy, and agricultural loans, and not from high yield debt. Yet, while regulators are concerned about real estate loans and other underperforming investments, their primary restrictions have been aimed at junk bonds, the very securities that provide the high risk-adjusted returns financial institutions need to compensate for their other loan losses.

In addition, investments in publicly traded corporate securities such as high yield bonds meet two other critical needs for financial institutions: liquidity, and the ability to match the maturities of assets and liabilities. The capital markets spread financing risk among a larger universe of lenders, ultimately making available more capital at better rates. While the high yield market—like all capital markets—has suffered periods of extreme volatility, it remains far more liquid than the interdepository secondary market for direct commercial credits. Securities investment provides a variety of yields and maturities, giving financial institutions unprecedented flexibility in tailoring a portfolio to match their asset base.

Given the increasing evidence that academic research and government investigation have provided for the positive economic impact of junk bonds, the continued misunderstanding of these securities remains a puzzling mystery. In order to find the solution, it may be helpful to examine the political and conceptual limits to the current policy debate about high yield securities.

Interest Group Politics and Capital Markets

The most obvious question in the debate surrounding high yield securities is: Whose ox was gored? It certainly was not the investors who enjoyed rates of return hundreds of basis points above those available from other financial instruments. It was not businesses hungry for flexible, long-term, fixed-rate capital and freedom from restrictive bank loans. It was not the employees who gained equity participation through ESOPs, or the customers and vendors who enjoyed heightened economic activity financed through high yield securities. And it certainly was not the shareholders whose equity values grew with debt-financed growth, or those who earned substantial acquisition premiums in transactions partially financed with high yield securities.

When we look at the facts, there were only two major groups that suffered setbacks with the development of high yield bonds: banks and large, established corporations. As William Carney has succinctly noted,

> There are two reasons why junk bonds have come under attack—other explanations are mostly window dressing. First, junk bonds have made it easier for new challengers to enter the market for corporate control. Second, they are a valuable financing innovation for midsize companies that were traditionally ignored by large underwriters and had to pay higher interest rates at commercial banks. To the extent that junk bonds compete with existing lenders, these institutions predictably have responded by seeking to regulate competitors who exploit this new tool.

When the General Accounting Office investigated problem thrifts and insurance company insolvencies, they could find no evidence that high yield defaults had affected the investment portfolios of those companies. As we noted a moment ago, problem banks and thrifts were the result of poor performance among loans for agriculture, energy, and real estate. In legislative hearings, however, it has become clear that commercial banks and insurance companies have been most interested in using regulations to restrict competition for loans and access to capital markets. In New York, for example, only two insurance companies exceeded the 20-percent limit on high yield investments, First Executive Life and Presidential Life—two insurance companies that were challenging more established names in the insurance industry. No wonder Equitable and Metropolitan Life led the effort to regulate high yield investment.

The use of political regulation to restrict economic competition has a long history in railroads, communications, energy, and other industries. It is ironic that during an era of financial deregulation, counterpressures from vested interests would seek to make our capital markets more rigid. Yet the high yield market provided the flexibility corporations needed to adapt and change, and undermining the flexibility appeared to be the only way for established companies and entrenched managers to protect their independence, preserve their supremacy, and maintain the vestiges of the old order.

Conceptual Limits to High Yield Regulation

While interest groups work to further a hidden political agenda, the expressed purpose of financial regulatory policy is to base transactions on legal and accounting standards derived from historical principles of safety, soundness, and financial prudence. It is hoped that these principles can counterbalance the risks inherent in our economy and assist in keeping our markets fair and equitable.

As Michael Milken suggested, recent regulations have confirmed the victory of form over content in public financial policy. A high yield security that is traded in public markets with considerable liquidity and rigorous due diligence has limited risk as an investment instrument. Commercial loans that accomplish the same purpose and have fewer self-regulatory provisions to insure safety and soundness are much more risky. In content, the financial instruments are essentially the same. But because they differ in form, high yield securities have been the subject of considerably more onerous regulation.

One factor contributing to the negative perception of high yield bonds has been an antiquated and static approach to risk analysis. By looking solely at the balance sheet, which is a snapshot of a firm's financial condition on a given day, it is easy to assume that highly leveraged companies are over-leveraged. But if those companies are putting their leverage to productive use, they can generate enough cash flow to service their debt and still earn attractive profits.

While balance sheets are static, the companies they picture are dynamic, continually adapting and responding to new market conditions, consumer preferences, and technological advances. As we have seen in the case of leveraged buyouts, a balance sheet with a large amount of debt is not always a negative factor for forward-thinking companies. Substantial leverage can provide incentives to increase productivity and profitability, and often results in improved operating performance.

The myth that additional leverage will slow productivity growth, cause rampant unemployment, and reduce R & D spending has been shown to be just that—a myth. If our public policy fails to distinguish between myth and reality, the United States may have to face the unpleasant realities that could follow from undue regulation of our capital markets.

If an army went to war but refused to let most of its soldiers carry weapons, it would almost certainly lose. Today, the United States is trying to compete in a global marketplace. Our corporations have taken their positions on the battle lines, yet the government is anxiously trying to regulate and restrict which companies can have access to the capital they need to succeed.

Who will win or lose the battle? Drexel Burnham is already a casualty. Only time will tell the full story. Perhaps the answer will not be so clear-cut. In economic competition, nations may show strength for a time, then fall by the wayside as their fundamental weaknesses are exposed. Mexico was a brilliant competitor in the 1970s, as long as the price of oil remained high. Today, it is struggling to pay the interest on its debt. The United States was once the leader of the industrial world. Today, we have lost much of our market dominance to Europe and the Far East.

The cost and availability of capital has been a primary factor in determining our competitive position in today's global markets. Whatever the critics may claim, high yield bonds have been a valuable tool, helping corporations meet the challenges of an increasingly competitive world.

We have seen that high yield companies are outperforming their industries in key performance areas. We have found that leveraged buyouts can have a positive impact on sales, productivity, and operating income. We have learned that leverage can produce positive results for companies, industries, and the economy.

Will regulators take these facts and findings into consideration in their policy decisions? Will America's small and medium-sized companies continue to have access to affordable capital? These issues are larger than partisan politics or the designs of special interest groups. They affect more than the companies that issue high yield bonds and the investors who buy them. The answers our legislators provide will determine the economic future of our nation.

11

Shake-outs and Showdowns in the Capital Market

A junk bond backlash in the courts, Congress, legislatures, and turmoil in the bond market itself has unfolded since most of the evidence in this book was gathered and analyzed. Does this mean, as some business writers have suggested, that the high yield market is dead? Has that market's explosive growth ended, and have we returned to the old economic order of static book accounting and the staid dominance of the country's largest firms? Was the high yield market a passing fancy of paper shufflers on Wall Street or has it become an institutionalized part of modern corporate finance and business practice to build a value-added economy?

This chapter addresses these questions, and also

- Reviews the major structural changes in corporate finance, business organization, and strategy promoted by high yield securities
- Examines the shake-out that occurred in the junk bond and LBO market during the Fall of 1989, why it happened, and what the consequences might be
- Explores the role of financial innovation in the 1990s and how high yield securities are evolving to adjust to the challenges of international competitiveness and the geopolitical shifts that are the centerpiece of our times.

The perplexity of keeping economic growth alive in new sectors and rebuilding old sectors remains with us. To mitigate a recession and counter future business cycle downturns will require ongoing availability and access to low-cost financing by firms that will generate high yield returns for investors. As discussed in Chapter 3, that capacity to innovate financially was true during earlier periods when high yielding securities were preferred stock or common stock. If the junk bond revolution achieved anything, it was the extension of access to capital to firms and sectors that suffered from chronic undercapitalization. The extension of that logic of economic growth to minorities, distressed communities, and underdeveloped regions (like Latin America, Eastern Europe, and the Soviet Union) is also to be discussed.

What Junk Bonds Wrought

The more than 800 companies that issued more than 2000 different high yield issues in over 100 different industries comprise the junk bond market today. By the end of 1989, the high yield market had topped $200 billion in total value and comprised 25 percent of the total corporate bond market (see Figure 11-1). Professional investors represent the largest segment of owners in that market. According to the General Accounting Office (1988), the breakdown of ownership of high yield securities was insurance companies (30 percent), mutual funds (30 percent), pension funds (15 percent), foreign investors (10 percent). Other individual investors or money managers owned the remaining 15 percent of those securities. The value of new high yield issues in the market peaked at $41.8 billion in 1986 and has trended downward since to $37.5 billion and $34.7 billion in 1987 and 1988 respectively.

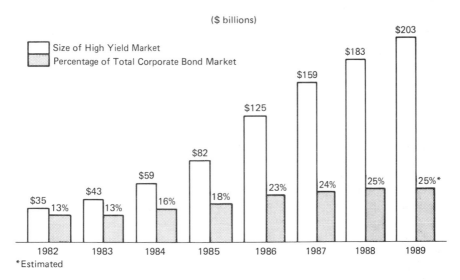

Figure 11-1. Public high yield market growth, 1982-7/31/89 (*Investor's Digest Daily*)

But, let us move beyond the numbers and summarize what these numbers and the empirical evidence presented in this book really mean. Basically, the high yield market created conditions for:

- The reintegration of financial and industrial resources and interests
- The reintegration of ownership and control
- Increased capital access for smaller companies
- The democratization of capital
- Increased competitiveness

Reintegration of Financial and Industrial Resources

With the high yield market, our financial institutions have begun to move toward the integration of industrial and financial resources enjoyed by our major foreign competitors in Japan and Germany. As Michael Jensen (1989) has convincingly argued, the high yield market and the growth of buyouts has eliminated the central weakness of large public corporations—the conflict between owners and managers over the control and use of corporate resources.

With the growth of the high yield debt market, investors became more active. Those that held large amounts of equity or debt sat on boards, monitored management, and generally were involved in the long-term strategic direction of the company. Active financial investors, as Jensen explains, were driven out of corporations during the 1930s and 1940s with the passage of legislation such as the Glass-Steagal Banking Act of 1933, the Chandler Bankruptcy Revision Act of 1938, and the Investment Company Act of 1940.

Under these measures, Congress limited the active participation of money managers or large owners of debt and equity on the boards of public corporations. Institutionally, this left corporate managers with greater autonomy and increasingly unmonitored by financial institutions or investors. The forcible separation of financial and industrial interests eliminated many shareholder rights and led to the insulation of management authority and decision making from shareholder scrutiny.

Without an active voice in corporate strategy, financial interests could only exit from their ownership position in their portfolio companies if they found management lacking on an ongoing basis. "Portfolio churning" and "stock flipping" became commonplace, as passive investors came to depend for their returns more upon short-term arbitrage than upon long-term value-generation.

In Japan and West Germany, our major foreign trading competitors, the integration of financial and industrial interests led banks and investment companies to promote lower costs of capital in order to maximize asset appreciation of their investment in industrial companies over time. Export financing, promotion of technological innovation, and other investments targeting long-term growth and competitiveness were more common.

With the rise of the junk bond market, the return of merchant banking, and the formation of investment companies (like LBO associations), active investors were financially empowered to take greater control in the strategic direction of corporations. Financial and operational concerns were not artificially separated or perceived as contradictory. Active investors like Carl Icahn, Boone Pickens, Irwin Jacobs, Carl Lindner, and Kohlberg Kravis and Roberts actually ran companies. Family funds (Bass, Pritzker, Bronfman), investment bank partners' funds (Lazard, Drexel, Morgan Stanley), pension funds, and law partners' funds became commonplace and controversial. In investment banking, it became a time to return to the merchant banking traditions that remained common in Western Europe or the Far East. No longer were investment bankers pursuing a passive role as financial intermediaries raising money for fee income alone; through junk bonds and bridge loans they took a more active role, investing their own capital to insure economic returns for issuers and investors.

Reintegrating Ownership and Control

The separation of ownership and control in the modern corporation as detailed by Berle and Means (1932), and the absence of competition in the market for corporate control, led to management being insulated from monitoring and resulted in enormous inefficiencies. In the movement toward professional management heralded in the 1930s and echoed in generations of business and economics textbooks, the diffusion of share ownership and the rise of professional managers separated corporate control from owners in many public companies. While shareholders assumed the financial risks of the company, their sheer numbers made it impossible for them to directly participate in corporate decision making regarding the day-to-day running of the company. As a result, technical and professional rationality, as opposed to ownership interest, were supposed to determine the course of business strategy. In short, managers were the decision makers whether those decisions were in shareholders' interests or not.

The reintegration of ownership and control was another aspect of the high yield challenge to established corporate and political power. To the extent that entrenched managers controlled corporations, high yield bonds enabled competitors to contest that control. This was done either through takeover battles and increased demands for shareholder rights by individual and institutional investors, or by building stronger market challengers. Following deregulation in the telephone industry, MCI Communications emerged as a strong competitor, primarily as a result of high yield financing. From 1981 to 1988, the company increased its employment from 1,952 to 14,236. During that same period, about 128,000 jobs were eliminated by investment grade AT&T and the seven Bell operating companies.

Increased Capital Access

Prior to the rise of the high yield market, corporate size and age was the greatest determinant of whether or not a company had easy access to capital. As we have seen, companies were hamstrung by restrictive commercial bank lending practices of the 1970s, the exclusiveness of bond rating agencies that discriminated against smaller companies in less established or troubled industries, restrictive private placements, dilutive common stock offerings, or costly variable rate bank loans. New technologies, services, or products produced or distributed by entrepreneurs seeking mobility outside established corporate channels were shunned by the capital markets or went begging. Whether firms pursued aggressive or defensive strategies to open new economic frontiers or defend old ones from foreign competition, however, one critical element was missing: capital.

Barriers of entry to the capital market and restrictions on capital access all contributed to increased costs of capital to U.S. firms. This was occurring precisely as global competition was heating up and U.S. economic hegemony was eclipsing rapidly. High costs of capital, as we have seen, were an additional burden, a factor contributing to U.S. industrial decline.

Junk bonds changed the rules of capital access. Size and age were less important for raising money in the high yield market than flexibility and speed in accurately developing and executing business plans that would open new markets, increase cash flow, and build equity values.

With the increased competition from the high yield market, commercial banks also eased up on access to senior and subordinated debt and adopted for broader business purposes securitization practices that had become widespread in mortgage banking. As with the liberalization of credit in the housing market or loans to support higher education, car ownership, or self-employment, credit enabled individuals to acquire and expand their economic resources for strategic goals. Capital access has enabled more active economic participation by owners, managers, employees, and investors.

Democratization of Capital

Companies leveraged through the junk bond market came to have an ownership structure fundamentally different from that of many more established public corporations. Owner-managers were more predominant and employee stock participation was more widespread among junk bond firms. Through expanded equity participation and pay-for-performance compensation plans, firms become more flexible in their ability to incite managers and employees to be responsive to growth and innovation, since the personnel now participated directly in the results of those changes. Rather than fearing and resisting the prospect of technological or organizational changes directed at enhancing productivity, workers and managers began to embrace them.

In traditional firms, wages were viewed as the central point where value was exchanged between workers and employers. Historically, struggles for access to economic benefits focused on participation in the labor market and the market price of labor—the daily wage. Participation in the capital market was not on the economic or political agenda.

With the proliferation of employee stock ownership plans and other equity participation arrangements by managers and employees, the wage contract was no longer the sole source of economic value for employees. Stock ownership gave managers and employees a new claim on the profit interests of the firm. Those who dedicated themselves to improving performance and productivity could look forward to appreciation in the equity value and increased income and wealth directly resulting from their efforts and rewards based on productivity. Bitter fights over how to carve up a shrinking pie became refocused on how to make it bigger. Companies like Healthtrust, Charter Medical, Avis, Unimar, Omak and many others witnessed major improvements in operating efficiency and productivity as employees became owners. As Quarry and Rosen (1989) have shown, employee-owned companies outpaced their competitors in operating margins, return on equity, and the ratio of book value to share growth. As with management buyouts, employee buyouts proved again a simple truth about new financial technologies that created more capital access—people with opportunities work harder.

Innovative high yield companies began to provide alternative means of compensation to their employees. Performance bonuses and incentive-based pay have replaced fixed wage structures in many firms. More established companies have began to emulate these strategies. In other high yield companies, ESOPs or other equity participation plans are supplementing wages with dividend income, performance awards, and capital appreciation, while providing tangible incentives to improve operating results. While fixed wage structures locked companies into high costs during economic downturns, more flexible pay arrangements enabled companies to retain jobs and avoid layoffs during difficult times.

The extension of ownership and, at times, control to employees represents another watershed contribution of high yield financial innovations. By definition, each employee buyout has been a leveraged buyout. The realignment between owners and managers under this form of ownership change extended to labor as well, and is perhaps a harbinger of important developments in the decades ahead. While organized labor and management seemed trapped in adversarial patterns of conflict from another century, the high yield bond market began to redefine the nature of labor-management relations. Louis Kelso, the father of employee ownership plans, described well the shift of management and labor's focus from distribution to production (1986). Given the possibility of becoming owners, managers and workers stopped asking how they should distribute income and began to ask how they could distribute ownership to maximize income and wealth. This shift of focus brought the productive capacity of capital into the limelight, eclipsing earlier issues about wages and labor relations. In short, the issue became not whether workers could rent their jobs, but whether they could own them.

Increased Industrial Competitiveness

The findings in this book contradict the misinformation and conventional wisdom about junk bonds and buyouts and the business strategies they have promoted. We have seen that high yield strategies were most intense in those industries that were restructuring or growing the fastest: manufacturing, finance, and services.

Generally, the use of high yield securities has been to build and rebuild companies. Junk bond financial technology found appropriate application in the following areas:

- Financing high-growth, innovative companies that are relatively smaller in size and have greater operating risk (e.g., communications, entertainment, health services, educational services, electrical machinery, computing equipment, and semiconductors)
- Restructuring ownership and strategy of low-growth companies through leveraged buyouts and recapitalizations (e.g., food processing, retail trade, textile industries, and transportation)
- Recovering equity through workouts and turnarounds of distressed companies (e.g., utilities, mining, finance)

To determine the effects of high yield financing on corporate performance, we examined data on employment, productivity, sales, capital investment, and capital spending. In Chapter 4, we found that junk bonds did considerably more than simply reconfigure a company's financial structure (as critics have charged). Instead, high yield firms when compared with their respective industries, deployed capital at much higher rates and more productively.

As Chapter 5 detailed, the positive impacts on job growth and retention, sales increases, increased capital investment, and spending were consistently demonstrated. Despite variations among firms and industries, high yield companies evidenced a greater capacity than U.S. industry in general to grow faster in growth sectors of the economy (health and educational services, trade, computing equipment), and to retain jobs and market share in declining sectors (durable and nondurable manufacturing), and actually reversed patterns of decline by companies in some industries (utilities, primary metals, mining, airlines, and communications). In those high-growth, innovative sectors that were the backbone of the high yield market, trade surpluses look in sharp contrast to the massive nonpetroleum merchandise trade deficits the U.S. experienced during the 1980s.

In examining a number of high yield companies in detail, we found that by accessing nontraditional sources of capital in the junk bond market, companies re-created their businesses and often reinvented their industries in the process. Stone Container consolidated a number of low-margin, low-market-share producers into a high-margin, high-market-share operation that modernized and reopened obsolete plants. Hovnanian redesigned family housing for higher-density development, applied innovative construction methods, and financed ownership. Smaller-scale manufacturers like Quanex, Worthington, and others moved from scale to scope economies in manufacturing, becoming niche manufacturers for new product markets. Cable, television broadcasting, resorts, and leisure services crossed industrial category lines to re-create the entertainment industry. New technologies were applied to mundane goods and services both in their production and distribution in apparel and fashion industries. The list goes on.

Chapters 7, 8, and 9 detailed findings about leveraged buyout firms and manufacturing plants that were involved in buyout transactions. Overall, leveraged buyouts reversed patterns of sales declines or increased low rates of growth. The growth in sales volume was extensive after firms went private through an LBO. Productivity also increased at a firm level. After the sell-off of assets that had greater value outside the company, LBO firms engaged in new capital spending to create a stronger, more productive economic base in their core business. Prior to their buyout, LBO firms experienced patterns of job loss that appear to have been reversed by the core business after spin-offs occurred.

In examining LBO firms in detail, we found that they were comprised largely of *strategic buyouts,* which resulted in realizing synergies through product extension or market acquisition, and *defensive buyouts,* which resulted from recapitalizations by existing companies when faced with takeovers, or spin-offs and divestitures. Strategic buyouts, for the most part, seemed to be most likely to succeed, while some defensive buyouts (e.g., Freuhauf) only further entrenched failing management.

Plant-level data from manufacturing establishments showed that LBOs had significantly higher rates of productivity growth than did other plants in the same industry. The productivity impact of LBOs was much larger than previous estimates of the productivity impact of ownership changes through merger and acquisition in general would have suggested. Management buyouts appear to have had a particularly positive effect on productivity change. This finding is consistent with earlier results on employee buyouts. Plants involved in management buyouts were less likely to close after the buyout than were other plants. Though LBOs have been concentrated in lower technology industries, we found that most LBO firms increased their research and development spending and employment by at least as much as, and in some years more than, the industry average.

Giving noninvestment grade companies access to the public capital markets has lowered their cost of capital, positively affecting virtually every demographic, industrial, and economic sector. Today, working families might leave their children in a daycare center financed by high yield bonds (Kindercare or Le Petite Academie); seek medical treatment through high-yield-financed health care (Maxicare, Salick, Charter Medical); read a "high yield" newspaper (Ingersoll) or book (Macmillan, Maxwell); go to work at any number of manufacturing or service companies financed by high yield securities (steel, paper products, chemical processing, financing services);

return to high-yield-financed homes (Hovnanian Enterprises); let their children watch cable television (almost exclusively financed in the high yield market), and go out either to shop (Macy's), eat (Chi Chi's, Denny's) or see a movie (Lorimar, Warner, Orion).

Junk Bond Jitters: Shocks and Shake-Outs in the High Yield Market

In spite of a constant barrage of political controversy, the high yield market demonstrated an enormous capacity to absorb bad news and still grow. As already noted, earlier shocks had been felt in the high yield market—including the 1981-1982 recession, the LTV default in 1986, the stock market crash of October 1987, and the investigation and litigation against Drexel Burnham Lambert, the market leader, and its most valuable player, Michael Milken. In each case, high yield bond prices dropped sharply on bad news, but as investors took advantage of lower prices, returns and prices rebounded (see Figure 11-2).

Through the Summer and Fall of 1989, the junk bond market experienced the most serious shake-out of its young history. After repeated regulatory assaults, market changes, and legal distraction in the market's leadership ranks, the market jittered. Alarmist talk about a handful of poorly structured and relatively recent transactions shook Wall Street's steadiest hands (see Figure 11-3).

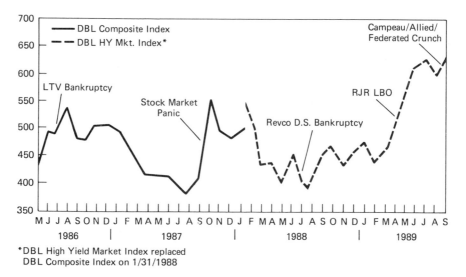

*DBL High Yield Market Index replaced
DBL Composite Index on 1/31/1988

Figure 11-2. High yield spreads—Index vs. Treasuries (Basic Points) (Drexel Burnham Lambert, High Yield Research).

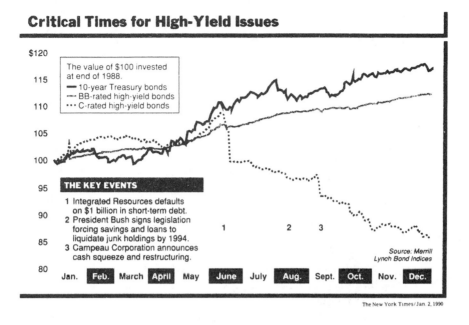

Figure 11–3. Critical times for high yield issues (*New York Times* 1/2/90).

The shake-out began when Integrated Resources defaulted on $1 billion in short-term debt in June 1989. By September, a cash-flow crunch at Campeau's empire, which had $2.6 billion in high yield debt outstanding (raised by First Boston), precipitated a further market decline. The high yield market reeled from news of other troubled transactions (Southland's default and Ohio Mattress's failure to bring a new issue to market). Corporate bond defaults more than doubled (from $4.96 billion to $11.05 billion), but still were less than 5 percent of total market value. The average price of bonds on the high yield market dropped 1.6 percent on average, but by more than 20 percent on more speculative issues. Compared to the stock market's 7 percent drop in a single day, the high yield market jitters disproportionately riveted the attention of market observers. The volatility was more than high yield investors had been used to. Financial Cassandras reveled in sucker-punching the junk bond market as it faltered.

Describing the turbulence in the junk bond market calls for explanation. In sifting through the shake-out, it is important to understand the structural market changes that led to weakness in the market, the impact of regulatory pressures, and the consequences for the debt and equity markets as we enter a new decade.

Structural Factors

By the close of the decade, the size and composition of the companies in the high yield market had changed. Signaling the contribution of high yield financial strategies, nearly $23 billion worth of original noninvestment grade issues were creamed from the junk bond market and upgraded to investment grade credit quality. Firms like MCI Communications, ITEL, Hasbro, Occidental Petroleum, Chrysler, and Enron became part of the investment grade market.

Though the quality sector of the junk bond market continued to grow, the increase in defaults and fears of recession received more visibility. Only nine companies (Eastern Air Lines, Southmark, Integrated Resources, LTV, Texaco, Revco, P.S. New Hampshire, Griffin Resorts, and SCI Television) made 44 percent of all defaults between 1977 and 1989. Most of the troubled credits hitting the headlines were transactions that had taken place in 1987 and 1988.

What had happened to the size and composition of the junk bond market that led to the most recent deals being the shakiest? As can be seen from Figure 11-4, the industrial composition of the high yield market shifted slightly as it grew. The energy, agriculture, and mining sectors which produced defaults in the late 1970s, were largely abandoned. Manufacturing and financial, insurance, and real estate issues increased significantly. Integrated Resources and Southland, two of the largest defaults, were in the troubled

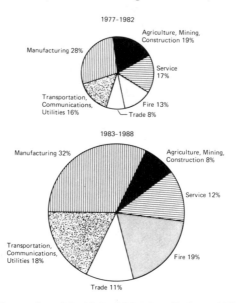

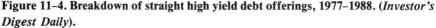

Figure 11-4. Breakdown of straight high yield debt offerings, 1977–1988. (*Investor's Digest Daily*).

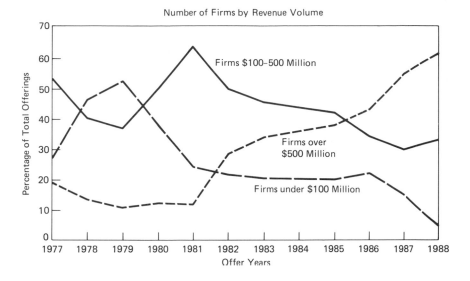

Figure 11-5. Distribution of straight high yield debt offering by firm, 1977–1988 (Drexel Burnham Lambert).

real estate sector. Figure 11-5 describes shifts in the high yield market that resulted from changes in firm size of issuers. With the growth of the high yield market, the new debt issues were increasingly by large firms. As we see in the graph, in 1979, firms with sales below $100 million comprised over 50 percent of the market. By 1988, the market share of these smaller corporations had dropped to below 10 percent. Corporations with revenues over $500 million averaged about 11 percent of the market at the beginning of the 1980s, but had over 60 percent of all the dollars raised in the high yield market by the close of the decade. Small and medium-sized firms, which were the backbone of the high yield market during its growth phase, became underserved in recent years. In short, the junk bond market was not being recharged by the new, dynamic firms that were its core business.

Another indicator of this shift was the relative share of high yield proceeds that went to finance LBO restructurings of low-growth companies as opposed to financing internal growth and strategic acquisition for high-growth innovative firms. As Figure 11-6 indicates, the high yield share of LBO financing increased dramatically in 1987 and 1988 (Paulus and Waite, 1990).

With more of the high yield proceeds going to larger firms or LBOs of low-growth industrial sectors, the absolute and relative deal flow from high growth innovative firms diminished. With deal flow declining and the supply of capital increasing, prices soared on junk bond transactions, and the margin for error became very thin.

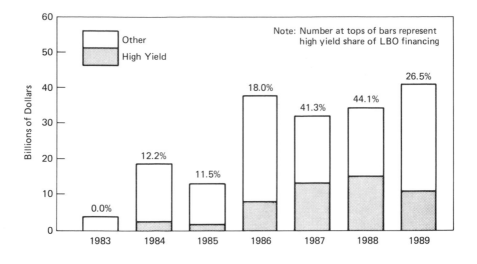

Figure 11–6. The role of high yield financing in LBOs (Security Data Corporation, and Morgan Stanley & Co., Inc.).

As takeovers and buyouts became fashionable during the late 1980s, special funds proliferated, with managers receiving large up-front fees plus overrides (typically of 20 percent). The charges of greed in the 1980s apply most appropriately to the fees charged by purely financial players in the numerous LBO funds that were created during this time. The LBO business became fee-driven with more of compensation taken from front-end fees than from the back-end profits generated by increased equity values. The situation of diminished flow of new, quality deals and increased supply of capital at higher costs is best described by Sir James Goldsmith:

> Huge amounts of equity deployed within a policy of maximum leverage created a pool of resources that swamped the available opportunities. For every billion of equity invested in the funds there were a further $9 billion available in the form of various kinds of debt. Another change was that the transactions became fee driven. Of course, some of the fund managers acted responsibly and did very well for the companies that they acquired and for their investors. But others were too keen to do deals at any price. In a normal acquisition, if the buyer pays too much he suffers. In these transactions, the higher the price, the higher the up-front fees. So the prices of businesses soared. (Sir James Goldsmith, November 1989)

By the late 1980s, as the pressure to "do deals" overrode discrimination, new issues flooded the market that were later discounted in the 1989 shakeout. As the prices of LBO deals soared, the entrepreneurial buyout that added economic value became superseded in the LBO market by defensive buyouts and friendly transactions. Increasingly, institutional investors and commercial banks let it be known that they would have no part of hostile transactions. For example, after Ron Perleman's attempt to buy Gillette and Boeing's panic that Boone Pickens was acquiring its stock, Citibank board members from both companies pressured the board to defer from participating in hostile transactions. Lazard Freres formed a "White Squire" fund for the sole purpose of providing equity capital to managers facing potential takeovers. The firm, whose eloquent partner Felix Rohatyn had coined the moniker "securities swill," issued junk bonds to finance this takeover defense fund. Through interlocking directorates on commercial banks and political pressure on pension funds (New York's governor recommended against investments in LBO blind pools), recapitalizations that resisted rather than promoted change in corporations became more common. Sir James Goldsmith elaborates:

> Following a hostile takeover, management is changed. In friendly deals, the old management is consolidated. In the worst, somewhat caricatural cases, the result is a company bought at too high a price, overleveraged and undercapitalized and managed by a team with a proven record of failure... instead of disposing of the diversified subsidiaries, those subsidiaries are retained and are leveraged at the maximum level, and without recourse to the parent.... The result is appalling. Instead of having a rich, tired old conglomerate, you have the same conglomerate, as diversified as before, but instead of being rich, each of its subsidiaries is leveraged to the maximum. So you end up with a conglomerate with a lot of hollow legs. (Sir James Goldsmith, November, 1989)

This seems to have occurred in companies like Fruehauf, Polaroid, and Goodyear, where existing management and corporate strategies dominated. Recent years have shown that the problems of bureaucratic waste first evident within diversified public corporations could also be re-created through leveraged buyouts and recapitalizations.

In summary, as the high yield market matured, many quality issues graduated into the investment grade market. As the high yield market drifted toward larger transaction size, it was not recharged by the smaller, more innovative firms in high growth sectors that had been its main engine of growth in earlier years. Coinciding with diminished deal flow was an increased demand for transactions by the new LBO investment pools that flooded the market. This created conditions that drove prices in the LBO market artificially high. The margin for error in cash-flow projections diminished as prices soared, and some companies got into trouble. This was compounded by a new-found use of leveraged and new financial technologies, not to promote changes but to defend managers in low growth sectors against them. All of these structural factors were seriously compounded by regulatory changes that artificially flooded the secondary market for high yield securities, thereby inhibiting demand for new issues.

Regulatory Factors

The impact of the public policy and public relations war against junk bonds became apparent in 1989. New regulations and a steady barrage of bad press generated additional selling pressure on the junk bond market. Under enormous pressure of a RICO indictment that would have frozen the firm's assets and possibly crippled it permanently, Drexel agreed to a settlement with the Securities and Exchange Commission that included a $650 million fine and Milken's departure from the firm he had helped build. Between the fine, legal fees, and lost business, Drexel estimated the cost of the "war," as it was referred to within the company, at over $2 billion.

More than money was lost. Between April and December 1989, facing higher costs in a declining market, Drexel reduced its employment by about 40 percent. Without Milken, facing widespread morale problems within the firm, and with a diminished capital base, Drexel could no longer lead the junk bond market as it had before. No longer could the firm support the market by committing funds to trading bonds in the secondary market, thus sapping liquidity in the market and generating further price volatility in thinner trading. As one trader told me, "We just can't afford to buy back the paper at any price; we can't afford to own it." Finally, in February 1990, Drexel Burnham declared bankruptcy, a result of its mounting problems, including its $650 million fine to the government.

Several corporate and state pension funds liquidated their junk bond portfolio as the legal and regulatory pressures increased. Fears of a recession drove other investors to think that many heavily indebted companies would be unable to pay interest on their loans in an economic downturn.

Some states limited the ability of state-chartered insurance companies and banks to invest in junk bonds. In September 1989, President Bush signed Congressional legislation forcing savings and loans to liquidate their junk holdings by 1990. This artificially increased the supply of bonds on the market and eliminated one of the few profitable investment the thrifts had made.

Although the September 1989 legislation technically gave the thrifts five years to sell their high yield paper, accounting regulations state that while a security that is to be held to maturity can be carried on an S&L's books at its purchase price or at par, securities that are to be sold before maturity must be "marked-to-market" by the end of the current quarter. Thrifts therefore had ninety days in which to sell their lower-quality paper.

The liquidation of high yield paper depressed the high yield market, forcing institutions that had not yet sold their bonds to mark down the value of their portfolios, impairing their capital positions and ultimately producing more candidates for the Resolution Trust Corp. (RTC), which may become the largest owner of high yield paper in the country.

The sell-off soon snowballed, causing a collapse in high yield prices that necessitated more selling on the part of the thrifts, which started a selling panic based on misguided regulation and fueled by ignorant media reports, all at a time when the market was least able to absorb the inventory: just after the government had taken $650 million out of Drexel Burnham.

Ironically, the paper that the S&Ls were selling was issued by companies that were still making interest payments and therefore providing the thrifts with solid income.

K.H. Thomas Associates, a Miami-based financial consulting firm, has estimated that the Federal Government held approximately 2 percent of the entire high yield bond market by early 1990. The face value of the bonds, $4.24 billion, represented 32 percent of all high yield bonds owned by the savings industry as of September 30, 1989.

Despite extensive empirical research on the performance of high yield bonds relative to other investments and the performance of junk bond issuers relative to their industries, and studies of the impact of a recession on default rates, the political environment in Washington and state capitals was largely poisoned against junk bonds. The perception that junk bonds were connected with scandals, hostile takeovers, and high risk won out over reality and led to political regulation of the market. Much of the motivation for misinformation and misperception about the junk bond market has been discussed in Chapter 10.

Additionally, the courts approved a panopoly of measures that further protected management from shareholders. Various poison pills, the use of minority ESOP as a takeover defense, and other protective measures were approved by the courts and contributed to a legal evolution transferring rights of corporate governance from shareholders to management.

In other proposed measures, Congress discussed reclassification for tax purposes of high yield original discount and pay-in-kind bonds with terms of five years or more as preferred stock. This would eliminate the interest deductibility of those types of junk bonds. Other bills proposed eliminating net operating loss tax carry backs in acquisitions, again eliminating a tax advantage available in financing ownership change.

Consequences

High Yield Market Segmentation: Quality Tiering

The structural shifts described earlier have led to segmentation in the high yield market by quality. The junk bond market was always very credit-specific. However, a tiering in the market between seasoned junk bond issuers with multiple issues on the market and a track record, new issues, and troubled credits has emerged. The first tier is comprised of issues whose yields range between 11 and 13 percent and comprise about $84 billion of the market.

Companies like Turner Broadcasting, Holiday Inn, and Viacom Media come to mind. The middle segment of the market is comprised of firms that are mostly new issues with about $72 billion of value, comprising 36 percent of the market. With the secondary market flooded by older issues divested by S&Ls and pension funds, the demand for new issues has diminished and the cost of capital to issuing firms has increased substantially.

Finally, troubled or less established credits grouped into the third tier—Pan Am, Western Union, and current defaults—comprise about 22 percent of the market or $44 billion in value, with yields over 16 percent.

The market corrected for overpricing of some junk bond issues through the shake-out and tiering, and it would thus be incorrect to assume structural weakness in the junk bond market. Just as the entire stock market reacted to rumors of trouble in one takeover (UAL, 1989), so, too, did the high yield market react to concern about troubled credits in its lower tier.

The risk of default among high yield companies is widely exaggerated. Failure rates of high yield issuers—and LBOs and their spin-offs—are remarkably less than for American businesses as a whole. Even one widely quoted study that claims a 34-percent default rate for new high yield issuers converts to a 2.8-percent annual average default rate over a period of twelve years, only slightly higher than previous studies. More to the point, perhaps, the study identified seventy-eight defaults out of a universe of 1,500. Yet, including the defaults, those 1,500 issues still provided investors with a positive return of 8.5 percent annually, a rate which over the same period compared favorably with Treasuries or high grade bonds.

Higher Costs of Capital? Dejunking Balance Sheets

The purpose of the high yield market, as explained in this book, was to lower costs of capital. Ironically, another market adjustment resulting from the high yield market shake-out could well be a return to equity. In a situation where the equity market continues to soar, the underlying equity value of high yield companies has continued to increase dramatically. The rise in market capitalization has coincided with a strong equity market and a troubled debt market. For new issues especially, buyers of high yield securities have been requiring enormous risk premiums, creating conditions whereby some companies could improve their capital structure by "dejunking" their balance sheet—refinancing higher-cost debt securities with new relatively lower-cost equity capital. This assumes, of course, that the new issue equity market recovers substantially enough to pick up the slack from a higher-cost junk bond market and that smaller firms can continue to afford the transaction costs of such refinancing (Yago and Tannenbaum, 1989).

Should equity markets falter or falter in general specifically for such refinancings, the consequences for sustaining economic growth could be serious. Existing and proposed restrictions on capital markets could strangle sources of growth capital that have fueled the expansion of new and renewing firms. Eliminating the tax advantages for employee buyouts, limiting deductibility of interest in LBOs, and other assorted limits on merger and acquisition activity would have severe consequences—inhibiting change in ownership and corporate strategies requiring business combination and competition. Combined, these assorted regulations of the capital markets could become a historical preservation act for entrenched managers, failing corporate organizations, and strategies and moribund industries that resist competition and change.

The only ones served by such restrictions on capital access are those interests threatened by the accountability that results from the reintegration of ownership and control in corporations. In some cases, smaller competitors sought more than market share; they sought control of other corporations. Political resistance in Congress and State Legislatures to structural changes in the (economy organized by large companies unable to compete economically) became rampant. The junk bond market became a convenient target to distract political hostilities from Congress itself and from uninspired corporate leadership by those President Roosevelt used to call "economic royalists."

With limited access to capital by small and medium-sized businesses (which have compensated for the contraction of the largest firms and their industrial sectors), the economy's ability to mitigate a recession will quickly atrophy. In short, economic growth has been kept alive through access to capital. Any restriction on that access or rise in the cost of capital will hamper firm and industrial capacity to counteract the challenges of an economic slowdown.

12

Toward a New Economy

In the 1980s, high yield securities played a constructive role in enabling the restructuring of companies in mature industries and the explosion of companies in new, innovative industries. As the 1990s begin, the future of high yield financing is uncertain. One thing is clear, however: Any actions that make it more difficult for small and midsized companies to obtain affordable capital also make it more difficult for the country's economy to grow and compete. If the political forces that shape regulations do so from a narrow economic perspective, their actions could have a devastating effect on the viability of U.S. firms in highly competitive global markets.

In concluding, it is important to review:

- barriers to continuing economic change toward equitable growth
- the new financial technologies from the high yield market that might overcome those barriers
- future sources of growth in domestic and foreign markets that might best benefit from high yield strategies in the 1990s and beyond by extending economic participation in capital markets and growth economies.

Barriers to Change

The signs of business barriers have begun to appear. New issue junk bond offerings have been withdrawn from the market; the initial public offering equity market has still not recovered from the October 1987 crash; and the funding squeeze for start-ups has tightened considerably (capital commitments to venture capital funds have fallen as investors have sold off their venture capital holdings and have withdrawn funds from start-ups).

Smaller companies are already feeling the pinch. A survey of fifty-eight banks conducted by the Federal Reserve in January found that in the past six months, 60 percent had tightened standards for loans "below investment-grade commercial and industrial customers"—basically, small and medium-size businesses (*Wall Street Journal,* March 18, 1990). It is not likely this trend will improve until the government realizes what its policies are doing.

To overcome these emerging business barriers will require the kind of ongoing economic experimentation that began in the 1980s. What form will twenty-first century companies take? Employee and management buyouts and buyins, takeovers and makeovers, start-ups, follow-ons, and turnarounds are all emerging in defining the strategic direction and financial structure that improves outcomes for workers and consumers, owners and managers, investors and companies.

The requirement for most companies over the next few years will be to move beyond dogmatic corporate financing decisions to more dynamic capital structures that blend debt *and* equity in their most appropriate combinations to raise capital and moderate costs. As the high yield market has grown in recent years, new structures of debt and equity securities (and combinations of both) have been devised to develop our financial technology and hence reduce capital costs. To sustain and extend economic growth in the changing global economy, we will need more high yield advances, not a return to rigid, costly, and restrictive credit and financial practices.

Innovative High Yield Instruments

A wide range of innovative financing instruments have developed within the high yield market. The focus of these innovations has been not only the restructuring of the ownership and organization of companies, but the current and future income-producing potential of a company's assets. The application of these innovations to new promising sectors of growth in the United States and in countries requiring restructuring and innovation, will be important in the years ahead to realize the economic potential of the political reforms in Latin America and Western and Eastern Europe. In developing new financial technologies, Milken countered the conventional wisdom of corporate finance that the choice of financing was a black or white decision between debt versus equity. The spectrum of securities in the high yield market contained significant equity components. As Milken described it, his role and that of other financiers, as one that, works with corporate balance sheets through an endless array of tools to create capital structures which facilitate corporate growth. As a company matures or the environment changes, its financial needs change. It is the financier's job to provide the relevant tools which enable a company to adapt to change. (Milken, 1990)

In short, straight debt and straight equity are antiquated financial categories that ignore the demands for flexibility in financing in an ever changing economic environment.

Table 12-1 reviews some of the innovative high yield instruments that have developed to produce flexibility and options for lowering capital costs. *Commodity-related* securities have allowed companies to borrow at substantially lower rates by tying their interest rates to their performance or to the commodity they produce. Silver- and copper-indexed bonds (Sunshine Mining, Magma Copper) were used to save and expand important mining companies. At Sunshine, the company's most important mine closed in 1986, due to depressed silver prices relative to labor costs. With new financing, the company also signed a new wage contract, which reduced operating costs through a flexible wage scale based on the price of silver and a profit sharing element for employees. Aligning the interests of management, labor, and bondholders to the income stream of the company enhanced flexibility. Similar financing was used in oil-indexed bonds, which securitized oil assets for NRM Energy and Texas International, enabling them to survive and recover.

Deferred payment securities—including zero-coupon bonds, split coupon bonds, and pay-in-kind bonds—enabled flexibility in payment schedules that financed growth and restructuring in a number of companies. Charter Medical is a good example of how these securities were used. Charter Medical, a pioneer in providing psychiatric care, early on perceived the severe problem of underbedding for mental diseases. Employment grew from 1,237 employees in 1970 to 17,000 in 1988, when these flexible securities enabled a management/employee buyout of the company. Duracell, Safeway Stores, and the RJR leveraged buyouts are other examples in which payment was deferred to accomplish financing and income growth.

Hybrid securities, including exchangeable preferred stock, various forms of convertible stock, and equity appreciation rights, have enabled companies to extend their maturities further out than had been available from more conventional straight debt. For most of the 1980s, costs of capital were lowered by nearly half when companies substituted convertible securities for equity. Companies like Farley, MCI, and Memorex used these instruments; troubled banks (e.g., Mellon) used stand-by equity as well. McCaw Communications, for example, used such securities to evolve from a collection of radio station assets and a tiny cable TV operation into the largest cellular telephone company in the nation. Assets grew from $14 million to more than $2.1 billion, and the company's cellular licenses represent a potential customer

Table 12-1. Innovative High Yield Instruments

Commodity–related debt

–silver–indexed bonds
 Sunshine Mining

–copper–indexed coupon bonds
 Magma Copper

–Oil–indexed bonds
 NRM Energy
 Texas International

Floating–rate debt

–adjustable–rate preferred
 Levitz
 Neoax

–variable rate bonds ($11 billion)*
 Knoll International
 Nortek
 Mesa Petroleum

Deferred payment securities

–zero–coupon bonds ($7 billion)*
 RJR Holdings
 Storer Communications

–split–coupon bonds ($32 billion)*
 Charter Medical
 Duracell

–pay in–kind bonds and preferred stock
 ($12 billion)*
 Charter Medical
 Safeway Stores

Hybrid securities

–exchangeable preferreds
 Farley
 Memorex Telex
 RJR Holdings

–high–premium convertibles
 MCI
 Storage Technology

–equity appreciation rights
 MSA Shopping Malls

–stand–by equity with puts/calls
 Mellon Bank

Multicurrency issues

–currency hedge bonds
 Fairfax

–dollar–denominated foreign issues
 Bond Brewing
 Linter Textiles
 Trans–Resources

–nondollar bonds
 Coastal (Yen)

Transition securities

–increasing–rate notes ($22 billion)*
 Anacomp
 Cherokee
 Kaisertech

–resets
 Jim Walter
 KinderCare Learning Centers

–extendibles
 Mattel
 Turner Broadcasting

Exchange offers

–debt for equity
 Teledyne
 Northwest Industries

–debt for debt
 Nortek
 Southland

–equity for debt
 Reading & Bates
 Western Union

Collateralized bond obligations

 WSGP
 Duff & Phelps

Asset–backed securities

–mortgage–backed bonds ($10 billion)*
 Bally's Grand
 Days Inns

–secured equipment trust bonds
 Eastern Air Lines
 Trans World Airlines

–liquidating trusts
 Grant Street

*Amount issued

base that is 70 percent greater than that of its nearest competitor. Employment has grown by 60 percent since the company's first high yield offering in 1986.

Multicurrency issues enabled cross-national merger or transnational expansion to occur. In some cases the issuing of non-dollar-denominated bonds (e.g., Coastal) took advantage of different currency conditions to lower overall capital costs.

Transition securities, including increasing rate notes, resets, and extendibles, added additional flexibility to corporate financing in the high yield market by adjusting repayment to anticipated changes in the income stream of the company. Using such high yield securities, KinderCare Learning Systems became the largest provider of child-care services in the country, responding to society's need for the professionalization and standardization of daycare. Sales grew from $137.1 million in 1982 to $653 million in 1988, as employment more than doubled (to 19,000). After a failed diversification strategy into home video and computers, Mattel used these types of securities to recapitalize and refocus on its successful toy business. Turner Broadcasting also used these flexible versions of high yield securities.

Exchange offers, including debt-for-equity and equity-for-debt swaps were used by troubled companies like Western Union and Teledyne. *Asset-backed securities* including mortgage-backed bonds (used by hotel chains like Day's Inn, Motel 6, and Holiday Inn) and secured equipment trust bonds (used by airlines like TWA and Eastern) offered investors security in restructured companies not obtainable otherwise and got needed capital to the companies to shift strategic direction towards new routes, service, and markets.

In response to problems of selling bonds in the depressed junk market, the repackaging and diversification of those securities has been made possible through *collateralized bond obligations* (CBOs). CBOs derive from additional securitization in order to attract investors. They resemble collateralized mortgage obligations, in which a pool of mortgages is turned into a security. In CBOs, a large, diversified group of high yield bonds are put into a pool that is overcollateralized (e.g., a $100 million CBO issue is backed by bonds with a face value of $150 million). The diversification and additional interest payments enable the pool of noninvestment grade bonds to achieve an investment grade rating any single issue would be unable to secure.

Future Sources of Growth

Where will economic growth come from in the 1990s? Restructurings of mature industries and high growth firms in new sectors will continue. Restructurings through LBOs will probably fall off during the 1990s. The focus will shift toward smaller transactions that are value driven and not fee driven. This will include an increasing number of workouts of troubled credits and transitions among family and closely held companies both in the United States and Western Europe that originated after World War II and whose management is nearing retirement age. Fast-growing, innovative sectors of the economy will continue to seek high yield financing.

As in the past, the greatest sources of economic growth could come from sectors currently excluded from the capital markets. Expanding economic participation in market economies is central to both domestic and foreign economic agendas for the 1990s and beyond. This is particularly true for minority businesses in the United States and the integration of regional economies in Latin America and Europe resulting from the geopolitical shifts of the post-postwar era.

Mainstreaming Minority Businesses

Evidence of alarming diametric trends in business and the economy abounds between the covers of accumulating U.S. data. A polarized economy is emerging, characterized by severe shortages in skilled labor and a broad class of structurally unemployed and increasingly unemployable persons. To further economic growth in the 1990s, participation in new markets, and technological innovation, revitalized and restructured industries must be expanded to include the growing African-American, Hispanic, Asian, female, and immigrant populations. Mainstreaming minority businesses is a central item for the economic agenda of the 1990s.

Business formation and survival rates remain low in many distressed regions and minority communities, as does job formation. Lack of equity and especially of debt capital (Bates, 1989) has been demonstrated to be a major cause of business failure and of the absence of economic value creation. Government has failed to initiate or successfully implement policies and programs to address these issues. Financial redlining, both by financial institutions and through state and federal regulations, has resulted.

Restricting access to capital could force us to face the twenty-first century with American labor and capital, business and markets, hopelessly in search of one another. It is axiomatic in business that equity and economic efficiency enhance one another. However, if we should fail to maximize both, too many people and too many communities will be left behind, increasing social and economic costs that will curtail our competitive strength and diminish our future.

Applying new financial technologies to grow businesses in the minority communities could democratize capital further, leveraging long-term investment strategies in support of what are the most pressing social and economic needs of the day. The application of new financial technologies reviewed in this book could carve new channels of capital to generate new waves of market creation and economic growth. The formula of fixed-rate, affordable, and flexible financing that was successful in the 1980s needs application to these sectors of the economy as well. Market-driven policies that focus on capital access and the production of wealth and income will move us beyond beggar-thy-neighbor distribution politics that hold economic progress hostage to the adversarial relations of a zero-sum economy.

Developing Third World and Eastern European Economies

The requirements for economic development for new entrants into the market economy differ little from those that have been discussed throughout this book. Access to capital, the development of human resources, and the creation and distribution of new products and services to solve social needs are the ingredients that proved successful in the high yield market of the past and will create the international high yield market of the future.

Transnational regional economies are integrating in Western and Eastern Europe and in North and South America. The European integration of 1992 is being rewritten to include Eastern Europe. The successful conversion away from a Cold War defense economy requires the economic development of the Soviet Union. The geographic destiny of integrating North and Latin American economies in order to create cross-national companies that can compete globally is critical to the prosperity and stability of this hemisphere.

The challenges of the geopolitical shifts of the post-postwar era are mind boggling. The political reforms and movement towards democracy in Latin America and Eastern Europe cry out for economic policies that are similarly pathbreaking. Though the differences between these situations are vast, several key issues remain common to countries and companies in both contexts.

With the macroeconomic reforms of budgetary and fiscal policies emerging in countries as diverse as Mexico, Bolivia, and Poland, taking the next step requires promoting microeconomic policies to encourage business development. In Latin America, the challenge of reversing capital flight and attracting the return of national capital also exists.

All of these countries have the common problem of monetarizing the currency, that is, insuring that currencies are backed by productive capacity in the market economy and not only by government printing presses. Solving this problem could be aided by creating secondary capital market instruments that will retain new capital, attract the return of national capital, and develop strategic foreign investment partners. This would build confidence in the economic system and generate new goods and services.

Creating effective capital markets within and between these countries to globally trade their securities would increase market liquidity and help promote economic participation by workers, entrepreneurs, and investors domestic and foreign. In all of these countries, economic reforms must now include restructuring large, inefficient economic units that have been nationalized and converting them into new privately owned centers of growth, income generation, and jobs. In short, the pattern of decentralization, deconglomeration, and democratization of the economy must now take place.

Where will the money to finance these economic changes come from? How can the changes be organized? First, social equity can be insured by creating economic equity. Developing the equity base of these countries can be achieved through privatization by employee and management buyouts and joint venture structures with foreign investors. Privatization through the democratization of capital combines the economic requirements of growth with the social and political goals of expanded market participation. The definition of economic participation can be extended to include cooperation of all sectors of the economy.

The types of cash-flow-oriented equity participating debt instruments that grew up in the junk bond market have clear-cut application here. Commodity-related debt instruments would work well in resource-rich countries such as Mexico, Venezuela, and the Soviet Union. Exchange-offer swap mechanisms could reduce debt in Poland and Bolivia as they have in Chile and Brazil. Asset-backed securities and other securitization mechanisms might have application in heavy industries in Eastern Europe and Latin America. Transition securities could finance commercialization of and exports from new scientific and medical technology-based companies in the Soviet Union. As in the United States, economic experimentation will accompany growth in the creative application of these new financial technologies to new forms of business organization.

High yield strategies of the future will continue to reintegrate ownership and control through a financial incentive structure that links investors and worker/manager-owners to spur operating efficiency and employee productivity, creating new economic value. This will restore the accountability that has been lost by corporate and government bureaucrats alike.

The evidence is coming in that the application of these strategies in other parts of the world works. In the United Kingdom, recent restructuring demonstrated the improved performance experienced by new takeovers, privatizations, and ESOPs. Similar evidence is available on formerly state-owned companies in the electrical and machinery industries in France.

In Italy, associations of small to medium-sized industrial producers in Emilia-Romagna and Tuscany are models of cooperatively financed manufacturing networks of globally competitive companies in industries as diverse as steel products and textiles. High risk is shared by financial institutions and companies with rewards similarly distributed. In Spain, the organization chart of the Modgragon Workers Cooperative, which owns 160 firms comprising 25 percent of the Basque country's employment looks a lot like an LBO association financed by a blind pool.

New corporate organizations and strategies engendered by high yield financing can continue to create opportunities for social and economic change. The definition of a new economy and new century hang in the balance.

Methodological Appendix

The data analysis chapters of this book are based upon extensive empirical research projects that began at the Economic Research Bureau in 1986. Chapters 4-6 are based upon a study we published in July 1988 entitled, "The Uses and Effects of High Yield Securities in U.S. Industry." In this study, I led a team of researchers including Drs. Gelvin Stevenson, Charlene Seifert, and Sen-Yuan Wu to examine the effects of high yield financing on employment, productivity, sales, capital investment, and capital spending in 755 public companies, which comprised a subset of the 1,200 companies that had issued high yield securities by 1987 for which we could find consistent data. In many cases, the data we were able to obtain required confirmation. Frequently, we had to confer with industry analysts, review prospectuses, examine 10-Ks, or study newspaper reports to fill in missing data, correct data anomalies, or cross check our findings. We also examined case histories of twenty-one high yield firms, to provide an in-depth perspective on how companies used junk bonds to achieve their corporate objectives.

In this study, information from a variety of data sources was assembled: COMPUSTAT, IDD Information Services, Securities Data Company, Inc., Moody's Investor Service, Standard & Poor's, U.S. Bureau of Labor Statistics, U.S. Survey of Current Business, Drexel Burhham Lambert, and the Federal Reserve Bank's Flow of Funds Accounts.

For the purpose of this study, we considered new issues that were below investment grade, including straight debt, convertible securities, low-rated preferred stock, and split issues. We also included nonrated issues with equivalent characteristics. An issue is considered noninvestment grade if it is unrated or rated below BBB by Standard & Poor's or below Baa by Moody's.

Aggregated data on all public high yield issues from 1980 to 1987 were utilized to assess the role of high yield securities in overall patterns of corporate debt. Federal Reserve Flow of Funds data were used to derive credit market information, and compared to data on the high yield market from Drexel Burnham Lambert.

After reviewing aggregate information on the size of the high yield market, the distribution of issues, and changes over time, we focused our study on issuing firms that reported employment, sales, and investment data. The purpose of the study was to investigate the impact of high yield financing on corporate economic performance.

Once we had determined the number of firms reporting information on our key performance measures, we pursued two major methods of investigation—cohort analysis for firms reporting available data from 1980 to 1986 and before/after analysis for the Class of 1983.

To correct for the addition of new issuing firms, we studied high yield firms using cohort analysis, i.e., analyzing the change in each variable (employment, sales, capital expenditures, etc.) from the year the firm first issued a high yield security until 1986.

By analyzing the behavior of annual firm cohorts, we were able to investigate the data reported on the number of firms appearing in our high yield data set for any given year and then track the performance of that firm's employment, sales, or expenditures, changing the number of firms on the changes of employment, sales, capital expenditures, etc. Cohort analysis allowed us to track the average annual changes among high yield issuing firms reporting data in consecutive years and correct for any aggregate bias or distortion of average annual changes by more summary analysis.

To further isolate the impacts of high yield financing, we separately considered those firms that issued high yield securities in 1983. This allowed us to track the impacts for three years before and three years after the issue. Although this before/after analysis is limited to 163 firms that issued high yield securities in 1983, it controls for time order and the effects of issues on corporate performance more systematically than even the cohort analysis.

Given the constraints of existing data as currently reported to the SEC and gathered by proprietary data base firms (e.g., COMPUSTAT, Dun & Bradstreet, Standard & Poor's, Moody's), we are not able to isolate impact of growth through acquisition from internal growth effects. The fact that rates of restructuring appear to be relatively consistent between investment grade and noninvestment grade firms, however, provides a control against any systematic variation or bias in our data. Also, even when growth resulted from acquisition, there is no apparent reason to discount its impact. Since employment appears to grow under new ownership, growth through acquisition would not necessarily have occurred under the firm's previous ownership or management. Our study does not correct for employment growth through acquisitions, nor does it correct for job loss through divestitures.

From the data base of high yield issuers from 1980 to 1986, we selected case study firms from each industrial category in order to obtain a variety of examples of how issue proceeds were used. We reviewed prospectuses, quarterly and annual reports (10-Q and 10-K statements filed with the SEC), along with investment analysis reports, new stories, and other corporate information available through DATEXT. To gather more information about the background of various companies and their use of high yield securities, we also conducted interviews with securities analysts and corporate representatives.

This first research project, however, told only one part of the high yield story. A large percentage of high yield financing is done privately, and a great deal of high yield debt is used to fund private companies or take companies private. While the absence of data on private placements is a thorny problem, enough data were available on LBOs to undertake two comprehensive studies of these transactions. The firm-level data on LBOs reported in Chapters 7 and 8 were based on work completed with Jeff Tannenbaum and Pamela Commeta-Berndt to review the effects of LBOs on a wide variety of performance variables in a study published in June 1989 entitled "LBOs in Focus: The Role of Debt in Ownership Change and Industrial Competitiveness in the Eighties." We examined pre- and postbuyout performance in net sales, market productivity, labor productivity, and operating income. We also considered the impact of the LBO on the firm's working capital position, interest coverage, capital spending, and employment. Aggregate data were gathered along with in-depth studies of specific companies. We selected ten case histories from a wide range of industries, covering strategic and defensive buyouts, including both successful and unsuccessful transactions.

Of the 169 LBOs during our study period, consistent data were available for only forty-three transactions. However, these forty-three transactions comprised over 65 percent of the total dollar value of LBOs during the study period. For many of the variables we examined, complete data were available only for a subset of our sample. Even then, Trinet and DATEXT figures often disagreed. Extensive research in 10-Ks and other SEC filing helped us fill in data gaps and resolve apparent conflicts.

Information from a variety of data sources was assembled for this study: Drexel Burnham Lambert, Mergers and Acquisitions File, DATEXT, Mergerstat Review, W. T. Grimm & Co., IDD, COMPUSTAT, Standard & Poor's, Survey of Current Business, DOC, Worldwide Economic Outlook, Morgan Stanley & Co, Inc., Department of Commerce, Trinet, and the U.S. Department of Labor.

Specific data on all public LBOs from 1980 to 1988 were utilized to assess the role of firms pre- and post-LBO. Information obtained electronically from DATEXT on firms' 10-K reports and hardcopy 10-Ks from disclosure were used to derive financial information. Electronic and hardcopy reports, 1981-1987, from Trinet were used to assess the role of LBOs on employment and sales data.

After reviewing aggregate information on the size of the LBO market, the distribution of buyouts, and changes over time, we focused our study on firms that reported management and operational performance, debt and investment performance, employment, and sales data. The purpose of the study was to investigate the impact of LBOs before and after on corporate economic performance.

Once we had determined the number of firms reporting information on our key performance measures, we pursued two major methods of investigation—cohort analysis for firms reporting available data from 1979 to 1987, concentrating on cohort years 1984-1986, and before/after analysis (pre/post LBO).

We studied LBO firms using cohort analysis, i.e., analyzing the change in each variable (employment, sales, capital expenditures, invested capital, debt and investment performance, management and operational performance, etc.) where data were available.

By analyzing the behavior of annual firm cohorts, we were able to investigate the data reported on the number of firms appearing in our LBO data set for any given year and then track the performance of that firm's employment, sales, capital expenditures, invested capital, debt and investment performance, and management and operational performance over time. This approach allowed us to eliminate the effects of the changing number of firms on the changes in the above variables. Cohort analysis allowed us to track the average annual changes among LBO firms reporting data in consecutive years and correct for an aggregate bias or distortion of average annual changes by additional analysis.

To further isolate the impacts of the LBOs, we separately considered those firms that went through an LBO in 1984, 1985, and 1986 exclusively. This allowed us to track the impacts for at least two years post-buyout. Although this before/after analysis is limited to forty-three firms that went through an LBO, 114 firms were analyzed for employment and sales data. Post-LBO performance data in some cases were not available due to the privatization of the firm, whereby the firm was no longer responsible for publicly reporting information to the SEC. From the data base of LBO firms from 1979 to 1987, we selected case study firms from each industrial category in order to obtain a variety of examples of how pre- and post-LBO performance affected the firms.

Chapter 9 was based on a follow-up LBO study in which I joined Drs. Frank Lichtenberg of Columbia University and Donald Siegel at the National Bureau of Economic Research, and now my colleague at the Harriman School of Management at Stony Brook, in examining changes in productivity, employment, and research and development in plants involved in major LBOs and management buyouts, a study completed in July 1989 entitled, "LBOs and Industrial Competitiveness: The Effects of LBOs on Productivity, Employment, and Research and Development." By studying plant-level data, we were able to provide fresh insights on the effects of these transactions and overcome some of the limitations of firm-level analysis.

We assembled our information from a variety of sources. Building on data from *Investors Digest Daily* and the Securities Industry Association, we accessed a Mergers and Acquisitions Data Base for a complete list of LBO transactions valued at over $35 million from 1981 through 1986. Since data on individual LBOs were not available for smaller transactions, we limited our investigation to major LBOs.

In examining total-factor productivity, we linked data contained in our list of major LBOs to an extract of data on manufacturing establishments in the Bureau of Census Longitudinal Research Data file (LRD). The last year for which Census data were available was 1986. This was unfortunate because most of the LBOs during our study period occurred in the last three years, and we were thus limited in our ability to measure behavior in the years following the LBO. Nevertheless, our sample was large enough for us to obtain reasonbly precise estimates for at least two years following the buyout.

One major advantage of the Census Bureau data set is that unlike publicly available data sources, they include observations on both privately owned and publicly held firms and establishments. Most LBOs are, at least initially, privately owned. Privately held companies are generally not required by the SEC to issue financial data, which clearly poses a problem for assessing postbuyout performance.

A second important advantage of the establishment-level Census data is that they allowed us to analyze partial-firm or subsidiary LBOs. Of the LBOs in our sample, 46 percent were of divisions of firms rather than entire firms. Since divisional or lower-level data are not generally publicly available, even for publicly held firms, previous studies have had to confine their attention to buyouts of entire firms. Not only do such studies ignore an important segment of the LBO market, their data may obscure the effects of divestitures and spinoffs on postbuyout performance. Fortunately, our plant-level data allowed us to circumvent some of these problems, tracing the performance of LBO plants regardless of whether or not they remained a part of their original parent companies.

We checked for LBO activity first at the firm level, and then at the partial-firm level, assigning appropriate codes to our variables based on whether the entire firm was included in our list of LBOs, or whether the establishment's SIC code appeared in our list of SIC codes for divisions of the firm involved in LBOs.

To determine the SIC code for a given establishment, we utilized a business description of the unit from the Mergers and Acquisitions Data Base provided by the Securities Industry Association. Additional information about the industrial activities of divisions or companies was obtained from *Standard & Poor's Registry of Corporations* and the *Directory of Corporate Affiliations*.

We tried to address potential measurement error problems systematically. If two subsidiaries of a firm both had plants in the same industry and only one was engaged in an LBO, we could erroneously assume that both plants were involved in LBOs. Fortunately, McGuckin and Andrews (1988) found that firms rarely divest only some of their plants in a given four-digit industry. And even if random errors did occur, they would simply reduce the magnitude and significance of the estimated differences in behavior between LBO and non-LBO establishments.

Our data allowed us to distinguish between management buyouts and other LBOs. MBOs accounted for 45 percent of the value of all major LBOs from

1981 through 1986. Among the major LBOs captured in our extract of the LRD, however, MBOs accounted for only 27 percent of total value, perhaps because management is less likely to participate in LBOs in manufacturing than in other sectors.

Our extract from the LRD contained data on 20,493 manufacturing establishments for the year 1981. Of these establishments, 1,108, or 5.4 percent, were involved in at least one major LBO from 1981 to 1986. Over 35 percent of the LBO establishments were involved in MBOs, and about 30 percent were involved in partial-firm LBOs. These two attributes are correlated: MBOs account for 47 percent of partial-firm LBOs, but only 30 percent of full-firm LBOs.

Bibliography

Abbott III, T. A. (1988). "Price dispersion in U.S. manufacturing," Center for Economic Studies Working Paper. Washington, D.C.: U.S. Bureau of the Census.

Abernathy, W. J., Clark, K. B., and Kantrow, Alan M. (1983). *Industrial renaissance: Producing a competitive future for America.* New York: Basic Books, Inc.

Altman, E.I. (1990). *"Measuring corporate bond mortality and performance,"* New York: New York University.

_____ (ed.). (1990). *The high yield debt market: Investment performance and economic impact,* Homewood, Illinois: Dow Jones-Irwin, pp. 41-57.

_____, and Nammacher, S.A. (1987). *Investing in Junk Bonds: Inside the High Yield Debt Market.* New York: John Wiley & Sons.

Amihud, Yakov (May 1988). "Management buyouts & shareholders wealth." Prepared for the Conference on Management Buyouts. New York: New York University.

_____, and Mendelson, Haim (December 1986). "Asset pricing and the bid-ask spread." *Journal of Financial Economics* 17, 223-249.

Asquith, P., Mullins, D., and Wolff, E. (September 1989). "Original issue high yield bonds: Aging analysis of defaults, exchanges and calls." *Journal of Finance,* 44-4, 923-953.

Atkinson, T. R. (1967). *Trends in Corporate Bond Quality.* Cambridge, Mass.: National Bureau of Economic Research.

Bartel, A. and Lichtenberg, F. (October 1988). "Technical change, learning, and wages." Cambridge, Mass.: National Bureau of Economic Research Working Paper No. 2732.

Bates, T. (1989). "Small business viability in the urban ghetto milieu." *Journal of Regional Science,* Vol. 29, No. 4.

Berle, A. Jr., and G. Means (1932). *The Modern Corporation and Private Property.* New York: Macmillan.

Bernanke, B., Campbell, J. (1988). "Is there a corporate debt crisis?" Brookings Paper on Economic Activity, 1. Washington, D.C.: Brookings Institution.

Bhide, A. (July 1988). "Causes and consequences of hostile takeovers." Unpublished doctoral dissertation, Harvard University. Cambridge, Mass.

Birch, D. (1979). "The job generation process." Program on Neighborhood and Regional Change, MIT. Prepared for U.S. Department of Commerce, Economic Development Administration. Washington, D.C.

_____ (1987). *Job Creation in America.* New York: The Free Press.

Birch, D. L., and MacCracken, S. (January 1981). "Corporate evolution: A micro-based analysis." Cambridge, Mass.: MIT Program on Neighborhood and Regional Change.

Blume, M., and Keim, D. (December 1984). *Risk and Return Characteristics of Lower-Grade Bonds.* Philadelphia: University of Pennsylvania, Wharton School, Rodney White Center for Financial Research.

_____ and _____ (August 1989). "Realized returns and defaults on lower-grade bonds: The cohort of 1977 and 1978," Rodney L. White Center working paper, The Wharton School, University of Pennsylvania, Philadelphia, PA.

"Born-again stocks," *Forbes* (March 20, 1989) 210-11.

Broske, M. S. (September 1987) "Do investment grade bonds differ from one another indefault risk?" Oklahoma State University, College of Business Administration Working Paper 87-18.

Brown, C., and Medoff, J. (May 1987). "The impact of firm acquisitions on labor." Washington, D.C.: National Bureau of Economic Research.

Bull, I. O. (May 1988). "Management performance in leveraged buyouts: An empirical analysis." Presented at the Conference on Management Buyouts, New York University, New York.

Carney, W. (March 30, 1987). "Examine the motives of junk-bond critics." *Business Week,* p. 18.

Congressional Research Service (Economics Division) (December 1987). "Leveraged buyouts & the pot of gold: Trends, public policy, and case studies." Washington, D.C.: Government Printing Office, 1-96.

DeAngelo, H., and DeAngelo, L. (May/June 1987). "Management buyouts of publicly traded corporations." Reprinted from *Financial Analysts Journal* 1-12.

_____, _____, and Rice, Edward M. (Summer, 1984). "Going private: The effects of a change in corporate ownership structure." *Midland Corporate Finance Journal* Vol. 2, No. 2, 35-43.

Dunne, T., Roberts, M., and Samuelson, L. (1987). "The impact of plant failure on employment growth in the U.S. manufacturing sector." Pennsylvania State University, University Park, PA.

Ellsworth, R. R. (April 1987). "U.S. business should take on more debt." Graduate Management Center. The Claremont Graduate School, Claremont, CA.

ERISA (1974). Employee Retirement Income Security Act of 1974.

Fridson, M., and Wahl, F. (July 1987). "Fallen angels versus original issue of high-yield bonds." *High Performance: The Magazine on High Yield Bonds.* New York: Morgan Stanley.

General Accounting Office (February 1988). "Financial markets: Issuers, purchases and purposes of high yield, non-investment grade bonds." Washington, D.C., General Accounting Office.

Ghemwat, P., and Nalebuff, B. (January 1987). "The devolution of declining industries." *Discussion papers in economics.* Princeton, N.J.: Princeton University, Woodrow Wilson School of Public and International Affairs, No. 120.

Gogel, D.J. (July 1987). "Corporate restructuring, management fights the raiders." *Management Review,* 28-34.

Goldsmith, Sir James (November 16, 1989). Speech given at the International Mergers & Acquisitions Second Annual Conference. London: Sponsored by the International Herald Tribune and Skadden, Arps, Slate, Meagher and Flom.

Grant's Interest Rate Observer.

Hall, B. (1988). "The effect of takeover activity on corporate research and development." *Corporate Takeovers: Causes and Consequences,* (ed.) Alan Auerback. Chicago: University of Chicago Press, 9-25.

Hatsopoulos, G. (1983). *High Costs of Capital: Handicap of American Industry.* Waltham, Mass.: Thermo Electron Corporation.

Herman, E., and Lowenstein, L. (April 1986). "The efficiency effects of hostile takeovers." New York: Columbia University Law School, Center for Law and Economic Studies Working Paper.

Hickman, W. B. (1958). "Corporate bond quality and investor experience." Princeton University Press and the National Bureau of Economic Research. Princeton, N.J. and Cambridge, MA.

Investor's Responsibility Research Center. (July 1989). "Review of state anti-takeover legislation." Washington, D.C.

Jensen, M. (May 1986). "Agency costs of free cash flow, corporate finance and takeovers." *American Economics Association Papers and Proceedings* 76.

Jensen, M.C. (January 1989). "Capital markets, organizational innovation, and restructuring." For presentation at the Board of Governors, Federal Reserve System, Washington, D.C.

_____, and Murphy, K. (March 1989). "Performance pay and top management incentives," unpublished working paper 89-059, Harvard Business School. Cambridge, MA.

_____, and Warner, J. B. (1988). "The distribution of power among corporate managers, shareholders, and directors." *Journal of Financial Economics* Vol. 20, 3-24.

Kaplan, S. (January 1988). "MBOs: Efficiency gains of value transfers?" Cambridge, Mass.: Harvard University, 1-39.

Kelso, L. O., and Kelso, P. H. (September 1987). "Leveraged buyouts good & bad." *Management Review* 28-31.

_____, and _____ (1986). *Democracy and economic power: Extending the ESOP Revolution*. Cambridge, MA: Ballinger Publishing Company

Kieschnick, R. (May 1988). "Management buyouts of public corporations: Analysis of prior characteristics." Presented at the Conference on Management Buyouts, New York University, New York, 1-43.

Kohlberg Kravis Roberts & Co. (with Deloitte Haskins & Sells) (Spring 1989). *Journal of Applied Corporate Finance*. Vol. 2, No. 1, 64-70.

Lehn, K., et al. (1986). "Noninvestment grade debt as a source of tender offer financing." Study commissioned by Securities Exchange Commission, Office of the Chief Economist. Washington, D.C.

Lehn, K., and Poulsen, A. (December 1988). "Free cash flow and stockholder gains in going private transactions." Washington, D.C.: Securities and Exchange Commission and University of Georgia.

Lewellen, W. G., and Kracow, W. A. (Winter 1987). "Inflation, corporate growth, and corporate leverage." *Financial Management* 29-36.

Lichtenberg, F. (June 1988). "The private R&D investment response to federal design and technical competitions." *American Economic Review* 78, 550-559.

_____, and Siegel, D. (January 1989). "The effect of takeovers on the employment and wages of central-office and other personnel." New York: Columbia University Graduate School of Business and National Bureau of Economic Research, 1-36.

_____, and _____ (1987). "Productivity and changes in ownership of manufacturing plants." *Brookings Papers on Economic Activity* 643-673. Washington, D.C.: Brookings Institution.

_____, and _____ (January 1989). "Using linked census R&D-LRD data to analyze the effect of R&D investment on total factor productivity growth." Discussion paper, Center for Economic Studies. Washington, D.C.: Bureau of the Census.

Lowenstein, L. (May 1985). "Management buyouts." *Columbia Law Review* Vol. 85, No. 4, 731-784.

_____, and Herman, E. S. (April 1986). "The efficiency effects of hostile takeovers." New York: The Center for Law and Economic Studies, Columbia University School of Law, Working Paper No. 20, 1-72.

McGuckin, R. H., and Andrews, S. H. (December 25-30, 1987). "The performance of lines of business purchased in conglomerate acquisitions." Presented at the American Economic Association meeting, Chicago.

_____, and Pascoe, G.A. (July 1988). "The longitudinal research database (LRD): Status and research possibilities." Center for Economic Studies Working Paper No. 88-2. Washington, D.C.: U.S. Bureau of the Census.

Marais, L., Schipper, K., and Smith, A. (June 1988). "Wealth effects of going private for senior securities." Working Paper.

Meltzer, A., and Richard, S. (1987). "Mortgaging America's corporations." Pittsburgh: Carnegie Mellon University.

Mergers and Acquisitions, various issues.

Miller, M. (Fall 1988). "The Modigliani-Miller propositions after thirty years." *Journal of Economic Perspectives,* Vol. 2, No. 4, 99-120.

Mitchell, M., and Lehn, K. (August 1988). "Do bad bidders become good targets?" Office of Economic Analysis, Securities and Exchange Commission. Washington, D.C.

Mitchell, M., and Netter, J. (March 30, 1988). "Stock market evidence from the October 1987 proposed takeover tax bill." Office of Economic Analysis. Washington, D.C.: U.S. Securities and Exchange Commission.

Modigliani, F., and Miller, M. H. (June 1958). "The cost of capital, corporation finance and the theory of investment." *American Economic Review* 48, 3, 261-97.

Murphy, D. M., and Topel, R. H. (October 1985). "Estimation and inference in two-step econometric models." *Journal of Business and Economic Statistics* 3, 370-379.

Neter, J., Wasserman, W., and Kutner, M. H. (1985). *Applied Linear Statistical Models,* 2nd ed. Homewood, Ill.: Irwin.

Pakes, A., and Ericson, R. (March 1989). "Empirical implications of alternative models of firm dynamics." Cambridge, Mass.: National Bureau of Economic Research Working Paper No. 2893.

Paulus, J., and Gay, R. (1987). "Is America helping herself: Corporate restructuring and global competitiveness." *World Economic Outlook.*

_____ (July 1988). "Permanent mass layoffs and plant closings, 1987." Washington, D.C.: U.S. Department of Labor, Bulletin #2310.

Paulus, J., and Waite, S. (1990) "High yield bonds, corporate control and innovation." Unpublished manuscript.

Perry, K., and Taggert, R., Jr. (September 1987). "The growing role of junk bonds in corporate finance." Working paper, Department of Finance, Boston University. Boston, MA.

Porter, M. (1983). Cases in competitive strategy. New York: The Free Press.

Pound, J. (March 1987). "Why corporations restructure." Working paper, Department of Finance, Yale University. New Haven, CT.

_____ (April 1988). "Debt and corporate performance: New theories and evidence on capital structure." Prepared for Drexel Burnham Lambert's 1988 Institutional Research Conference, 1-13.

_____, and Gordon, L. (April 6, 1989). "High yield placements and corporate performance." Presented at Drexel Burnham Lambert's Eleventh Annual Institutional Research Conference.

Porter, M. E. (May-June 1987). "From competitive advantage to corporate strategy." *Harvard Business Review.*

Pozdena, R. (April 1987). "Junk bonds: Why now?" *Federal Reserve Bank of San Francisco Weekly Letter.*

Rasky, S. F. (December 7, 1986). "Tracking junk bond owners." *The New York Times.*

Ravenscraft, D., and Scherer, F. (1987). *Mergers, selloffs, and economic efficiency.* Washington, D.C.: The Brookings Institution.

Roach, S. S. (Spring 1989). "Living with corporate debt." *Journal of Applied Corporate Finance* 2, 19-29.

Romano, R. (May 14, 1987). "State takeover laws." *Wall Street Journal.*

Rosen, C., and Quarrey, M. (September-October 1987). "How well is employee ownership working?" *Harvard Business Review,* pp. 4-7.

Scherer, F.M. (February 25, 1987). "Testimony before the Committee on Energy and Commerce." Washington, D.C.: U.S. House of Representatives.

Schrager, R., and Sherman, H. (Janury 1987). "Junk bonds and tender offer financing." Investor Responsibility Research Center. Washington, D.C.

Smith, A. (January 1989). "Corporate ownership structure and performance: The case of management buyouts." Chicago: University of Chicago, unpublished paper.

Sobel, R. (April 6, 1989). "Historical perspectives on the use of high yield securities in corporate creation." Prepared for Drexel Burnham Lambert's 1989 Institutional Research Conference.

Solow, R. M. (August 1957). "Technical change and the aggregate production function." *Review of Economics and Statistics* 39, 214-231.

_____ (October 1988). "Sources of value in management buyouts." Cambridge, Mass.: Harvard Business School, unpublished doctoral thesis.

Tufano, P. (August 1989). "Financial innovation in historical perspective, 1830-1930," Cambridge, MA.: Harvard Business School, unpublished paper.

U.S. Bureau of Labor Statistics (July 1988). "Permanent mass layoffs and plant closings, 1987." Washington, D.C.: U.S. Department of Labor, Bulletin #2310.

_____ (September 30, 1988). "Multifactor productivity measures, 1987." Washington, D.C.: U.S. Department of Labor, 88-478.

U.S. Department of Commerce (1986). *1986 U.S. Industrial Outlook.* Washington, D.C.: International Trade Administration.

U.S. National Science Foundation (February 1, 1989). "An assessment of the impact of recent leveraged buyouts and other restructurings on industrial research and development expenditures." Washington, D.C.

Wharton Econometric Forecasting Associates (WEFA) (September 1988). "The risk adjusted returns for major investments available to thrift institutions." Washington, D.C.

Waite, S., and Fridson, M. (January 1989). "The credit quality of leveraged buyouts." *High Performance.* New York: Morgan Stanley, 9-15.

Yago, G. (1986). "Plant closings in New York: Causes, consequences, and policy implications." Economic Research Bureau, W. Averell Harriman School for Management and Policy Working Paper HAR-86-001, State University of New York at Stony Brook.

_____, and Stevenson, G. (1987). "Employment impacts of mergers and acquisitions." Working paper, Economic Research Bureau, W. Averell Harriman School for Management and Policy. State University of New York at Stony Brook.

_____ et al. (July 1988). "The uses and effects of high yield securities in U.S. industry." Working paper, Economic Research Bureau, W. Averell Harriman School for Management and Policy, State University of New York at Stony Brook.

_____, Lichtenberg, F., and Siegel, D. (1989). "Leveraged buyouts and industrial competitiveness: The effects of LBOs on productivity, employment, research and development." Working paper, W. Averell Harriman School for Management and Policy, No. HAR-90-003. State University of New York at Stony Brook.

_____, Tanenbaum, J., and Cometta-Berndt, P. (July 1989). "Leveraged buyouts in focus: The role of debt in ownership change and industrial competitiveness in the eighties." Working paper, Economic Research Bureau, W. Averell Harriman School for Management and Policy, State University of New York at Stony Brook.

_____ and _____ (Summer 1990). "Employment impacts of mergers and acquisitions." *Journal of Applied Corporate Finance.*

_____. "Economic Impacts of High Yield Securities and Public Policy Response," in E.I. Attman (ed.) *The High Yield Debt Market* (Homewood, Ill.: Dow Jones Irwin), 1990.

Index